Along *the* Way

A Green Beret shares stirring stories of those he met and those who supported him in Vietnam — Tet 1968

FOR ROGER ... ANOTHER SUPPORT UNIT !!
THANK YOU FOR ALL YOUR SUPPORT OF MY JEWELRY CAREER THOUGHOUT THE YEARS.
WARM REGARDS,
Paul
"DE OPPRESSO LIBER"

Along *the* Way

A Green Beret shares stirring stories of those he met and those who supported him in Vietnam — Tet 1968

by

THOMAS A. ROSS

Atlanta, Georgia

American Heritage Publishing - Atlanta
Peachtree Corners, Georgia

Along the Way

Published by
American Heritage Publishing
5710 Mt Repose Lane NW
Peachtree Corners, GA 30092-1428

First Edition - Privileges of War, 2004
Published by American Heritage Publishing - Atlanta
5710 Mt. Repose Lane, NW
Peachtree Corners, Georgia 30092-1428

Second Edition – Along the Way, 2020

Book design by Jill Dible & Antonio DeRosa
Editing by Robert O. Babcock & Robert L. Hawley, Jr.
Cover design by Creativindie Book Cover Design

For legal and other reasons, some names in this book have been changed.

Library of Congress Control Number: 2020923942

ISBN: 978-0-9754859-1-0

Printed in the United States of America

Dedication

To the more than three million who served, and, especially,
to each of the more than fifty-eight thousand who died or
were declared missing in action in the Republic of South Vietnam.

To my teammates on Special Forces Detachment A-502
and those encountered while there—you inspired this book.

To those who wear an American military uniform today.
Thank you for your service.

To the memory of my friend, Ngoc,
to his wife, Kim, and their four children; Chau, Bau, Hieu, and Nga.

And, finally . . . with love,

To Amy, my inspiration and—the light of my life,
my four children; Angie, Brian, Allison, and Lindsay,
my grandchildren, and my friends,
who all give me many good reasons—to live and enjoy life.

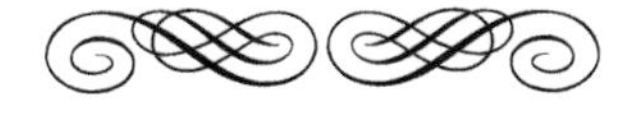

CONTENTS

FOREWORD

THIS IS A REAL STORY. It is told by a real soldier about one of the most incredible moments in the Vietnam War. It is a story of the energetic innocence of youth, the craving to be a patriot, the anguish of war fought on the other side of the world. Yet, even in the despair amongst demons of horrific proportions, heroes were bred.

On one mission of mercy to save others described in his second book, *Rescue in the Valley of the Tigers,* Tom Ross shows us what it means to be a positive American. He makes us all proud. He doesn't ask that you understand all the real pain of triumph and fear that he experienced. He only hopes that you won't forget what happened, or the men and women to whom it happened.

Tom Ross's *Along the Way* makes me glad to have served in Vietnam and proud to be an American.

Max Cleland
CPT U.S. Army, Ret.
Author, *Strong at the Broken Places*
Former U.S. Senator (1997–2003)

Preface

AS A YOUNG BOY, I was healthy, very happy, and blessed with more than my share of vim and vigor. As a result, I gave my parents a run for their money while they did their best to raise me to be centered and have good moral values. To direct my energy constructively, my parents got me involved in Scouting at an early age. I became a Cub Scout and later a Boy Scout, ultimately earning the rank of Eagle Scout. My parents also made sure that I was in church every Sunday, where I served as an altar boy and choir boy.

My rearing took place in Pensacola, Florida, which was also home to the Navy's flight demonstration team, the Blue Angles. I used to watch them practicing out over the Gulf of Mexico while I fished from the Pensacola Beach Pier. They were magnificent and inspiring, so it was easy for me to grow up a patriot. I always thought of myself as a good kid, an All-American kid. No one special, just someone who loved the country where he was growing up.

Later, during what had been carefree college days, I would find myself unexpectedly called to demonstrate my patriotism. The calling was so strong that I would be compelled to leave college behind, join the U.S. Army, and volunteer for service in Southeast Asia.

After nearly two years of exceptional training, I became a part of the Vietnam War as a military adviser. During my time as an adviser, I was privileged to meet and work with individuals who didn't hesitate to risk their lives for things they believed. Not all were military and not all had combat assignments, but they shared a common bond—all of them were Americans.

It may be hard to believe and difficult to understand, but my time in Vietnam was an incredible adventure. It wasn't something one would choose as an exotic vacation, but still an adventure. While it was full of both good and bad experiences, it was also full of challenges that tested my ability to respond. Any of those challenges could have abruptly ended my existence on God's green earth, so I came home with a very special appreciation for life. But I wanted my service in Vietnam to be about more than simply fighting and surviving the war.

When I left home, besides my duffle bag, I carried the hope of doing something good, achieving something meaningful during my time in Vietnam. While I had no idea what that might be, the hope still went with me.

When my tour of duty ended and I returned to my Northwest Florida home, I was shocked and deeply saddened to learn that American civilians were routinely spitting on the uniforms of returning servicemen while hurling hateful epithets at them. I couldn't believe this was happening in my country. *Surely,* I thought, *those spitting on our troops have no idea what they faced or how they served.*

To me, the spitting incidents were disgusting, shameful, and significant enough that, within days, I drafted an outline and the first pages of a manuscript for this book and my second book which covers one specific experience in Vietnam.

My goal was to share inspirational stories of some extraordinary men and women and the remarkable deeds that I witnessed during my service to the country I loved. The experience of serving with those men and women and the memories of their courageous and selfless actions—will remain with me forever.

Ultimately, the purpose of this book is to provide a different perspective of the Vietnam War—and those who fought it.

INTRODUCTION

ALONG THE WAY is the first of two companion books that represent the 2nd Edition of *Privileges of War*, a 1st Edition book by Thomas A. Ross.

When Tom completed the manuscript for the second edition of his first book, the word count and page count were so high that the decision was made to divide the manuscript into two separate books.

This is *Along the Way,* the first of those two books and it describes selfless and courageous deeds performed by some of the individuals Tom met while serving his tour of duty in South Vietnam.

Rescue in the Valley of the Tigers is the second book and it describes Tom's long-held hope to do something good, something meaningful during his time in Vietnam, and what happens when that opportunity presents itself.

While serving as an officer and military adviser with the U.S. Army 5th Special Forces, the elite unit also known as the "Green Berets," it was my honor, my privilege, to witness American men and women in action.

Along the Way is a collection of positive stories about wartime service during one of the most negative and controversial periods in American history. While the stories told here are relatively simple and straightforward, they are also meaningful, with the potential of changing viewpoints and opinions—some have already changed lives.

Soldiers did not commit the U.S. military to war in Vietnam, our government leadership did. However, those who fought the war bore the burden of that commitment both on Vietnamese battlefields and in their hometowns when they returned. Not only did American soldiers fight horrific battles against an enemy who hated them, but upon returning home they often faced fellow countrymen who seemed to hate them as well.

Few of the Americans who served in Southeast Asia were pot-smoking, cursing, killing machines, as they have so often been portrayed—I certainly wasn't. As a young boy, I served my community. I was no angel, but neither was I a devil. I didn't go to Vietnam to kill anyone. Rather, I went to serve my country—I went to help another country in its fight for freedom.

It is my opinion that the great majority of the more than three million American men and women who served in Vietnam were decent individuals who believed in the principles of freedom. Whether or not they agreed with government policies regarding the war, they either demonstrated their patriotism or respected constitutional law by responding as either an enlistee or a draftee. They either wanted to serve in Vietnam and found a way to get there, or they had absolutely no desire to be there—but went anyway. Most of them were young, either still in or scarcely out of their teens when they were asked to shoulder heavy responsibility and face life-or-death situations, many of them daily. I know. I was there. I was one of those soldiers, and *Along the Way* is my story—a firsthand account of the many acts of selfless heroism and courage witnessed during my tour of duty.

Many of the books currently in print, movies, and so-called "documentary" films about the Vietnam War tell provocative stories with messages that are dark, brooding, and often flagrantly biased. While many ugly and brutal events took place in Vietnam, with the atrocities at My Lai being perhaps the most notorious and most widely known—good things happened too.

This book shares a very different perspective of the war in Vietnam and those who served half a world away from their homes. *Privileges of War* treats neither the politics of the war nor the conflict itself. Rather, it depicts some of the individuals who were there and demonstrates the spirit-lifting manner in which they served. This detailed, action-filled account gives readers a real, often frightening idea of what it was like to be on the ground or in the air over the Vietnamese jungle during that conflict.

Stories related on the following pages could be about a relative, friend, or acquaintance you know who served in Southeast Asia. These are factual accounts of persons who could have, or maybe still do, live in your community or—in your own home. Most of those portrayed in this book were warm, very real, and wonderfully full of life. Many were individuals who could smile and display a bright sense of humor under the most difficult circumstances. Those I encountered never failed to meet their challenges in the face of danger. In fact, many raced into danger headlong, often placing personal safety at risk to help or protect others. They served with honor and distinction and were men and women of whom this country can be very proud.

The American public deserves to hear all the stories, not just the ugly ones. In this book, you will read some of the many bright accounts of dedication and patriotism that I was privileged to witness. They are not offered as a sanctimonious gloss over of ugly occurrences that took place during the Vietnam War. They are presented simply because I feel that a vital piece of the American historical puzzle is still missing. Stories of heroism, courage, and commitment demonstrated by U.S. troops and other Americans in Vietnam deserve to be shared as well.

Sad, but many of the men and women who served in Vietnam are still reluctant to discuss their wartime experiences for many reasons. Some fear they might be viewed negatively, may offend others, or still other reasons. During the more than fifty years since I served there, I have encountered countless other veterans who exist in every socioeconomic level of our society. Because the war was so divisive, and the controversy over it so bitter, many veterans remain secretive about their service, unwilling to discuss or mention it even with those closest to them. My greatest sorrow has been encountering spouses or children who have far too often said, "He has never spoken to me about the time he spent in Vietnam."

Over the years that the first edition of the book was in print, I hoped it would help dispel some of the negative myths about our involvement in Vietnam, redefine the image of the Vietnam veteran, and encourage other men and women who served there—to tell their stories. There are more than three million others with stories to tell. In sharing their experiences, I continue to hope that the sheltered pride they have felt compelled to conceal for so many years can, at last, be shared. I also hope this new edition helps move the discussion of the Vietnam War beyond the war itself—to those who served in it, largely without thanks.

When I began writing, this book was for my wife, Amy, and our children. I wanted them to know why I went to Vietnam, what I did there, and what I saw others do. However, as the manuscript developed, the last of those three things became its focus; its purpose grew far more important. The book took flight in a quiet and very personal way for my country, a country I care about deeply. I wanted to share rarely told, and often, uniquely American stories about those I met—Along the Way.

My sincere belief is that the men and women portrayed in this book asked nothing for themselves beyond the opportunity to serve their country and help the people of South Vietnam in their fight for freedom. Many Americans were so committed to the effort that they volunteered to serve multiple tours of duty there. Like the first edition, this one provides the reader with the opportunity to learn about the many challenges faced by young men and women in Vietnam at a time when support for them was deteriorating back at home.

This book is not a macho, shoot'em-up, war tale. It is a sensitive factual story of the inspirational dedication displayed by American men and women who served our country during an unpopular war. And it was written so that it could be read and easily understood by women and other family members of veterans who may not have military experience. Finally, the book was also written for those born long after the Vietnam era so they may have another insight to compare with things they may have heard or read or were taught in school.

Hopefully, you will find the book exciting with highs and lows that will tug your emotions in different directions. You may read parts that make you laugh and others that cause you some distress, emotions similar to those I experienced.

Ultimately, I hope that what you read in *Along the Way* will make you proud of all those who served our country with honor and courage while in Vietnam—as well as those who serve in other places around the world today.

If you enjoy this book, I hope you will consider reading *Rescue in the Valley of the Tigers*. In my next book, you will follow me on a daring rescue of mountain villagers, Montagnards, who were held and used as slaves deep in enemy territory. While I had always hoped to do something meaningful during my time in Vietnam, it would take many others to help me to accomplish that mission and—it nearly cost me my life.

AUTHOR'S NOTE

THE ORIGINAL DRAFT of this book contained much more about a unique relationship that developed between my Vietnamese Special Forces counterpart, Major Nguyen Quang Ngoc, and me.

When the first edition of this book, *Privileges of War,* was ready for publication in 2003, I wanted Ngoc to review pages of the draft where he was mentioned to make certain that he was comfortable with what I had written. Unfortunately, with the multiple family and business moves that both of us made, we lost contact. The last I heard from him; Ngoc had moved to Hawaii. I knew that because one day a coconut with my address and his return address carved on it was delivered to my front door. That was it—just the coconut.

Ngoc was an extremely intelligent man and at the time Vietnam fell, he had been promoted to colonel and was serving as the head of what amounted to the Vietnamese Veteran's Administration. He also had a bright sense of humor. As you will read, we often shared witticisms during our time together. Often, it was a way to lessen tension or divert from the distasteful aspects of war. In this case, the coconut was his way of sharing a smile.

After removing the outer husk, I bored a hole in the coconut shell and drained the coconut milk. Next, I cracked the shell and harvested the coconut meat. Then, I gathered my family and introduced them to the joy of fresh Hawaiian coconut.

Despite a diligent effort, which included contacting Vietnamese organizations in Washington, D.C., and other parts of the country, I was unable to locate Ngoc or any of his children.

Years earlier, in 1975, and for reasons you will read later, Ngoc and I were sharing a bottle of wine at my Gulf Breeze, Florida home. That evening, he confided to me what seemed a deeply emotional hope that he could one day take his family and—return to Vietnam.

So, believing there was a real possibility that Ngoc may have returned to what had become a Communist Vietnam, I feared the repercussions he and his family might suffer if Vietnamese authorities read what I had written about his fight against them. So, to protect my friend and his family, I went back through the manuscript, changed occurrences involving Ngoc, removed all but the most innocuous references to him, then published the book in 2004.

Unexpectedly, in November 2015, Ngoc's daughter, Hieu, located me and called my office. I was extremely excited to receive her call. It was a wonderful moment that reunited me with the Nguyen family. And, as it turned out, Ngoc hadn't gone back to Vietnam but had still been living with his lovely wife, Kim, in Hawaii. While I was sorry that my many calls to "Nguyen" listings in the Hawaiian phonebook had somehow missed Ngoc, it was good to know that he had decided to stay in the USA.

Now, with this 2nd Edition, newly titled *Along the Way,* it is with great pleasure that I can tell the entire stories as they occurred and appropriately recognize a man who courageously fought for the freedom of his country. And, I know first-hand that Ngoc also deeply and genuinely appreciated the Americans who joined and supported him in that fight.

This edition also includes more stories, general information, detail, and pictures, than the first. Nothing helps tell a story like pictures. So, in many chapters, there are pictures of individuals and places you will read about—I wanted you to feel as if you are there with me as you read each story.

Abbreviations

AHC	Assault Helicopter Company
AIT	Advanced Infantry Training
AO	Area of Operation
ARVN	Army of the Republic of South Vietnam
ASAP	As Soon As Possible
CAV	Cavalry
CIB	Combat Infantryman's Badge
Chopper	Helicopter
CIDG	Civilian Irregular Defense Group
CO	Commanding Officer
COC	Combat Orientation Class
DI	Drill Instructor
FAC	Forward Air Controller
FDC	Fire Direction Center
GI	Government Issued/General Issue
HE	High Explosive
KIA	Killed in Action
LLDB	Luc Luong Dac Biet (Vietnamese Special Forces)
LRP	Long-Range Patrol
LT	Lieutenant (Pronounced "ell-tee" in conversation)
LZ	Landing Zone
MEDCAPS	Medical Civic Action Program
MIA	Missing in Action
NCO	Non-Commissioned Officer
NVA	North Vietnamese Army
OCS	Officer Candidate School

Abbreviations

PIO	Public Information Officer
Psy Ops	Psychological Operations
ROK	Republic of Korea
RPG	Rocket Propelled Grenade
S2	U.S. Intelligence
S3	U.S. Operations
SF	Special Forces
SFC	Sergeant First Class
SFG	Special Forces Group
Sit Rep	Situation Report
SPC4	Specialist fourth class
Spooky	Modified C-47 aircraft gunship
SRAO	Supplemental Recreational Activities Overseas
TAOI	Team Area of Influence
TAOR	Team Area of Responsibility
UH-1	Huey helicopter
VC	Viet Cong
WIA	Wounded in Action
XO	Executive Officer

The Setting & Flags

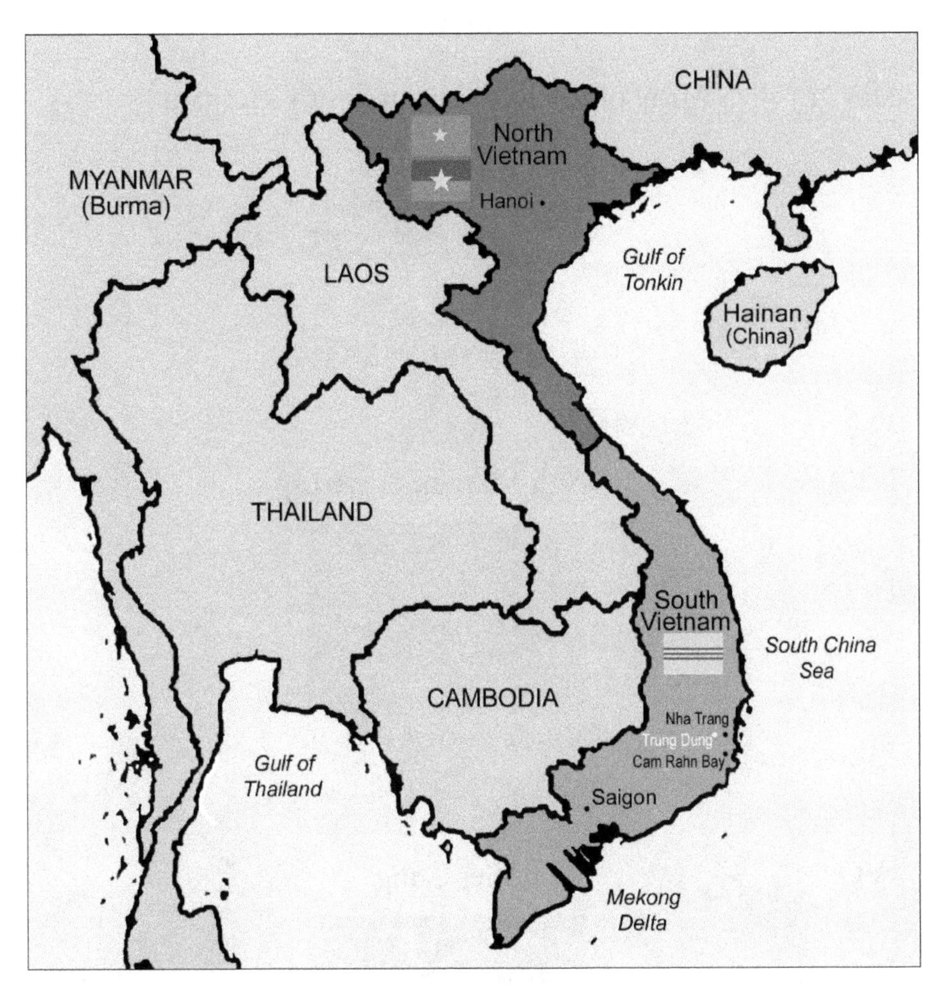

North and South Vietnam (now, Vietnam) were both parts of the area known as "Southeast Asia." Surprisingly, many people weren't and still aren't sure exactly where the area is located. Southeast Asia is situated on the Asian continent and consists of countries located east of India, south of China, west of New Guinea, and north of Australia.

This map is provided so you will know where key cities and my base camp, Special Forces Detachment A-502, and Trai Trung Dung, were located within the overall arena of the Vietnam War.

The Setting & Flags

FLAGS

ARVN — Army of the Republic of South Vietnam

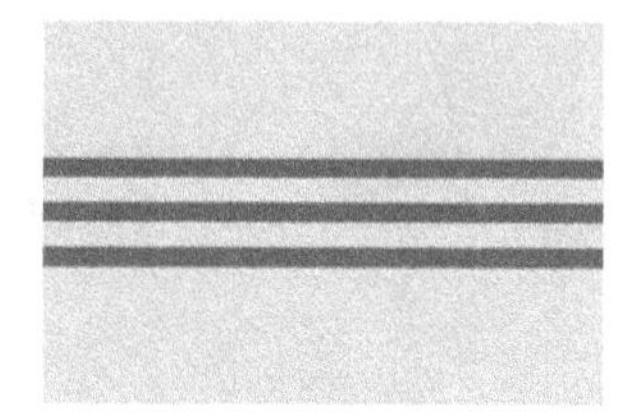

(Yellow Background with Red Stripes)

NVA — North Vietnamese Army

(Red Background with Yellow Star)

VC — Viet Cong

(Red Top, Blue Bottom Background with Yellow Star)

Chapter 1

Arriving in Nha Trang

MIDDAY, EARLY FEBRUARY 1968—*This looks as if it could be the beginning of a fantastic tropical vacation*, I thought. And, the magnificent scenery below certainly made the thought a plausible one.

With an index finger, I eased my sunglasses up above my eyes to have an un-tinted view of the spectacle passing beneath me. The landscape was even more beautiful with its vivid natural colors exposed. It could easily have been the edge of paradise.

We were flying low over sparkling blue-green water that flashed and glittered as it rolled gently onto a long, narrow, light-brown beach. The natural piping of lush green palm trees that decorated beaches swayed slowly in warm tropical breezes. Coral heads blossomed from beneath crystal-clear water and bright green mangroves grew thick along waterways that led to winding inland rivers. Occasionally, the beach dissolved into massive rock outcroppings that rose to meet us. Off in the distance, dark green inland mountains were visible against a bright blue sky, which played host to a few randomly scattered, fluffy white clouds.

The panorama before me, a true masterpiece of nature, was surely meant for the cover of an exotic travel brochure—this was exactly the way I imagined Tahiti would look.

As any other healthy young male might, I had daydreams of someday traveling to a faraway tropical island, which I would share with at least one stunningly beautiful woman. Now, barely a few hundred feet below me was at least part of the dream—the tropical island. The view was so hypnotically captivating that I could even hear the rhythmic beating of island drums. I began to wonder, *Will the rest of the dream come true?*

Still peering beneath my sunglasses as we crossed over the shoreline, I could see what appeared to be a native village in the distance. Here and there, over and through the thick growth of tropical vegetation, I caught an occasional glimpse of shapes that perhaps were island huts. As we neared them, and then swooped almost directly over them, I saw that the hut-like shapes weren't truly huts at all. Rather, they were large military tents that had absolutely nothing to do with a romantic island village, Tahitian, or otherwise. We were arriving in Nha Trang and the tents were part of a military base camp position for a U.S. Army artillery battery.

The imagined sound of island drums quickly faded as I once again became conscious of the synchronized *whop, whop, whop* sound of the churning helicopter blades above me. I let my sunglasses fall back to the bridge of my nose and settled back into my seat.

In reality, this wasn't the beginning of a fantastic vacation at all, and no beautiful woman waited on the beach to welcome me with a cold tropical drink. The unexpectedly beautiful terrain I had just flown over was at a point where the eastern coastline of South Vietnam met the South China Sea. Exotic, but certainly no vacation—at least, not in 1968.

The helicopter on which I was a passenger was a military shuttle on its way to Nha Trang from Cam Ranh Bay, an arrival and departure point for U.S. troops serving in Vietnam. Those of us on the shuttle had been in Vietnam for only a day or two—just long enough to be officially processed "in-country." Now, we were all on our way to duty stations.

Since volunteering for this duty, my eventual assignment with the 5th Special Forces Group had been one I anticipated. I had trained hard for the assignment and had tried to prepare myself, both physically and mentally, for the day I would become a part of the Vietnam War. But the day that began to unfold wasn't at all what I had envisioned. I had expected a dark and ominous setting, not a place that looked as though it might be a vacation destination or part of a pleasantly remembered daydream.

Upon reaching Nha Trang, I was to report to 5th Group Headquarters where I would receive my assignment as a military adviser, one appropriate for my rank of 1st Lieutenant. The flight north along the coast didn't take long, only about twenty minutes. Shortly after flying over the artillery battery we reached the outer edge of Nha Trang Air Base and began our landing approach to runway Zero-Five.

After almost two years of intense military training, I had finally received orders in January 1968 that directed me to service in the much-talked-about country of South Vietnam. Now, I was just one in the very long line of approximately 3 million men and women who had received or would receive similar orders, whether they wanted them or not.

During our approach to the airbase, and even as the chopper came to rest on a pad at the edge of the base runway, it was still a bit difficult to believe that we had been flying over—Vietnam. Maybe I had seen too many old black-and-white war movies, but my image of Vietnam was of a dark, war-torn place in varying shades of gray. Surely too, recent war damage would be easily visible, with smoke rising over a not-too-distant battlefield. Instead, the sky before me that day was clear and bright, and the landscape was a mixture of colors as vibrant and beautiful as any back home in Pensacola. However, in mere moments, things would begin to change dramatically.

The helicopter blades were still spinning over my head as I jumped down onto the hot asphalt runway. Once on the ground, it didn't take long for me to realize that I had indeed reached Southeast Asia. As soon as I carried my duffel bag far enough away from the chopper for the smell of exhaust to dissipate, a distinctly new odor filled my nostrils. Coming from every direction and permeating the air, it seemed to be a mixture of fish and fowl being cooked together and was as foreign to me as the ground on which I then stood. The odor wasn't at all offensive, but it was certainly new and distinctively different. I had never smelled air like that before. Other sights and sounds around me offered additional evidence that I truly was in a country halfway around the world from home. Asian people were performing various tasks as their supervisors shouted directions in a language I recognized as Vietnamese.

As I stood there looking, listening, smelling, absorbing it all, little doubt remained about my exact location on the Earth. Suddenly, the only things that didn't seem foreign to me were the military equipment and the familiar humidity, which reminded me of the Florida Gulf Coast.

Turning a 360-degree circle, I continued to survey my new surroundings with every one of my five senses more acute than I could ever recall. *So, this is it,* I thought. *This is the place creating so much controversy back home.*

Then, beginning to mentally prepare for the months ahead, I watched troops as they came and went, moving all around the runway. I wondered if any of those who were arriving felt the same strangeness that I did. As for those who were departing, I could only guess about their feelings. Some looked very excited and discernibly glad to be going home; others looked very worn and tired, while still others appeared expressionless.

Examining some of the passing faces, I wondered—*Does even one of these men feel he has accomplished anything during his tour of duty?* I was searching for the slightest evidence that any of these men might have felt as if he had accomplished even the smallest good, but I just couldn't tell.

Watching as the last man in one group boarded a homeward-bound shuttle, I began to wonder what my feelings of accomplishment might be in twelve months. *Will my presence here have made a difference? With the dissension over the war growing back in the states, will anyone ever know or even care that I was here?* Of course, I had no way to know the answers. But making a personal contribution and accomplishing some good had been among my reasons for coming to Vietnam. I hoped to do something, anything, that would make a difference to someone, even if that someone were only me. Having volunteered for this assignment, I didn't want my time in Vietnam to be meaningless or inconsequential—especially if it cost me my life. And, yes, I had considered that possibility.

While I couldn't at that point know why the men around me had come, as 1968 unfolded I would learn much about others who were there. In many cases, their presence was no more complicated than a simple, but strong, patriotic desire to contribute—to make a difference.

In my case, the desire to make a difference had been so strong that, counter to my parents' pleas, I decided to leave college and join the service. Now that I was actually standing on foreign soil, about to begin making that contribution, my mind began to race and fill with thoughts and questions. *Have I made the right decision? Am I truly where I want to be?*

Strange, but those questions seemed to answer themselves as quickly as they formed. But there was one that gave me pause, *now that I have reached Vietnam, will I make it back to this spot in twelve months to catch the return shuttle to Cam Ranh Bay and my flight home?* I purged that thought almost as quickly as it had developed.

Certainly, I didn't want to consider the prospect that I might be killed, however real that possibility. However, I know my father had considered it, though, because on the day I left home his eyes were filled with tears when we said good-bye. My Dad was a big man and a veteran of World War II, and I had seen him that way only once before—the day his father died.

Blue Skies and Puffy White Clouds — Could be Paradise

Above: My view the day I arrived in Nha Trang. The ride brought me up the coast and around that point in the distance—Could there truly be a war here?

Below: The crew chief's .60-caliber machine gun in the picture below suggested that the answer to my question was—yes. But that was still difficult to believe.

CHAPTER 2

Leaving College Behind

AFTER CARRYING MY DUFFLE bag to a small operations building and checking in, I was told that a call would be placed to 5th Group Headquarters to let them know I had arrived. They would send someone to pick me up.

Going back outside to a pickup area at the edge of the runway, I dropped my duffle beside me and began the wait for my ride to headquarters. Again, observing the activity around me, I began to reflect on my decision to join the service and volunteer for duty in Vietnam.

The scuffed, olive-drab green duffel bag at my feet had been carried from base to base for over two years. Glancing down at it, my thoughts began to drift to the evolution that had taken me from college student to professional soldier.

Perhaps the drift was simply an endorsing review of experiences that had led me to where I stood at that moment. Whatever the reason, I felt a smile ease onto my face as recollections of college days began to develop. Then, memories focused so quickly it was as if I had been awakened by the snapping fingers of one of my college professors. He used the crisp loud sound to regain the attention of a daydreaming student.

During the two and a half years spent in college, I changed majors five times. No, I wasn't a professional student. I simply had an interest in a great many things while lacking a bit in direction and decisiveness. I had begun in pre-med then envisioned myself as an architect, a business executive, an attorney, and so on. All were worthy professions, but the changes in major required significant course changes. In reality, my academic performance was fairly lackluster primarily due to a preoccupation with the coeds around me.

One of my fondest recollections of early college days involved an encounter with an organization of young women rather than academics. The smile-creating recollection centered on a party arranged for my fraternity with the most popular sorority on campus.

Since our fraternity had a loveable, but somewhat "unruly" reputation on campus, and closely resembled the one portrayed in the movie "Animal House," there was only one way the sorority would agree to a joint party. I had to promise them a refined location, an array of sophisticated refreshments, and a "live" band, a record-player wasn't going to make it happen. So, without consulting my brothers who *will surely agree*, I thought—the deal was struck.

We must have washed and/or waxed over two hundred cars to earn enough money to pay for that party. We even had a bake sale and all the work was well worth the effort. We hired one of the hottest bands around and they played in a party room at the poshest hotel in town. In return for serving as the fraternity's Chief Negotiator, I had also negotiated for the right to escort the sorority's president as my date for the party. She was gorgeous!

What a great and wonderful time it was—just to be alive! We were young, happy, generally full of a little harmless nonsense, and we looked forward optimistically to the prospect of long bright futures.

During those relatively carefree days, the opportunities to fish off the Pensacola Beach Pier and just spend time with my friends were all that I needed to find great pleasure in life. My greatest responsibility was simply to finish college. And, the only thing I anticipated needing after college, besides a job, was someone special with whom I could share life.

Sometimes, I sat in the student union building with my face buried in a course catalog in my latest attempt to figure out how my many majors could be merged to achieve a single degree and graduation. At times, my gaze would rise above the pages. Looking out across the other tables, it was easy to become captivated by the attractive young southern women seated around me. And occasionally, I wondered if my someone special were somewhere there in the gathering. If she were there, I wondered how I would find her. Yes, I know—a bit romantic, but that's exactly the way I was in those days.

Eventually, I did find that very special someone, but it wasn't until many years later in 1978 and her name was—Amy. Strangely enough, and even though I didn't meet her until long after I had left Vietnam, it was the shadowy image and promise of Amy that helped me through many long days and nights during my tour of duty. Wondering about her filled the spaces of time when I felt far from home and a little lonely. As of this writing, Amy has been at my side for over forty years and, as I wrote in the Dedication, she has been—the light of my life.

Considering my days in college, they seemed like a distant part of a very innocent past. Many things had happened since deciding to enter the service, a spontaneous decision, and one that would change my life forever.

Standing there on the runway apron under a hot Southeast Asian sun, there was no avoiding recollection of the event compelling me to interrupt my college education and choose military service. It occurred one evening in

January 1966 while at my parents' home for dinner. My mother and sister, Polly, were busy preparing dinner while my father and I watched the evening news on television. When a news segment began that was reporting on an unfortunate gunshot taken by a young Marine, I was immediately and unexpectedly drawn to what was happening. The report struck me so forcefully that I would never forget its effect on me. The broadcast marked a specific point in time that brought maturity, decisiveness, and focus to what had otherwise been a happy-go-lucky college lifestyle.

In 1966, reports regarding the Vietnam War were typically the lead story or major report for almost every news program on the three major television networks, ABC, CBS, and NBC. That unforgettable evening, I sat and watched, absorbed by the report focusing on three young American Marines. They appeared to be about my age, or maybe even younger. Two of them were desperately trying to drag another Marine out of the line of fire after he had been seriously wounded.

Suddenly, and without any warning, as I watched the desperate struggle to save the downed Marine's life, I felt as if I had been drenched with ice water. The experience was remarkably intense and was accompanied by a wave of goosebumps that swept over my body. The strange moment was bizarre and might be more accurately described as a remarkable epiphany.

In an instant, there was a connection with the desperate situation of the young Marines and I found myself yelling at the television screen,

"Get him out of there! Get him out of there!"

I was stunned by the awareness and reality of what was occurring so far away from the safety of my family's home. I was immediately embarrassed by the thought that other young American men were fighting and dying while I attended school and enjoyed fraternity parties.

Television news programs had depicted countless other reports of war action, but none had affected me as powerfully as that one. Perhaps it was their terrible situation or the look on their faces, I don't know. For whatever reason, I remembered thinking that I could no longer stay at home to attend college and date girls while others did what I felt I should also be doing.

Other men in my family had served their country or community. My father flew in B-17s with the 100th Bomb Group of the Eighth Army Air Force in Europe during World War II. After surviving being shot down over Belgium, he was rescued by the French underground. My grandfather had worked long shift hours as a metallurgist, turning out needed supplies for the same war effort. And, my great-grandfather served as the chief of police in Proctorville, Ohio. Unfortunately, his service had cost him his life. After responding to a call for help, he was ambushed and killed.

I certainly had no desire to be killed as my great-grandfather had been. But, after considering what other men in my family had done, I couldn't imagine doing any less. And, I knew I couldn't ignore what I had just watched on television. As the TV anchorman turned to other news, a recently read quote came to mind, one discovered during research for a college literature class. Daniel Webster wrote, "There is no evil we cannot face or fly from, but the consciousness of duty disregarded." That quote seemed to sum things up for me perfectly. The decision was made. I would leave school and join the service—as soon as possible.

Paul A. Ross

My Dad during flight school training in 1942.

Chief Bias's Badge

Chief William W. "Boss" Bias This is my great-grandfather's badge.

Welcome to the U. S. Army

After taking the Army enlistment oath, I would begin three of the most extraordinary years of my life.

CHAPTER 3

Taking the Oath

STILL REMINISCING ABOUT FONDLY remembered college days, I chuckled out loud as I thought about my day at the draft board. When I went to collect my records and classification card, they had a difficult time finding my file. Unbelievably, I was told that no draft records existed for Thomas A. Ross. However, the clerk told me that they would continue to search and she asked that I return the next day.

The next morning when I arrived, a sweet older woman emerged from a rear area. She smiled and seemed excited as she walked to where I was waiting at the counter and said, "It's a good thing you came in young man." Then, she happily announced, "We found your records! They had been improperly filed. You would probably never have been drafted."

I laughed and said, "I wonder how many men have prayed that such a thing might happen to them."

Upon leaving the draft board office with records in hand, I mused about the irony of the situation and wondered how many of my contemporaries might have hoped the draft board would lose their records.

A few of my fraternity brothers and several of my friends had wished that something, anything, would happen to prevent them from being drafted. They had many reasons for not wanting to join the military. Some, who were committed to their education, wanted to finish college first. And, others were beginning to have questions regarding our country's involvement in the Vietnam War. While their motivations and feelings were different than mine, I bore them no ill feelings for not wanting to be drafted. For me, there was no remorse when my draft records were discovered in the wrong file. On the contrary, I would have been disturbed only if they hadn't been found. In reality, the one-day delay in finding my records had caused me to only become impatient and irritated. So, now, with records found and a 1-A classification card in hand, I was ready to explore the options of military service.

Flight school was my first consideration. I had grown up in Pensacola, home to Navy and Marine aviation, and flying had always been appealing to me. Unfortunately, because I hadn't completed my college degree, military flight school possibilities were very limited. If I were going to become a pilot, there was only one possibility and it wasn't with the Navy, Marines, or Air Force—it was with the Army.

After expressing my interest in flight school to the Army recruiter, he offered me the opportunity to take their flight school tests under the warrant officer program. With that being the only offer on the table, I accepted.

On the morning the flight school aptitude tests were given in Montgomery, Alabama, there were about fifty to seventy-five people scheduled to take them. Of that number, only about seven or eight of us passed the written portion. After my most recent performance back at school, I remembered how happy I was when told I had Passed.

The next morning, we were loaded into a van and driven to Fort Rucker, Alabama, for the flight physicals. When my physical was finished, I wasn't sure how I had done because, after my eyes were dilated, I couldn't have read an eye chart ten feet tall. I was sure I had failed the tests and had been blinded as well. But as it turned out, late in the afternoon, only three or four of the others and I, were told we had passed our physicals. By the time I learned the exam results, my eyes had cleared up enough to dial a phone number. I called my family to tell them I was going to fly. Was I excited and proud? You better believe it.

Within days of passing the flight school test and physical exam, the recruiter called to tell me that everything was official, I had been accepted for flight training. He said I had been assigned to a class and he gave me the date on which my training would begin. But, when he gave me the date, there was a problem. The problem was that my class date was over three months away.

When I asked why the delay, he explained the more current class dates were being given to personnel already in the service. Fair, but not at all what I wanted to hear and I had no interest in waiting that long.

After expressing the desire to begin my service sooner, I asked if there were any other options. The recruiter told me that to go sooner, I would have to go "on the ground" as an infantryman. Then, he mentioned the possibility of OCS (Officer Candidate School) but quickly cautioned that, without a college degree, he couldn't guarantee OCS to me, only the opportunity to take the test.

Then, continuing his explanation of that option, the recruiter told me that the OCS test would be given to me at the reception center after I arrived, along with a standard battery of tests. The reception center was usually the first place new troops reported after enlisting or being drafted.

Continuing his sales pitch, the recruiter said, "Based on your flight school tests, which were very good, you will have no problem with the OCS test . . . if that's an alternative you want to consider. But, again, you will have to enlist . . . with no guarantees."

I wasn't sure if he honestly believed what he had said or if he was just trying to meet his enlistment requirements for the month. I stopped and thought for a moment, then decided that the Army, and hopefully OCS, was probably the best of my options. With a committed determination, I said, "Get my papers ready . . . I'll be there to sign them shortly."

Then, as millions of soldiers before me—all the way back to the Roman

Legions and beyond, I signed papers that obligated me to military service. After that, things began to move very quickly.

Three days after signing enlistment papers, I was at the induction center in Montgomery, Alabama. The induction center was the facility where enlistees and draftees took the oath that formally committed them to military service. I suppose it was a lot like reciting marriage vows. In this case, only one person was speaking and the marriage would be a one-sided affair—if the Army were to be the wife, she would have her way all the time.

Inside a large auditorium at the induction center, a spit-and-polished looking Army sergeant walked to the center of the stage and called the room full of young civilian men to attention. They were of nearly every race, physical description, and attire. I was right in the middle of the crowd when the sergeant told everyone to raise their right hands. Once all hands were in the air, he administered the oath, which we all repeated, more or less, in unison. The oath committed those taking it, not only to military service but also to a strict code of conduct. Then, when the room fell silent, we were told to lower our hands—and congratulated on our membership in the United States Army.

As my arm fell back to my side, I wasn't sure what to expect of my new military career. I suspect others in the room with me may have felt the same uncertainty. But I did expect and felt fairly certain that my life was about to change dramatically—I had no idea how much or how soon.

After the induction ceremony and during the long overnight bus ride to the reception station, there was plenty of time to visit with fellow inductees. During that time, it became apparent that among the group of young men who were inducted that day, there existed many reasons for joining the military. Obviously, for those who had been drafted, their reason was that they hadn't been given a choice. The others, though, had varied motives for joining voluntarily. One had joined simply to flee a bad home life. Others had left poor rural countrysides or inner cities in hopes of finding a better life. And, some joined because a friend was joining or because a relative had or was serving in the military and they wanted to serve as well. Among some of the remaining reasons, were those of joining because of moral or political beliefs, or out of a sense of duty.

As the convoy of buses raced southwest down the long, dark, two-lane highway toward the reception station at Fort Polk, Louisiana, there was the realization that, for whatever the individual reasons, we were all about to begin a common experience. An experience that might eventually take many of us farther away from our homes than we had ever been before.

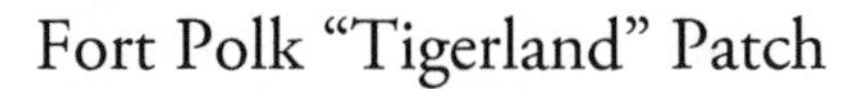

Fort Polk "Tigerland" Patch

In early 1962, the Army began transforming Fort Polk into an AIT (Advanced Infantry Training) facility. In 1966, when I arrived there, the humidity was very familiar to me. It was nearly identical to that in Pensacola. And, like Florida, parts of Fort Polk were filled with dense, jungle-like vegetation. So, with the Vietnam War in high-gear, Louisiana's heat, humidity, and rainfall were similar to that of Southeast Asia. That made Fort Polk an ideal location to train and acclimatize newly arrived inductees to become infantry soldiers destined for service and combat in South Vietnam.

With both basic and advanced infantry training at Fort Polk, specifically designed for service in Southeast Asia, the base became known as "Tigerland." Over the next several years, more soldiers were sent to Vietnam from Fort Polk than from any other American training facility.

Fort Polk – Joint Readiness Training Center Patch

Tigerland was a part of the Joint Readiness Training Center, so this is where I would spend my first eight weeks in the U.S. Army.

CHAPTER 4

You're a Soldier Now

WHILE WAITING FOR MY ride to 5th Group Headquarters, I once again thought about the recruiter who had enlisted me and wondered if he truly believed that the OCS test would be *no problem*. Or, with Vietnam-era enlistment quotas to meet, I pondered the question—*could he have simply been a slick salesman in a nice-looking well-pressed green uniform?* The answer was of little consequence at that point. But I clearly remembered my arrival at the reception center. It was there that I took off my civilian clothes and put on the OD (olive-drab) green Army uniform for the first time.

When I woke to the shifting gears of the Greyhound bus, the morning sun was just beginning to break through the tall trees that filled the swamp along the eastern side of the road. Spanish moss hung from almost every tree and diffused the sunlight into hundreds of golden beams of light that fell throughout the swamp. It made the still water glisten and illuminated early rising swamp critters. Turtles lined logs and tall cranes waded in shallow water searching for an early breakfast.

The swamp was still visible as far as the eye could see on both sides of the road, almost until the moment our convoy of buses passed through the main gates of the U.S. Army's Joint Readiness Training Center in southeast

Louisiana. As we continued on our way to the reception station, the fellow sitting next to me pointed to a sign. It read *FORT POLK, the birthplace of the infantry soldier.* Seemingly, I was about to be reborn in— "Tigerland."

When we arrived at the reception station, the birthing process and in-processing began immediately. Individual identities dissolved as heads were shaved and the identical OD green uniforms were distributed. In-processing also included the standard battery of Army tests and, among them, my promised OCS test.

My new GI (Government Issued) haircut didn't bother me a bit. After all, they gave one to Elvis when he joined the Army years earlier. And, the poorly fitted fatigues didn't bother me quite so much when the OCS test scores were posted and I found the word "Passed" beside my name. My trust in the recruiter was immediately confirmed, or maybe, restored. I'm not sure which.

Before reporting to OCS, though, I was told that it would be necessary for me to complete both Basic and Advanced Infantry Training. That would be a total of at least sixteen weeks. The recruiter hadn't told me about this requirement. I could have been in flight school in twelve weeks. Since no one had forced my decision, I was content to stay on the ground and began Basic Training at Fort Polk.

As thoughts of Basic continued to race by in rerun, I remembered what a change of pace the first few days in the Army were for all of us, then referred to as *Trainees.*

For me, the difference between civilian life and the military was nearly immeasurable. Basic Training was every new trainee's first taste of military life, a life devoid of any feminine touches. The United States Army certainly wasn't coed then and I couldn't even recall seeing a girl before my first night on the town in Leesville, Louisiana, and that wasn't until weeks after training had begun. However, before that first hint of relief from an exhaustive training schedule was to occur, we would be exposed to a profusion of new sights, sounds, and experiences.

Some of those first new sights, sounds, and experiences my fellow trainees and I encountered were all found in the form of some truly unique individuals. They looked strange in their flat-brimmed hats and reminded me a little of Smokey the Bear. They were often loud, frequently degrading, and added many unexpected new twists to the art of education. Those individuals were called DIs (Drill Instructors) and they possessed an unusual combination of qualities and skills.

Drill Instructors were a lot like having your mother, a teacher, and a warden all rolled into one physical presence. It was a frightening concept and, at first, they seemed to be doing their very best to intimidate all of us. Later, though, I came to another conclusion about their true purpose.

To this day, I remember the first DI I met, Sergeant Frederick E. Register. Sergeant Register presented himself in a crisply starched uniform and had his Smokey the Bear hat tilted slightly forward on his head. He was solidly built with a triangular frame and a matching angular jaw. His demeanor suggested that he was a no-nonsense kind of guy.

When he introduced himself to me and a few other early arrivals on our first full day at Basic Training unit, E 1-1, he informed us that he would begin teaching us *the fine art of military movement*—marching.

Sergeant Register was only a step or two away from me as he sounded out his cadence of, "Left, right, left . . . your left, right, left."

Whenever I was out of step, he would rush to within about six inches from my ear, maybe closer, and would scream at the top of his lungs, "Your left, son! Your left!" If I didn't immediately pick up the step, he'd yell, "Your other left, son! Your other left!" When I laughed at his new and unusual teaching method, he acted as though he'd been struck crazy and, then, I'd do push-ups. Push-ups were considered a form of punishment that would also build a trainee's body. So, there was a method to what seemed like madness. In time, fairly short order, I learned not to laugh, and—I learned to march.

Despite their yelling and often abrasive demands for discipline, I didn't dislike or have any problems with the DI's. Their task of turning, sometimes highly undisciplined, civilians into soldiers was a daunting job, and recognizably, not an easy one.

The DIs in charge of my training company seemed to be very dedicated men who liked what they were doing. As a result, I came to like and feel close to a couple of them, particularly my own platoon's DI, Sergeant Calderin. He was a big Latin man, from Puerto Rico I believe, who didn't look or act like one but had the first name of Angel.

On the night before graduation ceremonies, Sergeant Calderin took me and a couple of other trainees to town for beer. He said it was a graduation celebration and all evening he acted as though he knew something we didn't.

Some of the trainees had a difficult time with the DI's and their new Army life. The ones who had the toughest time at Basic were those who had been drafted and truly didn't want to be in the Army. It was my opinion that a few of them thought the DI's were trying to *break* them. A couple of the trainees reacted by becoming defiant—and regretted it. The others became determined and survived the training.

For me, the training that took place at all times of the day and night and under all kinds of weather conditions was exciting, amusing, and challenging. We hadn't joined or been drafted into a peace-time Army, this one was fully engaged in the real preparation for combat. It was clearly understood that any or all of us could eventually see duty in Vietnam. For me, it was a certainty because I planned to volunteer for duty in Southeast Asia. That realization was motivation enough for most of us to pay very close attention to everything we were being taught. It seemed to be a common-sense thing to become as well trained as possible and give myself every chance of returning from the war—alive.

Basic was also an endurance test. I could easily remember how tiring the training had been. On some days, we returned to the barracks so exhausted and worn out that we were quickly asleep as soon as falling into our bunks. Training on any given day could consist of an array of military topics including such things as marksmanship, demolitions, hand-to-hand combat, bayonets, pugil sticks, chemicals and gases, first aid, physical training, and much more. We ran and crawled under, over, around, and through all descriptions of obstacles. On one very memorable night, we crawled under a line of machine guns that were firing live ammunition. About every fifth round out of the machine gun was a red tracer round. The tracers caused the ground to glow an eerie red color as they streaked overhead. There were rumors, which I never believed, that someone panicked on a similar training exercise and had been killed when he stood up. True or not, for that reason, the sound of the machine guns and glow of the tracers were an exhilarating, heart-pumping experience. I loved it all! It was like being able to go to a very exciting adult amusement park—for free.

Finally, though, at the end of nearly eight weeks, the experience was almost over. The only thing left was the proficiency test. The test involved both written and hands-on testing to evaluate every new soldier's proficiency in the military skills taught during the past many weeks. To graduate, everyone in our two hundred twenty-two-man training company was required to take and pass the series of "proficiency" tests. If you failed, you repeated Basic Training.

On graduation day, we were all glad that Basic Training was over. But, as we fell into formation for the graduation ceremony, I felt different than when I arrived. Some of the physical differences, like a thinner and more muscular body, were obvious. But there were other mental differences, changes more difficult to articulate. While I wasn't quite sure what those differences were, it was certain I had begun to change in many ways.

During the graduation ceremony certificates and trophies were awarded for various achievements during training. The last trophy was for the highest score on the Proficiency Test. That was one I felt sure would go to one of the college grads.

Due to the draft during the Vietnam War era, it was not unusual for basic training units to have college graduates in them. There was at least one in ours who also had a graduate degree. Most of those guys, unlike me, were fortunate to have had OCS guaranteed.

When the results of the Proficiency Test and Highest Score Award were announced, I was watching one of my platoon-mates coming down off the platform with his trophy. So, I was distracted when the name was announced over the old loudspeakers that squealed, crackled, or popped with nearly every word that reverberated through them.

"Ross," the guy standing next to me said.

"What?"

"That's you, buddy."

"What's me?"

"The CO just said your name. Go get your trophy, man!"

I was sure he was just taunting me until I heard the Company's Commanding Officer, Captain Graciani, announce my name again.

It may have been a small event in the scheme of things, but I certainly felt proud when the trophy was placed in my hands. My proficiency scores had been the highest in the company. Consequently, they had won me a promotion from "Private Nobody" to "Private E2," one rank higher than Private Nobody. And, I had also won an appointment to one of the Army's Leadership Preparation schools. That was exciting news to me.

Graduation day from Basic Training was memorable and it marked a very important point in my life—the point at which I discovered focus.

It was my award that Sergeant Calderin had known about the night before when he took us to town to celebrate. He was a very good man who I believe was extremely dedicated to his job. He seemed at least as proud of my achievements as I did.

When I left Fort Polk, I realized that Sergeants Calderin and Register, and the other DI's had sent me away from Basic Training with more than a trophy, a promotion, and an appointment to a leadership school. They had sent me away with not only confidence in the newly acquired basic military skills they all helped teach me, but also greater confidence in myself.

Some had accused DIs of simply trying to *break* trainees and their screaming nose-to-nose confrontations had made that believable in the beginning. But, by the end of the training, I had a very different opinion. It was clear, at least to me, that their aggressive, abrasive tactics were simply methods to instill the discipline military service would require. They had a hell of a job with tremendous responsibilities and I believe that they all knew that most of the young men they trained would one day end up in Vietnam.

After packing my duffle bag, I walked out of the side door of the barracks to catch the bus that would take me to the airport. I had a two-week leave before having to report to leadership school and was looking forward to seeing my family.

As I started down the barracks steps, I noticed the massive presence of Sergeant Angel Calderin standing at the bottom. He smiled and seemed to be waiting for me. When I reached the last step, he extended his hand and said, “Congratulations Private E2 Ross . . . you’re a soldier now. Take good care of yourself.”

I was now an official member of Uncle Sam’s Army Infantry. It wasn’t much and it wasn’t far, but it was a start and I was proud of it.

Infantry Branch Insignia

Crossed Rifles

Later, after being commissioned, I would wear these crossed rifles of the infantry on my uniform collar until exchanging them for the Special Forces crossed arrows.

"Leadership"

Before going to a "leadership school," I thought I should be prepared when I got there. I wasn't sure what was going to be taught, but I felt I needed to know something about the subject and what others thought about leadership. So, I went to a bookstore and looked for a book on leadership. A woman at the store suggested a book of quotes on leadership by people who had left a mark in history.

The following are just a few of the quotes that held meaning for me.

He who has never learned to obey cannot be a good commander. —Aristotle

Anyone can hold the helm when the sea is calm. —Publilius Syrus

I am not afraid of an army of lions led by a sheep, but I am afraid of an army of sheep led by a lion. —Alexander the Great

If your actions inspire others to dream more, learn more, do more, and become more, you are a leader. —John Quincy Adams

A good leader inspires people to have confidence in the leader, a great leader inspires people to have confidence in themselves. —Eleanor Roosevelt

Leadership is the art of getting someone else to do something you want done because he wants to do it. —General Dwight Eisenhower

Leadership and learning are indispensable to each other. —John F. Kennedy

And, this one was my personal favorite.

Lead me, follow me, or get out of my way. — General George Patton

---

While I loved General Patton's quote, I decided to follow JFK's suggestion. When I arrived at the leadership school, I was prepared to listen and learn.

CHAPTER 5

Taking the Lead

THE LEADERSHIP PREPARATION SCHOOL to which I had been assigned was located in Fort Ord, California. There were only thirty students in the class and, while training lasted only two weeks, it was intense. As had been the case at Basic, I thoroughly involved myself in the training to learn anything and everything that might help me survive whatever experiences were yet to come my way.

After only the first few days at the school, it became more apparent that positive things were happening to me since joining the service. With each passing day, the nature of change and how it was affecting me became clearer. The qualities of decisiveness and focus were replacing the indecision that had marked my college days. And, as they developed, they were making me more confident and determined in my military skills.

Awareness of my evolution made me feel good and I vowed to make the evolving changes permanent.

A key part of leadership training that is still easy to recall involves a day spent at a unique obstacle course dealing with problem-solving. I would have paid for the opportunity to enter the course because, again, it was like going to an amusement park for grownups. That day took place near the end of our first week of training.

Our class bus entered a large fenced-in complex where there were ten or twelve individual obstacle or problem areas. As soon we were off the bus, the class was quickly divided into five six-man groups. Then, each group was assigned a different beginning problem that they were expected to solve. At each problem, a student would be selected as the "Leader" of his team. All the problems were unique, but each involved a realistic battlefield scenario. After an allotted amount of time, each group would rotate to a new and different problem until each student had a turn at leading a problem.

There were catwalks around and/or over the various problems. The catwalks were used by school instructors with clipboards who would grade each student leader. Each leader knew he was being observed and graded, so the heat to perform well—was on.

When my group of six arrived at our first problem, a student leader was selected, thankfully, I wasn't the first.

Then, the instructor for that particular problem read a scenario. Essentially, each problem was a giant puzzle that had to be solved. It's been over fifty years since I attended the school, so I will simply provide a "for example" description of a typical problem, based on memory.

On one problem we were faced with a wooden structure that was painted white with a few key areas painted red. The structure represented a row of blown out-buildings. We were told that the red areas were contaminated with radioactive fallout and couldn't be touched. If they were touched by a team member, that member would be considered dead and would be removed from the problem and no longer allowed to help. Then, there were areas on the ground that were painted yellow, these areas represented minefields. The results for team members touching yellow areas were the same as for the red areas. There were several other hazards noted, then we were presented with the overall problem to be solved.

In the case of this problem, we were told that there was a large enemy ammunition depot located on the other side of the structure. We were then told that our team was carrying demolitions and our mission was to cross the structure and destroy the ammunition depot. If we could cross the structure in time with our demolitions and destroy the depot, the enemy would be prevented from distributing ammunition to its units. If we were successful, several allied units would be saved and the battle won and—the problem solved.

To make each problem a bit more interesting, several miscellaneous items could be found lying around on the ground. For instance, there might be boards of various sizes, pieces of pipe, a length of chain, a bucket or a barrel, a length of rope, tubing, wire, and similar items. One or more of these things might help solve the problem while others were there simply as distractions.

Once the scenario was read, the instructor would ask the leader if he had any questions. After his questions had been answered, if he had any, the instructor said "Go!" and pressed the button on a stopwatch.

Once the exercise started, the leader would begin the task of solving the problem. He would quickly assess the situation and immediately begin giving his team directions.

The problems were often more complicated than the one I described. And, for those that seemed to have a straightforward solution, the actual execution of a solution could be very difficult.

Our team failed to complete any of the first four problems, but we came within a couple of minutes or less on the last two.

When we moved to problem number five, my name was called as the leader. It was my turn and—I was ready.

I realized that we had gotten close to solving the last two problems only after the leaders became frustrated and either began listening to suggestions offered by fellow team members or they outright asked for suggestions.

It occurred to me that because the school was a "leadership" school, each man might believe that, if he were the leader, he was expected to come up with a plan and solve the problem on his own. And later, several of my classmates told me that was exactly what they believed. And, that seemed a logical assumption.

Since we had been given no information about how the exercises were scored or leadership evaluated, I had absolutely no clue what instructors were looking for. But solving the problem seemed to be a fairly important aspect of each exercise, so I decided to try a different strategy. As I considered my plan, I mused—*What can they do . . . throw me out of the Army or keep me a private forever for not being a good leader?*

After I stepped to the front of our team, the instructor read the problem to me. When he finished, he asked, "Do you have any questions?"

I held up my index finger as if he should "wait one" (abbreviated military jargon for—*Give me a minute*) and I immediately turned to my team asking, "Does anyone have a question?"

There were three or four very good questions and I had a couple of my own. After our questions had been answered, the instructor said, "Go!" and started his stopwatch—we were on the clock!

Quickly, I turned back to my team and asked, "Who has a solution for the problem? If you have one give it to me quickly." Nearly every man had a suggestion and some were better than others. As soon as I had heard each, I said, "Great ideas! We're going to do this, that, and this." Combining some excellent suggestions from my team members with ideas of my own, we solved the problem in what the instructor claimed was record time.

No, I wasn't a genius or a wizard in solving complex military problems. But—I had been observant.

The night before graduation, I was walking back to the barracks after dinner when I heard my name called. It was the school's commanding officer, a captain whose name I have forgotten. He walked over to me and said, "I've been looking for you."

Oh, God . . . what have I done? I wondered.

Then, he continued, "I don't usually tell anyone in advance, but I want you to know that at tomorrow morning's graduation ceremony you will be awarded the class 'Honor Graduate' trophy. The reason I'm telling you this is because I have a question for you."

"Yes, sir?" I responded.

He then posed his question, "I wonder if you know why you are receiving this award?"

I wanted to give him a thoughtful response, so I considered his question for a moment. Then, responding, I told him that after all my training was complete, I intended to volunteer for service in Vietnam. I explained that, for that reason, I had studied very hard and tried to learn all that I could. "For me, it's all very simple, sir. I want to make it back home from Vietnam," I said, finishing with, "So, I know my grades were good."

"Yes, your grades were excellent. You had the highest academic score in the class, but there's another very important reason," he said. "Do you remember the day at the obstacle course complex?"

When I said that I did, he explained that the school had been instituted to teach good leadership practices to both soldiers new to the service as well as those already in the service who were in or about to assume leadership positions. The intention was that graduates of the school would go on to accept greater leadership responsibilities as they continued their military service. The captain continued saying, "That day at the obstacle course, you used all of the resources available to you. And, besides your initiative, one of the most important resources available to you was your team members. And, you used them very effectively. If you learn from your time here and continue to perform as you did here, I have little doubt that you will return from Vietnam."

He finished his remarks by saying, "Your records indicate that you are going to OCS. So, as one officer to a future officer, I want to wish you good luck, Ross." With that, he offered me his hand.

Some have served who found their time in the military to be difficult and distasteful. For me, the experience had been tough at times and always strict but supportive from the first day I enlisted. There was no requirement for the CO of the leadership school to so seek me out and encourage me—but he did. And, his few moments of encouragement were worthwhile and very much appreciated because, as you can see, I have not forgotten them. As I consider that brief encounter now, years later, it seems to me that the CO was the right man for the position he held.

Trained and Ready to Serve

This is how I was dressed as I stood on the runway apron in Nha Trang waiting for my ride to 5th Group Headquarters, musing about all the things I had experienced since joining the military. I was in Cam Rahn Bay and this picture was taken just before I boarded the helicopter that took me to Nha Trang.

When you read about what happened after I was picked up and on the way to Group Headquarters, keep in mind that this is how I was dressed. And, as you can see, I was unarmed—something that would become a serious disadvantage.

CHAPTER 6

AIT and Kowalski

THE PROMOTION PAPERS, CERTIFICATES, and trophies I had won since entering the Army were spread out on my bunk as I packed. They were satisfying to look at and I was proud to have them. But I had the presence of mind to know they wouldn't keep me alive in Vietnam—I hoped the training would.

From the leadership school, the others and I who were destined for OCS moved to a different part of Fort Ord for what we expected to be eight weeks of AIT (Advanced Infantry Training). Upon reporting at our respective AIT companies, we were assigned to various leadership positions because of the training that we had just completed. My assignment was Trainee Platoon Leader, a position that led and coordinated various aspects of training for a platoon-size unit (about 32 men) of one of the training companies, Company E 2-2.

When training began, as its name suggested, it was more advanced in every regard. Besides the training, my clearest memory of AIT centered on one private nobody, Howard Kowalski.

The episode with Kowalski began one evening after training. We had barely passed a week in AIT training. I was going over the next day's training schedule when an office clerk from the company headquarters came in and said the CO needed to see me.

When I walked into the headquarters office the clerk said the CO was on the phone, but wanted to see me as soon as I arrived. While I waited, I noticed a trainee with a packed duffel bag sitting in a chair next to the CO's door. He was a big guy and sat expressionless staring at the floor. Suspecting that he was a new man to be assigned to the company, I greeted him, "Hello, . . . how are you?"

There was absolutely no response. He didn't even look up at me.

Just then, the CO emerged from his office.

"Good evening, sir," I said, snapping a salute to the CO.

"Good evening, Ross. Come in and have a seat."

"Yes, sir."

Settling back into his leather chair, the CO folded his arms across his chest and began, "Ross, I've got a problem and want you to help me with it."

"Yes, sir. I'll do anything I can."

"I know that. That's the reason you're here. Your CO over at Leadership said you were the person we needed for this job. Ross, they've just transferred a disciplinary case into us from another unit."

"Yes, sir. Let me guess . . . he's sitting outside your door right now."

"That's him. His name is Howard Kowalski and, now . . . he's yours. We're transferring him into your platoon."

"Fine, sir. What do you want me to do with him?"

"Here's the situation. He's been transferred a couple of times for fighting and causing problems. He's been given many opportunities to get with the program, but this is his last chance. If he doesn't make it this time, he'll be deemed unfit for the military and will be booted out of the service."

"I see."

"So, I want you to take him with you when you leave. The first time he gets into a fight or screws up, he's gone. It's that simple. Can you deal with it?"

"Yes, sir."

"Fine, then . . . he's yours. Go get him and take him with you."

"I'll take care of it, sir."

I got up, saluted, and went to collect my new trainee. As I passed through the CO's door, "Come on Kowalski. You belong to me now."

He didn't utter a word, but slowly reached for his duffel bag and, as he stood, I glanced at the name tag on his field jacket. I was checking the spelling of his last name so that I could add it to my roster. It was then that I noticed there was something different about his field jacket.

Did he do that on purpose as some particular act of defiance or simply as a gesture of nonconformity? I wondered.

"Kowalski, did you do that . . . or did the seamstress do it when she put the tags on your jacket?" I asked.

"Do what . . .?" he queried in a deep contemptuous monotone.

"Come on . . . don't tell me no one else has said something to you."

"About what . . .?" his irritation now growing with my seeming harassment.

"Your name tag . . . it's on the wrong side of your jacket. You've got U.S. ARMY where your name tag should be . . . and your name where the U.S. Army should be."

"Oh, yea . . . "Kowalski responded, obviously aware of the mistake. No, . . . they did that on their own. I guess it was their way to say they didn't want me here."

"Who . . . the seamstresses didn't want you here?" I said, challenging his set-upon attitude.

"No, not her . . . the Army."

Such was my introduction to Private Howard Kowalski who seemed destined for nothing but trouble and, ultimately, separation from the Army. Hoisting his duffel bag up over his shoulder, he followed me across the street to our platoon barracks. I looked back once as we walked and noticed that he towered over me like a huge angry grizzly bear.

And they gave him to me, I thought.

Frequently, I tried to engage him in conversation, but Kowalski didn't say much the next couple of days as if resigned to a brief career in the Army. He never smiled and remained generally expressionless, except to occasionally give someone an intimidating glare. But then came the day—he exploded!

We had just come back from training and in the process of putting gear away, someone accidentally hit Kowalski with a backpack. I heard the commotion and went running to see what was happening. By the time I got to the center of the activity, Kowalski had another trainee pinned to the floor with one hand while the other hand was around his throat.

Grabbing the hand that was around the trainee's throat, I yelled, "Let him up!"

When he didn't respond, I jerked his arm and again demanded, "I said . . . let him up!"

Well, that action got a response. Kowalski jumped up, pulled his arm back, and squared off at me. There was total silence as Kowalski just stood there looking down at me with his fist clenched and his arm cocked.

I reached down and pulled the other guy up off the floor.

"Are you okay?" I asked.

"Yea, I'm okay. I didn't mean to hit him with the pack. Damn! It was just an accident Kowalski," rubbing his neck as he walked back to his bunk.

Turning back to Kowalski, "So, are you going to hit me or what Kowalski?" I asked.

Slowly, he relaxed and let his arm fall to his side.

"Good," I said, "Come on . . . let's go visit in my room. You just won a ticket home."

On the way back to my room, one of my squad leaders asked, "Do you want me to come with you?"

"No, let's see where it goes. But if you think you hear him pounding my head against the wall, you may want to come check on me."

He smiled and said, "Okay. I will."

When we got to my room, I sat on my footlocker and had Howard sit in a chair. There was no chance that I expected the scenario about to unfold.

"So, do you want out of the Army? Is that what this is about, Kowalski?"

Again, absolutely no response and he just stared at the floor.

"Kowalski, give me some sign that you hear my voice. If you want out, I will take care of it for you right now. That's why they sent you to me. Believe me, if you truly don't want out . . . I am your very last chance to stay in. But, if you do want out, you don't have to fight, you don't have to do anything else. Just tell me you want out and I'll go to the CO's office right now."

His head was hung and there was no suggestion of a response.

"Kowalski, do you want out?!"

As he lifted his face to look at me, I couldn't believe what I saw. Tears were streaming down the face of this big tough guy.

"No . . . I can't get out. I have to stay in . . . I have to take care of my grandmother. She depends on the money I send her. I'm the only person she has to take care of her . . . and she's the one who wanted me in the Army. She thought it would keep me out of trouble."

"Well, she missed on that bet, didn't she?"

"Yea, I guess she did."

Kowalski wiped the tears from his face obliquely as if they had never been there. But, at that moment, he looked as if he carried the weight of the world on his shoulders.

"So, Howard . . . can I call you, Howard?"

"Yea, sure."

"So, Howard . . . what do we do now?"

"Punish me. Do whatever you need to do . . . but, please, don't let them throw me out of the Army."

"I don't know Howard . . . it might be too late."

"But you don't understand. I grew up in Hell's Kitchen in New York. I had to fight all the time just to survive."

Then, for the next hour, Howard Kowalski poured his guts out. His had been an extremely difficult life except for the grandmother who had raised him and loved him.

After listening to his story, I could almost feel Kowalski's inner pain. I'm not sure I could have survived what he had lived through. But, more important, I better understood his difficulty in adjusting to a strictly disciplined military life.

"Okay. Howard . . . here's where we are. What happened this evening . . . can never happen again. You'll need to go apologize to the guy you just tried to choke to death. If he accepts your apology, then we're back on level ground. But if something like this does happen again, I won't be able to save you. Do you understand?"

"Yea," he grunted.

I continued, "And, Howard, you will have to become a model soldier. But, my promise to you is this . . . if you keep your nose clean and train hard, I'll stick with you and I'll help you. I won't let them throw you out. But, stumble just once and . . ."

"Yea, I know. I'm gone. Right?"

"You've got it."

"O.K. . . . that's fair," he said, "Thank you. I'll straighten up . . . and that's a promise."

"Good, I hope so. I'd truly like to see you make it, Howard."

As he got up to leave my room, I said, "Howard, do me a favor. Go over to Supply and ask the seamstress to switch your name tag. It's making me crazy."

For the first time, he smiled and said, "Yea, okay. I'll do it as soon as you give me the time to go."

Sure enough, Howard was true to his commitment. I don't believe I've ever seen such a dramatic change in anyone in such a short period. The very next morning, Howard was the first person in formation. When I walked out it was still pitch-black dark, but there he stood—all by himself.

As everyone else began to fall into formation, I walked to my usual position in front of the platoon. On the way, I passed Howard. As I walked by him, I heard him mutter in a low voice, "I told you I'd straighten up."

I looked back at him, smiled—and took my position.

Three weeks later, my OCS orders arrived. With little more than four of my eight-week AIT training program complete, the orders directed me to report to the Infantry School at Fort Benning, Georgia, where my class was being formed.

Two days later, I was gone. But when I left, Howard Kowalski had turned himself into the model soldier he had promised to become. In fact, he had been promoted and was wearing the armband of a trainee squad leader.

Officer Candidate School

OCS would be the next phase of military training for me and it was both an opportunity and an experience I had looked forward to since enlisting. However, within days of reporting, my career with the U.S. Army was very nearly ended when I shouted an unorthodox command to my training company.

Military Class Picture — AIT at Fort Ord

This was our AIT training platoon. I am holding the "guidon" to the right of our training staff corporal who is wearing a black helmet. Kowalski is also in the picture. He was assigned to the platoon just a couple of days earlier. He's easy enough to find even though the picture is relatively small—Howard is the one with the emotionless scowl on his face.

Howard Kowalski had grown up on the mean streets of New York City and he brought the "mean" with him when he joined the service. Howard and the U.S. Army were at war when I first met him in 1966. Fortunately, his was a truly remarkable transformation and I was honestly very happy for him—in the end, Howard had made peace with the Army.

Chapter 7

I am the Infantry!

TO UNDERSTAND THE ENERGY with which I and other young Army officers would enter the Vietnam war, you need to continue with me through the training that we would receive in preparation for that day.

During our first days at OCS, our class, along with a couple of others, was taken to Infantry Hall for a unique stage production. In 1966, Infantry Hall was the center of activity at Fort Benning and its theater was impressive. Once everyone was seated, lights slowly dimmed until the theater was dark, dramatic music rose in the background, and a deep distinctive voice began to recite a dramatic reading of the poem, "I am the Infantry!"

As the unseen reader continued to recite the poem, theatrical lighting illuminated portions of the stage in deep colors. Then actors, mostly in silhouette, began to reenact the poem as it was read.

"I am the Infantry" is a poem chronicling the U.S. Army's Infantry history from the nation's founding until today. It was written by Lieutenant Colonel Stephen H. White in 1955.

While I can't adequately describe the stage production as stirringly and dramatically as it occurred, I can share the poem as it was read in 1966. It begins on the following page.

I am the Infantry—Queen of Battle!

For two centuries I have kept our Nation safe,
purchasing freedom with my blood.
To tyrants, I am the day of reckoning;
to the suppressed, the hope for the future.
Where the fighting is thick, there am I.
I am the Infantry! — FOLLOW ME!

I was there from the beginning,
meeting the enemy face to face, will to will.
My bleeding feet stained the snow at Valley Forge;
my frozen hands pulled Washington across the Delaware.
At Yorktown, the sunlight glinted from the sword,
and I begrimed . . . saw a Nation born.
Hardship . . . and glory I have known.
At New Orleans, I fought beyond the hostile hour,
showed the fury of my long rifle . . . and came of age.
I am the Infantry! — FOLLOW ME!

Westward I pushed with wagon trains . . .
moved an empire across the plains . . .
extended freedom's borders and tamed the wild frontier.
I am the Infantry! — FOLLOW ME!

I was with Scott at Vera Cruz . . .
hunted the guerilla in the mountain passes . . .
and scaled the high plateau.
The fighting was done when I ended my march
many miles from the old Alamo.

From Bull Run to Appomattox, I fought and bled.
Both Blue and Gray were my colors then.
Two masters I served and united them strong . . .
proved that this nation could right a wrong . . . and long endure.
I am the Infantry! FOLLOW ME!
I led the charge up San Juan Hill . . .
scaled the walls of old Tientsin . . .
and stalked the Moro in the steaming jungle still . . .
always the vanguard, I am the Infantry!

At Chateau-Thierry, first over the top,
then I stood like a rock on the Marne.
It was I who cracked the Hindenburg Line . . .
in the Argonne, I broke the Kaiser's spine . . .
and didn't come back 'till it was "over, over there."
I am the Infantry! FOLLOW ME!

A generation older at Bataan, I briefly bowed,
but then I vowed to return.
Assaulted the African shore . . .
learned my lesson the hard way in the desert sands . . .
pressed my buttons into the beach at Anzio and bounced into Rome with determination and resolve. I am the Infantry!

The English Channel, stout beach defenses
and the hedgerows could not hold me . . .
I broke out at St. Lo, unbent the Bulge . . .
vaulted the Rhine . . . and swarmed the Heartland.
Hitler's dream and the Third Reich were dead.

In the Pacific, from island to island . . .
hit the beaches and chopped through swamp and jungle . . .
I set the Rising Sun. I am the Infantry!

In Korea, I gathered my strength around Pusan . . .
swept across the frozen Han . . .
outflanked the Reds at Inchon . . .
and marched to the Yalu. FOLLOW ME!

Around the world, I stand . . . ever forward.
Over Lebanon's sands, my rifle steady aimed . . . and calm returned.
At Berlin's gates, I scorned the Wall of Shame.
I am the Infantry! FOLLOW ME!

My bayonet...on the wings of power . . .
keeps the peace worldwide.
And despots, falsely garbed in freedom's mantle, falter . . . hide.
My ally in the paddies and the forest . . .
I teach, I aid, I lead. FOLLOW ME!

Where brave men fight . . . there fight I.
In freedom's cause . . . I live, I die.
From Concord Bridge to Heartbreak Ridge,
from the Arctic to the Mekong . . . the Queen of Battle!
Always ready...then, now, and forever . . .
I am the Infantry! FOLLOW ME!

How could any young American be exposed to such a piece and not be inspired to serve our country? Especially, a group of young men hoping to become infantry leaders.

When the production at Infantry Hall ended, lights in the theater came back on to the thunderous applause of hundreds of Army officer candidates. At that moment, every candidate seemed ready to find an enemy to defeat.

The production of "I am the Infantry" had certainly moved me. I couldn't wait to become a part of the tradition the poem represented. I hoped I could live up to what my father, grandfather, and great-grandfather had done.

The next chapter describes my arrival at OCS and significant experiences there in more detail. Before arriving, I expected the training to be exceptional and I was determined to learn as much as I could. What I didn't expect was having my spirit stirred by my experiences there. And, you just read one of the ways that was accomplished by the Infantry School.

Next Stop — Home of the Infantry

Camp Benning was founded in 1918 and the "Infantry School of Arms" was constructed. The camp was made a permanent installation and renamed Fort Benning in 1922.

The base was extremely active during World War II and it was during that period when the "Officer Candidate School" and the "Airborne Training Center" were established and opened at Fort Benning.

Since the end of World War II, Fort Benning remained highly active by promoting training, testing, and military demonstrations. I was about to become involved in all three—the training, testing, and would I witness many of those demonstrations.

"Iron Mike"

There are symbols and statues in many places around Fort Benning to inspire both leaders and soldiers. Above, is a statue called "Iron Mike" by many.

Officially titled, "Follow Me" this statue was one of the first things I noticed when I rode by Infantry Hall. The sculpture was created by two Army privates in 1959 and an OCS candidate served as their model for the piece.

The statue depicts a 1950s-era infantryman charging forward and gesturing for other soldiers to follow him into battle.

The two men who created the statue originally called it "The Infantryman" and it was first installed on Eubanks Field in 1960. Later, in 1964, it was moved to the front of Infantry Hall and was renamed "Follow Me." Students and staff at the Infantry School called the statue "Iron Mike," after Lieutenant General John W. "Iron Mike" O'Daniel. However, most soldiers use the term "Iron Mike" in reference to the "Airborne Trooper" statue at Fort Bragg, North Carolina. In only months, I would have the opportunity to see the other Mike.

Chapter 8

Follow Me!

IT WAS EXCITING TO finally be on my way to OCS, but it had been a little difficult to leave California. While there only about six weeks, I had made many friends and had been, more or less, adopted by the family of one of my fellow trainees. Almost every weekend until leaving, his family had invited me to spend time at their ranch in the mountains above Salinas. The ranch overlooked Monterey Bay and the view was magnificent. In the mornings, clouds over the Pacific Ocean often pushed their way in against the mountains. When the front door was opened, the clouds seemed to come right up to the base of the door—it looked like heaven. So, it wasn't easy to leave such a beautiful place and people who had been so kind to me.

OCS was yet another unique experience in what had become a series of such experiences. It would be six months of mental and physical training aimed at turning out an Infantry Officer in a relatively short period. My time at OCS would build on and refine things already learned and I looked forward to both the opportunity and training.

Still waiting for my ride to group headquarters, I reached up and felt the gold 2nd Lieutenant's bar on my collar. It was one given to me at OCS and was almost as hot as the runway asphalt. If the jeep didn't arrive soon, I was going to start looking for some shade, another ride, or begin walking.

Then, continuing to recall my days at OCS, one of my first memories of Fort Benning was of the day I arrived and saw the Infantry School's crest for the first time.

It wasn't long after passing through the gates of Fort Benning that my taxi dropped me off at my OCS class building. Outside, there was a sign that featured the Infantry School crest. The crest was a royal blue shield with the white "sword of leadership" in the center and, above the sword, were just two words. The crest appeared confident and noble, like something you might expect to find in King Arthur's court, where gallantry was ever-present.

As I continued to study the elegant, but uncomplicated crest, my focus returned to the two words above the sword. As I thought about their meaning, I began to realize that they and the crest represented a great deal of responsibility.

I was looking forward to becoming an officer, so for a moment, I considered the responsibility embodied in the Infantry School's crest and the two very simple, but powerful words. The two words, now full of meaning for me were—Follow Me.

On the day that 80th Company, Infantry Officer Candidate class number 10-67 began its first classes, few class members had any significant prior military experience. Less than six months earlier, most of us were working civilians, college students, or both.

At OCS, discipline, responsibility, and leadership were daily topics. With only six months to create a military officer out of individuals with little more than a few months of training, it was easy to understand why those topics were so important. It was also easy to understand the need for daily testing and pressure to perform. I had overheard one of the training officers telling a classmate that if a candidate (trainees were called *candidates*) couldn't keep up with the training, he would be—out. That was clear enough to me, so I made certain that I was never behind and, whenever possible, I tried to be ahead of the training.

The testing was indeed both mental and physical. It took many forms and could be thrust upon an individual or the group at any time. The most difficult test I faced at OCS occurred early in our training, during my three days as Candidate Company Commander. The incident very nearly cost me the opportunity to remain a part of the program.

Training had begun at a quick pace and became intense so quickly that, after only three weeks, nerves and tempers wore thin. There were occasional fights and un-tempered remarks exchanged in the barracks and on the various training fields. It seemed there was an ample supply of testosterone in class 10-67 and its presence was affecting morale negatively.

Sometime during the six months at OCS, each candidate was required to command the company of approximately one hundred eighty men for three days. During that period the candidate was evaluated for leadership and command qualities. The evaluation could weigh heavily on whether or not a candidate would be graduated and receive a commission as an officer.

As luck, or misfortune, would have it, I was selected for the next three-day command period. And, I knew that if the disruption which had been occurring continued, it would not speak well of my leadership or command ability. Something needed to be done to release the tension and pressure that had been so quickly built up. More pressure in the form of threats of discipline from me wasn't the answer in my opinion. There had to be another alternative and it needed to be discovered soon. The next day was my first day of command. And, it was also very nearly—my last.

As on the days prior, training on my first day was long and tiring. A couple of candidates were already talking about resigning. As I marched the company back to the barracks from training, another alternative occurred to me. However, I was concerned about how my plan to deal with the situation might be received by the company's Training Commander, Captain Wayne Byrd, and the six platoon training officers.

After considering the possibilities of their response, I decided that they would either see the intent of my action and approve or the opposite would be true and they might take disciplinary action against me. One thing was fairly certain, whatever the response, it wouldn't be mediocre. Either way, whether the response was positive or negative, I felt something of note had to be done. Otherwise, I might easily have been perceived and evaluated as *ineffective*. Well, I wasn't about to let that happen.

Follow Me! was our motto and, already, the expression, "Do something—even if it's wrong," was well known to all the candidates. So, I prepared to lead and do something, even if it turned out to be wrong.

As the company marched toward the barracks, the unit banner and the six-platoon guidon flags fluttered in the hot afternoon breeze and the chrome spear caps atop the guidons flashed in the bright Georgia afternoon sun.

When a change in the direction of march was required, I shouted a command which was echoed by all of the platoon leaders simultaneously. Then, the long green column would respond and the new direction was taken. I have to confess, marching the company to and from training was one of my favorite parts of my command period. My least favorite part was just about to occur.

Normally, when we reached the barracks my commands would form the company into a large 'U' shaped formation in the assembly area. The last command would be, "Company, halt!" the traditional military command to stop a moving unit of that size.

Instead, on that day, the command that echoed between the buildings when it rang out loud and clear was, "Hip, Hop . . . Company, stop!"

The command wasn't original, I had heard several of the other candidates laughing at lunch one day about the idea of someone actually using the command. It was the laughter generated by their discussion that had given me the idea. My thought was that some humor might be exactly what was needed to loosen things up a bit.

With the command still echoing in the closed quadrangle, I anticipated a couple of possible responses and waited for the fallout. But the actual results of my absurd command were remarkable and completely unexpected.

After the company halted in response to my command there was some spontaneous laughter and, then, utter silence. For a moment or two, maybe it was only a second or two, there wasn't a sound. The lack of sound made me think that maybe I was so scared that I had gone deaf. Still, without a sound in the air, I stood at rigid attention facing the company as I had early that morning—waiting. I didn't have to wait very long.

"Ross," shouted Captain Byrd, "What did you say!?" as though he couldn't believe what he had heard. "Do you think this is a joke!?"

"No, Sir!" I shouted as loud as possible. By the time I got those words out of my mouth he was looking at me face-to-face and his was very red. His eyes glared as if searching the very center of my soul.

"Are you crazy, Ross!? OCS was not established for your entertainment and amusement!"

Now, along with Captain Byrd, all six platoon training officers gathered around me, including my own platoon's Training Officer, 2nd Lieutenant Denton Eister. They were all ranting and raving. I could hear them saying things like, "This is serious, Ross!"— "You're in deep trouble, Ross!"— "You're out of here, Ross"— "What kind of a commander do you think you are!?"

Some used more expletives than others, but none seemed to recognize the intention of the command I had given. Amidst all the screaming, I wondered, *Have I made a really serious mistake?*

As things seemed to calm down, the commander stepped almost nose-to-nose with me and said, "Ross, I want to watch you do one hundred push-ups and I want to see you do them right now!"

I stepped back and got ready to drop down into a push-up position. As I did, I glanced down at the asphalt and it looked very hot. But, without saying a word, I continued down into the push-up position. Just as I began placing my hands, palms down, on the assembly area asphalt, which was indeed hot, I detected movement out of the corner of my eye. That's when the "remarkable" began to happen.

When I saw what the movement was, it very nearly made me forget about the heat beneath my hands as I began my hundred push-ups. My entire platoon, without direction, was dropping down to do push-ups with me.

The action of my fellow platoon members immediately drew the attention of the commander and the other training officers.

"What do you people think you are doing?!" Captain Byrd demanded. Outraged, he walked briskly to my platoon area. The others followed close on his heels to help fling at my platoon members the abuse that only moments before had been directed at me.

"Have you all lost your senses?" one of the training officers demanded. As the others joined in on the verbal assaults and while I continued doing my push-ups, I could see something new happening that I wouldn't have thought to wish for. All of the other platoons were dropping down to do push-ups with me and my platoon. Every candidate in the one hundred eighty-man company was doing push-ups.

When that happened, the screaming and abuse stopped and my push-ups became almost effortless. The sensation of hot asphalt under my hands seemed not so unpleasant.

My hundred pushups finished, I stood up and, again, assumed the position of attention. Captain Byrd stood with the tactical officers and they spoke among themselves until my classmates completed their push-ups. Then, Captain Byrd walked up in front of me and stopped at a normal distance.

"Candidate Ross!" he snapped.

"Yes, Sir!" was my reply as I waited for the punishment that was sure to come. But, instead of punishment, the "real" commander stared me straight in the eye and in a slow deliberate tone ordered, "Take command of your company."

Again, "Yes, Sir!" was my only reply as I responded with a crisp salute. Then, still looking me eye-to-eye, he took a half step closer to me. In a voice only loud enough for the two of us to hear, he said, "Ross, this is the first thing this company has accomplished as a team . . . luckily for you."

He returned my salute, turned, and marched away. As he left, I dismissed the company—very glad still to be a part of it.

When I first considered giving the absurd and highly inappropriate command, it was my hope the action would draw enough laughs to relieve some tension, as it had at lunch. I expected to be disciplined, possibly severely. But I believed the command would be a tension reliever and that, surely, with some explanation, Captain Byrd and his training officers would understand the purpose of what I had done. They were aware of the existence of a moral situation.

As it turned out, there was laughter, there was discipline, and there was relief, but no explanation had been necessary. My command period ended successfully because of the support of my fellow candidates.

Memories of my remaining time at OCS are far less dramatic. Most involve long challenging days of training and late nights studying.

Due to an intense schedule, the days, nights, weeks, and months of training seemed to pass fairly quickly. We trained at countless locations around Fort Benning in all types of weather and we attended innumerable classes in the field and at Infantry Hall on a surfeit of subjects including nuclear warfare. And, regardless of the time, location, weather, or class, we were rarely without frequent reminders of what would be expected of us as leaders and officers.

Finally, as the Fall of 1966 approached and the air turned cool, graduation became a not-too-distant possibility that glittered with thoughts of gold 2nd Lieutenants bars. At the same time, it became necessary for each candidate to choose the Army branch in which he wanted to serve. Some chose Armor, some Artillery, others selected MP's, but most chose Infantry.

Recently, though, a number of my classmates and I had been talking about a relatively new unit of the Army whose military tactics and techniques were supposed to be very different from those we'd been taught at OCS. The unit, which had captured the interest of and had been supported by John F. Kennedy, was called Special Forces.

Special Forces won President Kennedy's support because he believed it could be used as a means of combating guerrilla insurgencies, insurrection, and subversion in various locations around the world. With the ability to conduct unconventional warfare, the mission of Special Forces was to infiltrate by land, sea, or air deep into enemy-controlled territory. Then, from behind enemy lines, its members would organize, train, and direct indigenous personnel in the conduct of unconventional operations.

To attract individuals to the unit, which was an all-volunteer force, it was promoted and even romanced as the U.S.'s newest and most elite fighting force. The unit had been nicknamed the "Green Berets" because of the distinctive green headgear President Kennedy had authorized its members to wear. In addition to the beret, Special Forces had a morally noteworthy motto, "Free the Oppressed."

The unit, its mission, and its motto were all appealing to me and— where I wanted to be. But not for a superfluous reason, mine was more important and meaningful. Special Forces also touted its members to be the world's best-trained soldiers. That was the real attraction for me. Since I planned on serving in Vietnam, I wanted to be as well trained as possible.

However, when requesting more information and applications about Special Forces, some of us were told that it might be difficult for a 2nd Lieutenant to be accepted due to the number of applications from that level. Still determined to try, I asked a post recruiting sergeant if it would be possible to obtain the application forms anyway. "Yes, but obtaining the applications isn't going to be the problem and doesn't guarantee consideration," the sergeant told me.

When the application arrived, I read it very carefully. Toward the bottom, there were several blocks where a choice of duty station was requested. Some locations looked more like offerings by a travel agency than the military. But the very last entry was *Vietnam*, definitely not a tourist destination. Below *Vietnam,* there were two empty blocks into which the applicant was to write any choices of duty stations other than those listed.

Considering the application, it seemed to me there might be a way to, at least, have it considered. So, I began to fill it out.

Upon reaching the duty station choices, I checked the block marked *Vietnam*. And, in the two empty blocks beneath it, I wrote "Vietnam." Would it work? —who knew? But at least the effort had been made. I considered that they would either believe I was as committed as I truly was—or they would think I was nuts, a classic "Section VIII."

Within about ten days from the day the application had been turned in, my response came in my mail. Opening the envelope slowly, I wondered if my strategy had worked or if they had decided I was a mental case. But even before the one-page response was fully opened, the word "accepted" burst from the page. My application had been approved!

While I had been accepted for Special Forces training, it wasn't time to pack just yet. There were still a few weeks of OCS training and the formal graduation ceremony remaining.

When graduation day finally arrived, everyone still a part of the company was relieved that the six-month ordeal had finally come to an end. We were all looking forward to being commissioned as new 2nd Lieutenants. But, of the one hundred eighty men who started, only one hundred twenty would receive a commission.

Family members and friends had come from all over the country to attend graduation. The ceremony was held at Infantry Hall where families were given the opportunity to see the production of "I am the Infantry." For me, it was as stirring as the first time I saw it. Not surprisingly, even families and friends seemed moved by what they had seen.

When the stage production ended, diplomas were awarded and we were sworn in as new 2nd Lieutenants. After the traditional tossing of hats in the air, everyone went outside to find their families.

Outside Infantry Hall, I walked through the crowd of new lieutenants and family members looking for my own family. When I found them, I handed my new gold bars to my mother and grandmother who pinned them on. It was a proud day for all the new officers, their families, and their friends.

When my family left and I was alone back in the barracks, the pageantry and excitement of the day were tempered by thoughts of the responsibilities I had just accepted and the things I might be called upon to do. The already raging Vietnam War was escalating. I couldn't yet imagine the circumstances under which I might have to issue it, but I now felt extremely well trained, confident, and fully prepared to give the direction to, "Follow me!"

By the time of commissioning, I had evolved as a military man and personally changed a great deal. Lack of decisiveness was no longer a part of my character.

And, when I returned home and went back to college, I had a much greater appreciation of the important things in life, and education was one of them. I collected three separate degrees. Two were undergraduate, one was a Master's, I held membership in a national honor society and had graduated with honors—I had found focus.

After publishing the first edition of this book, I was invited to speak in many settings. I was interviewed on approximately sixty radio stations all across the country, those were exciting. But my favorite invitations were to in-person events where I could speak directly to and interact with the audience. And, of those, schools were a highlight because I could speak about finding *their* focus.

After explaining how dramatically finding focus had changed my life, I explained how important it was for them to do the same. When speaking to students now, I do the same thing and hope I've helped direct at least one student toward success.

Infantry School Crest

The Infantry School's motto is obviously "Follow Me," which simply means that a leader should be out in front of the troops—you don't lead from behind them.

Graduating from OCS under the shield of the Follow Me crest meant that I had been trained to lead. Confident that I had those skills, it became more important to me to have the courage to lead.

Asking other men to follow you into combat and giving that direction in such a way that those men jumped to their feet in preparation to follow the direction is a critically important skill for a leader to possess. But everyone needs to have the courage to face life's challenges, not just the leader.

As you have already learned, I have always been fond of quotes about some of the important aspects of life. They have given me inspiration when standing at a crossroad and a decision was required or when I faced a serious challenge and had to decide how to respond.

There are countless quotes on courage by many well-known individuals, such as Socrates, Aristotle, Napoleon Bonaparte, Winston Churchill, and many more. But, one of my favorites quotes comes from the man who created Tom Sawyer and Huckleberry Finn. Mark Twain was a character and a perfect example of classic Americana. About courage, he said, "Courage is resistance to fear, mastery of fear—not absence of fear."

In the next chapter, you will read about a young soldier who didn't let fear stop him. He recognized it, admitted it, resisted it, and continued through it to do what was expected of him. I witnessed his battle with fear, beginning to end. His courage inspired me and I have never forgotten our brief time together.

Fort Benning Parachute Training Towers

These are the parachute training towers at Fort Benning. In the next chapter, you will read about the day a young Army private and I were dropped from one of them in preparation to jump out an airplane door into a bright clear Georgia sky. Each tower was 250 feet high—we were lifted to the top of the tower, then released. This was another one of those times when I would have happily bought a ticket to be strapped into the parachute harness. It was great fun!

CHAPTER 9

The First Brave Man

NOW A COMMISSIONED OFFICER, it was time to begin work on what would become my specialty, unconventional warfare. That training would take place at Fort Bragg, North Carolina. However, before reporting for duty at the John F. Kennedy Center for Special Warfare, I was required to become parachute qualified. I would learn to leap from perfectly functioning aircraft right there at Fort Benning. So, the morning after OCS graduation, I packed my duffle bag and simply walked the short distance to the Jump School.

The next year of training would be far more intense than any I had yet experienced. But, before that training began, I would be given an unexpected opportunity to learn a very simple lesson in courage.

There were only a few things I recalled about Jump School. Most of it was just a blur of blue sky, white silk, hitting the ground, and rolling in the dirt. And, it was always a welcomed interruption when the white silk blocked a jumper's overhead view of the blue sky. That meant the parachute, which had been abruptly yanked from the pack on his back, had been successfully deployed. The rest was left to the laws of gravity and the wind.

One of the first thoughts that quickly sprang to mind regarding Jump

School was the recollection of my first look out the door of the airplane just before we jumped. It felt like my stomach had backed up against my spine and was trying to hold on to it. It was a long way down and to use a recognizable expression, people looked like ants. In reality, they looked smaller than ants to me.

The other memory was a warm one and revolved around a young Army Private who distinguished himself in my mind on the first day we met. His name, one of the only foggy parts of the encounter, was Gomez. While there is some uncertainty regarding his name, there is no uncertainty that he was the first of many brave people who would cross my path during my time in the military.

The encounter with Private Gomez occurred on the day of our first parachute training jump, the same day that my stomach discovered my spine. It was a winter day in Georgia, the sky was clear, very blue, and very cold. It was a perfect day for our first jump they told us.

Exiting the hanger where we had donned our parachute equipment, we could see and hear the planes that were to carry us aloft. They were lined up on the runway apron with their huge prop engines already spinning.

We approached the planes in single file formations called "sticks." I, other officers, and some senior enlisted men had been assigned as "Stick Leaders." That required each of us to lead one of the sticks onto a pre-designated jump aircraft. When we boarded, my position as Stick Leader would also place me first in line to jump when we reached jump altitude.

As we continued walking along the runway, my position at the front of the stick did have an advantage, it provided an unobstructed view of the airfield. I watched the reflection of the bright morning sun run along the smoothly curved edges on one of the big silver planes. When we got nearer to them, I pointed toward ours. We filed through the hot engine exhaust and walked up onto the plane where we sat on webbed canvas seats.

In only moments, the engines were powered up and we began moving down the runway. The engines roared and the plane heaved when it lifted off with its load of would-be Airborne soldiers. As we pulled up into a climb away from the runway, I looked around the plane at the other jumpers.

Looking along the line of faces, one by one, there were many different expressions. I took particular notice of the young private sitting next to me. He appeared to be of Latin descent and had been directly behind me in the stick. He hadn't said a word since we left the hanger. On the plane, he had drawn my attention because his head was down.

While I was watching him, he reached behind the front harness of his parachute and took a small crucifix from his shirt pocket. He didn't look up or say anything, but trembling, he gripped it tightly in his hand and kept his head down as if in prayer. *I should probably be doing the same*, I thought.

After the plane leveled off and its flight sounded less strained and a little smoother, the private seemed to relax. He turned toward me and noticed that I was looking at him. He forced a smile but still seemed very nervous.

"How are you doing?" I asked.

"Okay, sir," he replied, in a soft voice with a Spanish accent.

I looked at the name tag on his shirt and said, "Your name is Gomez?"

"Yes, sir . . ." he said. Then, he quickly added, "I'm from Texas."

His trembling stopped and he seemed to relax as we talked. And, our conversation kept my own apprehension from growing, so I continued, "Have you ever jumped out of an airplane before Gomez?"

"No, sir . . . and I don't want to jump out of this one."

I laughed as he continued, "But, I want to join the 82nd Airborne, so . . . I guess I'm gonna have to jump, right?"

Shaking my head affirmatively, the answer I offered was, "I guess so."

Gomez looked back down at the crucifix in his hand and relaxed his grip on it so that it fell to the palm of his hand. As he closed his fingers over it again, he looked over at me and saw I was still watching him. He leaned toward me and said in a quiet voice, "My father sent it to me . . . he said it would protect me."

Having grown up Catholic and, having even been an altar boy, I had an understanding of his father's sentiments. I told him I was sure that the crucifix would protect him and was sure that he would be fine.

It was just about then that the jumpmaster who had been sitting near the rear of the plane stood up and moved toward the jump door. This drew my attention as well as Gomez's.

When the jumpmaster reached the door, he put his head out and seemed to be checking our line of flight to the drop zone. The wind made his face ripple like a rubber Halloween mask. I looked over at Gomez whose face was distorted almost as much as the jumpmaster's.

As he watched the jumpmaster's face being twisted in the wind, Gomez began saying, almost in a chant, "Mother of God, Mother of God. . ." over and over in Spanish.

I patted him on the shoulder and told him everything would be all right.

"But, sir . . . we'll have to go out there. I never thought there would be so much wind."

"After you get past that first blast of wind Gomez, everything will calm down," I said, trying to reassure him.

"Oh, God, sir . . . please don't say *blast.* I don't wanna get blasted outta anything."

I couldn't help it, I laughed out loud and assured him that he wouldn't disintegrate when he went out the door and, after his parachute opened, he would just float down.

Gomez looked back down at the floor, took a tighter grip on his crucifix, and shook his head.

The jumpmaster pulled his head back in the plane and saw me sitting near the door. Then, to be heard over the engine noise, he shouted, "Sir! Would you like to look out the door? You can see where we're headed."

Now, I thought to myself, *with all of these men around me, what choice is there?* I wasn't going to say, "No, I'm fine right here where I am," even though I was. So, the only response to be given was immediate, "Sure, Sarge, that would be great!"

I stood up and moved confidently towards the door, but took a firm hold on everything along the way. It was important to me not to fall out of the door before having the chance to jump of my own free will.

"Look up along the side of the plane, sir, and you'll see the DZ (drop zone) up ahead."

He backed away from the door and indicated it was my turn to stick my head out. Leaning out the door, I looked ahead toward the DZ. Then, I looked straight down. It didn't look that far down, but I could feel the muscles in my stomach and behind tighten. So, despite the short distance to the ground, about 1,200 feet, some parts of my anatomy were getting a serious message of concern from my brain.

When I looked back up toward the DZ, the wind rippled my face as it had the jumpmaster's. I glanced over at Gomez and could tell he was watching my face twisting in the wind—his was becoming pale.

Pulling my head in, I told the jumpmaster the view was great, thanked him for the opportunity to look, and walked back to my seat.

"Gomez, we can do this," I encouraged him.

Then, as I took hold of an upright pole next to my seat, "It isn't that far down."

He shook his head as if he understood my attempt to make him feel better.

"I'm really scared, sir. Are you?"

This was my first jump, too. I was going to tell him the truth. So, looking him as squarely in the eyes as he was me, I said "Gomez, look at me, I have no wings . . . I can't fly. If I could fly, I wouldn't have any reason to be scared. But, since you can see I have no wings, yes . . . I'm scared just like you."

One corner of his mouth turned up into a cockeyed smile as I continued, "Listen . . . the engines are still running. Why would anyone possibly *want* to jump out of a perfectly good airplane except to be an airborne trooper!?"

Then, a full smile made its way onto his face.

"Yea, you're right, sir."

Then, he paused, looked down at his cupped hands.

"Here, Sir . . . would you like to hold my crucifix a little bit? It really helps."

"Yes, I would . . . and I'm proud that you would share it with me."

Just as Gomez dropped his crucifix into my hand, the jumpmaster shouted the command we all anticipated loud enough for everyone in the plane to hear.

"Red Light!"

That announcement meant that we were approaching the drop zone. So, after momentarily squeezing Gomez's crucifix, I dropped it back into his hand saying, "Thank you, it did help . . . it helped me a lot."

Then, came the command, "Get Ready!"

That meant exactly how it sounded. Get ready—we are about to do the deed.

"Stand up!"

Obvious, but that command meant we were almost over the drop zone and about to make our first jump.

"Hook-up!" came the jumpmaster's next command.

With that, everyone attached his static line to the overhead cable that ran the length of the plane. The static line would pull each jumper's parachute out of the pack on his back as he fell away from the plane.

"Check equipment!"

This command was important and meant we were to check to make sure our parachute was firmly attached to our bodies.

Then, came the command that once again made my stomach muscles and those in my behind draw tight. The feeling was similar to the one you may have experienced when you looked over the edge of a tall building or were at the top of the highest rollercoaster you've ever ridden.

"Stand in the door!"

That one meant the first man in the stick was to move to the doorway and get ready to jump. I was the first man. So, with Gomez and the rest of the stick right behind me, we did the "airborne shuffle" toward the door.

Upon reaching the door, I grabbed both sides and rested my right boot on the base of the door frame, about halfway out the door.

The wind and engine noise sounded louder than at any time since we had taken off. It couldn't have been easing Gomez's nervousness about jumping because it sure wasn't helping mine. But I looked over my shoulder and shouted, "Good luck, Gomez!"

"Good luck, sir! I'll see you on the ground . . . I hope!"

"Green Light!" the jumpmaster shouted!

This meant we were over the drop zone, but it didn't mean *jump*. For me, it meant—you are now in God's hands.

Then, with a hard slap on my pack, the jumpmaster yelled, "Go!"

And, with that, I jumped out the door—into thin air.

Gomez was scared, maybe even terrified, but when the time came to jump, he didn't stop or even hesitate. He went out the door right behind me, just as he had been trained to do.

After our parachutes had opened and we were floating down, he waved to me and yelled, "I made it, sir! . . . I'm okay!"

A week later, alive and uninjured, Gomez and I finished Jump School and were both awarded our silver wings.

Still being baked by a relentless Vietnamese sun, I would have welcomed some of the cold air Gomez and I passed through that day in February 1967

on our way to the ground. Recalling the very brief encounter and experience with Private Gomez, I recognized that it had not been an insignificant one for me. And, I was sure that it meant far more to me than it had to him. The meeting had provided my first opportunity to witness a man confront fear, then—overcome it. I don't know if anything I had said or done helped Gomez that first day, but his conduct had inspired me.

Even though he was afraid and confessed his fear openly, when the time came, Gomez had done exactly what had been expected of him. He had been as brave as any man who faces a fearful challenge and musters the courage to surmount it. I hoped I would respond as he had to the challenges that awaited me.

My last thought of Private Gomez was to muse about how proud his father would have been if he could have seen him as I did.

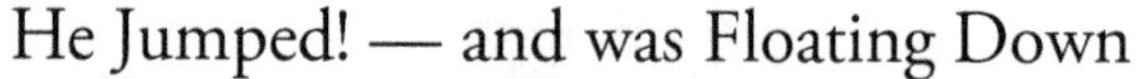
He Jumped! — and was Floating Down

After my parachute opened, I looked at the ground to see how far away it was, then I looked for Gomez. My view of him was similar to this one and I could hear him yelling, "I made it, sir! I made it!" And, he did indeed—make it!

United States Army Parachute Wings

These are the silver wings that Private Gomez and I earned after going through Jump School together. And, the training we received was taught in two phases.

First, we received Ground Training, which taught us how to re-engage Mother Earth when we hit the ground. Flexing and rolling when you touched down would prevent breaking ankles, legs, arms, or your face. This maneuver was called a "PLF" (Parachute Landing Fall).

After ground training, we were required to leap out the side door of an old C-119 aircraft—five times.

As my military training evolved, my jump experiences became varied and included propeller-driven fixed-wing aircraft, rotary aircraft (helicopters), and even jets. My most memorable jump was from a C-141 "Starlifter" four-engine jet—a real monster. The jumpmaster told me that our jump speed would be 140 miles per hour. You had to make certain that all portions of your harness, especially those running between your legs, were properly situated before you went out the door.

As noted earlier, among other prerequisites, Special Forces-qualified soldiers were required to complete parachute training. So, these are the "silver wings" that former SF soldier, Barry Saddler, sang about in his "Ballad of the Green Berets."

The Green Beret

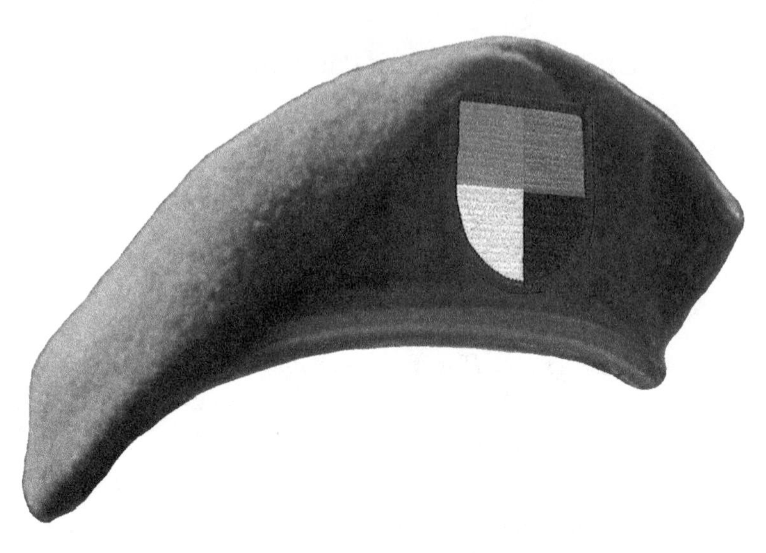

This was the prize for all those who volunteered to serve with the Special Forces.

Special Forces Crest

If the beret were earned, NCOs (Non-Commissioned Officers) would wear the Special Forces crest on the unit flash (patch) on the beret. Commissioned officers would wear their rank insignia on the flash.

Emblazoned on the distinctive black and silver crest worn by SF soldiers is the Special Forces motto: De Oppressor Liber, a Latin phrase that means To Free the Oppressed. Two crossed arrows symbolize the Special Forces' role in unconventional warfare. A fighting knife is attached over the arrows, which reflect the qualities of a Special Forces soldier – straight and true. The knife, a silent deadly weapon, was used by the American Indian.

Chapter 10

Earning the Green Beret

WITH JUMP SCHOOL FINISHED, I packed my bags one more time and headed for Fayetteville, North Carolina, and Fort Bragg. I had looked forward to Special Forces training since receiving my acceptance letter and couldn't wait for it to begin.

Strange, I thought, *the January sun in Vietnam seems as hot as the July sun back at Fort Bragg*. I reached up, took my beret off, and wiped the dripping perspiration from my forehead with my shirt sleeve. Repositioning the beret on my head, I remembered the sweat required to earn the right to wear it and how proud I was the first day I put it on.

Modern-day Special Forces began to gain prominence in October of 1961 when President John F. Kennedy visited Fort Bragg and the U.S. Army Special Warfare Center, then and still, the home of Army Special Forces. While at Fort Bragg, President Kennedy noticed that all of the Special Forces soldiers were wearing a green beret and he liked the look. At the time, the distinctive headgear was worn unofficially. Impressed by the demonstration of their capabilities during his visit, the president would later authorize the green beret as the "official" headgear of the U.S. Army Special Forces. From that point forward, the unit and its members would become forever known worldwide as— "The Green Berets."

Pleased with what he had seen at Fort Bragg, the president further demonstrated his support for the Special Forces and its unconventional warfare program. On, April 11, 1962, the president published an official White House Memorandum to the U.S. Department of the Army. In part, the memorandum read, "The Green Beret is again becoming a symbol of excellence, a badge of courage, a mark of distinction in the fight for freedom."

Because of the relationship that developed between President Kennedy and the Special Forces, the U.S. Army Special Warfare Center was renamed the John F. Kennedy Special Warfare Center.

I suspect that one of the reasons Special Forces got so many responses to its recruiting brochure was for much the same reason young boys responded to dares or any other challenge. The same reason they played war games or got involved in other rough, but generally non-injurious, contests like King of the Hill. They wanted their peers to believe that they were at least as tough or as brave as anyone else. As a youth, I got my share of bruises and abrasions trying to prove just that. I also suspect that the spirit of a young boy dwells somewhere deep within almost every man, still waiting, even in adulthood, for the challenge that will test his metal.

The Special Forces brochure that prompted my application featured a picture of a green beret on the cover. Above the beret, jungle green copy posed the question, "What does it take to rate a beret?"

Inside the cover, bold copy taunted the reader. "SO, YOU WANT TO WEAR THE GREEN BERET?" Sounded like a challenge to me.

Smaller white type against a wooded background explained what it would take to earn the beret and become one of the men who wore it. Again, the explanation read like a challenge, but more than idle boyhood taunts.

Four paragraphs from that brochure are reproduced on the next page so you will know what it was that attracted those who accepted the challenge and duty of a Special Forces assignment. When you read it, it will become clear that the message contained within the following paragraphs could evoke the production of testosterone, but beyond that, there is a call that beckons patriots.

The paragraphs read as follows:

It takes a special man to wear the green beret, a man of courage, dedication, and ideas. Let this be clear to you at the outset: Special Forces service is limited to those few men who want to be nothing less than the best . . . and can prove it both physically and mentally.

Special Forces is for men who love their country and the ideals for which it stands. Men who can teach as well as fight and for men who can think for themselves.

The job of a Special Forces soldier isn't easy. You may be asked to go into action anywhere in the world to help defend freedom. You may have to work alone, or with a small group of men for long periods of time. You will be expected to solve some of the most difficult problems that fighting men anywhere ever faced.

This is why it takes a special man to wear the green beret. This is why it takes dedication and maturity; brains as well as brawn. This is why only a comparatively few make the grade. But, to those who make it, there's nothing like it. And there's a knowledge that says: I have served my country and the cause of freedom and I'm proud of it! Those who wear the green beret are proud men and justly so. Do you think you have what it takes to become one of them?

There was certainly a challenge to my manhood, but it was the call to patriots that I heard.

When accepted for training, I wanted to believe I possessed what it would take to earn the beret. It was easy to believe and share the ideals of serving the country and the cause of freedom mentioned in the brochure. That's exactly why I had joined the service. And, possessing those ideals taught to me by family and community, they were already a part of who I was as a person.

It is one of the major points of this book and my firm belief that the great majority of the men and women who served in Vietnam were patriots who felt that they were serving their country while fighting for the freedom of another.

During my entire time in Vietnam, there were only three or four men who I thought might have felt differently. Had I been their commander, I would have sent them home without prejudice. They were the type of individuals who could cause other dedicated men to lose their lives and they are not the men and women discussed in this book.

It was late afternoon when I pulled into the parking lot at the 3rd Special Forces Group Headquarters, the unit to which I had been assigned for training. While I didn't know it at the time, my effort to "rate a green beret" would put me in a position to meet the men and women about whom this book is written and dedicated.

Upon reporting to B Company, 3rd Special Forces Group, to begin SF training I was initially assigned as the company's S2, Intelligence Officer. When I reported, I already felt well trained. The next day, when my training unit began the JFK Center qualification ("Q" Course) program, I anticipated SF training to add refinements to things already learned. I was also prepared to be taught some unique SF tactics and techniques. But what I certainly did not expect was being very thoroughly—retrained. Unconventional warfare would become my primary skill.

The focus of SF training involved unconventional warfare as well as counterinsurgency tactics and strategies. It was all new material and very different from what my classmates and I had previously been taught. However, the training we had received before arriving at Bragg wouldn't be wasted. It would be used to teach, train, or advise foreign military units on the subject of conventional warfare tactics in countries where a conventional war might be fought. There were also aspects of our previous training that applied to both conventional and unconventional warfare. Communications, demolitions, and weapons use are just a few of those things.

Getting up off my duffel bag, I hoisted it up on my shoulder. The jeep still had not arrived, so I decided to move to the shade of the nearby Ops (Operations) building.

As I walked and thought about my training and experiences at Fort Bragg, it was a sure bet that they could easily fill the pages of a book someday. But it was only impressions and highlights of SF training that flashed through memory.

When an officer or enlisted man reported for Special Forces training, he was issued a standard dark green beret and given a training flash to have sewn on it. The training flash was a patch that was as wide as a full flash but only about a half-inch high. The thin patch displayed the colors, but, not the design, of the wearer's assigned Group. The patch indicated that the individual wearing the beret was in training to become Special Forces qualified. Only after successfully completing training would that person have earned the full-flash and the right to wear it on the green beret he had earned.

The road from training flash to full flash was a long one and not everyone reached the end of that road. But those who made it rarely forget the sense of accomplishment they felt the day they donned their full-flash green beret.

SF training began in JFK Center classrooms and, as it progressed, it included several unique classes that required security clearances. At those classrooms, signs outside the room listed class title and instructor, just as with every other class. However, on these signs, there were large bold lettering that indicated the material to be presented was either CONFIDENTIAL or SECRET. In the cases of the "Secret" classes, it was not uncommon to encounter armed guards with class rosters posted at the doors to the classrooms. If you were in line and your name wasn't on the list, you were sure to need a very good reason for being there.

Among a host of other topics, the "Classified" courses included subjects on special weapons and equipment, surreptitious methods of entry, and methods of prisoner interrogation.

During classes on special weapons and equipment, we were shown pieces of equipment and gadgetry that looked as if it had come straight from the imagination of a filmmaker. The amazing thing was, they were all real, and—they worked. I *loved* those classes.

The classes on interrogation techniques were not a part of the normal SF qualification training. Those classes were additional training for those already assigned, or about to be assigned, to an "Intelligence" position. Intelligence training was conducted at the Army Intelligence School at Fort Holabird, Maryland, and it was so sophisticated that they used civilian actors in makeup and costume to play the parts of Vietnamese villagers, captured Viet Cong, or North Vietnamese Army soldiers.

As training advanced and the potential for exposure to more sensitive material became increasingly likely, so did the requirements for security clearances. Those of us involved in Intelligence or other sensitive areas were required to be cleared to a level of TOP SECRET.

During Special Forces training, the classroom sessions were the easy part. The bulk of the training, however, did not involve exotic weapons or high-level security clearances. It involved an abundance of very long days filled with a great deal of hard work. It also included bruises, abrasions, and occasional lacerations, much like the ones I had gotten as a boy when falling out of a tree. But these were a result of things like a rainy night parachute landing into trees or slips and falls off rock faces during mountain climbing classes. I also got a severe case of poison ivy that disfigured my face for three days. My face looked like something from a horror movie.

Special Forces training exercises were designed to be as realistic as possible. Authentic Vietnamese villages had been constructed to enhance the realism of our training. And, if you had the misfortune to be captured by an aggressor unit during a field exercise, you could expect to be sent to a POW (Prisoner of War) camp. There, with some distress, you would learn realistic enemy methods and philosophies on prisoner interrogation. Theirs were different than ours.

One sergeant who was captured on a training exercise was nailed into a half-buried coffin. When he wouldn't divulge requested information, guards took turns pounding on the coffin with sticks in an attempt to make him talk. Of course, the sergeant knew the mild form of training torture would stop and that he wouldn't be killed, something about which real POWs could never be sure.

While the heat radiating off the hot runway asphalt in Vietnam wasn't nearly as uncomfortable as things endured back at Fort Bragg, I thought about some of the tougher parts of the field training exercises.

One of the things that came to mind was the eighty-to ninety-pound rucksack we were required to carry in the field. Instructors would weigh packs to make sure they were heavy enough. If they weren't, rocks would be added to compensate for any weight discrepancy. Then, more likely than not, extra rocks would be added. So, I didn't take any chances, the bottom of my pack was loaded with canned fruits. At least, I wasn't going to be hungry. Worn out, maybe—but not hungry.

Other things we endured in the field included cold and, sometimes, wet rainy nights without shelter, wading around in ice-cold water up to our chins, blistering hot days with little or no food, nights with little or no sleep, and insect bites. Those things were all thought of as routine experiences. And, if they weren't enough, there was the unspoken promise of SF training that was known to every Special Forces soldier. It was the promise that anything could happen next—and you'd better be ready for it!

Special Forces training was extremely difficult at times and was conducted under less-than-ideal conditions most of the time. But, on the day we were awarded our full-flash berets, we all knew what we had accomplished by completing the training successfully. And, at the end of the training, there were fewer of us than at the beginning.

When a "Green Beret" left Fort Bragg, it was with very special pride and considerable confidence. It was certain he left with a good deal more than he had taken there.

At Fort Bragg, we had been taught how to help foreign governments build both small units and large armies, then, teach them how to function as a coordinated military team. We had been trained to increase our endurance and tolerance of discomfort in order, not just to survive, but to carry on and succeed in our mission. The training had not only given each of us confidence in ourselves to function alone when necessary, but also confidence in those with whom we would serve. You knew you could count on your teammates in difficult times, no matter how difficult those times became.

If personal changes had multiplied since leaving college, then by the time I left Fort Bragg, they had increased exponentially. And, that was a good thing because my next duty assignment would take me—to the war."

From TrainEE to TrainER

After arriving in Vietnam, one of my many jobs would involve training Vietnamese troops. Pictured above is a parachute training exercise that was conducted not far from the base camp where I would be assigned in Khanh Hoa Province.

As a part of the training, I jumped with the troops who were being trained. So, that could be me up there under one of those chutes.

After completing the Special Forces Qualification "Q" Course, I was awarded the 3rd Group flash (above L). This was the first full flash I wore, so I was extremely proud the day a seamstress removed the narrow training flash and stitched the full-flash onto my first beret. Since her shop was on Fort Bragg's main post, the seamstress understood the significance of what she was about to do for me. So, when I handed her my beret and the new flash, she smiled and said, "Congratulations! Now, you stay right here, lieutenant. I'll do this for you while you wait, I know this is an important day for you"

The 3rd Special Forces Group was activated on December 5, 1963, at Fort Bragg, North Carolina. The four colors of the quadrants of the 3rd Group's beret flash were inherited from the flashes of the pre-existing SF units from which 3rd Group's members were initially drawn. For this reason, the unit adopted the motto: "From the Rest Comes the Best". The four colors represent—yellow (1st SFG), red (7th SFG), black (5th SFG), and white (Special Forces Training Group).

The 3rd Group was originally oriented toward the Middle East and Africa during the 1960s. The unit trained the armed forces of Mali, Iraq, Ethiopia, the Congo, and Jordan. The 3rd also supported the Gemini 6 and 7 space launches in 1965. And, 3rd Group worked with the 5th SFG, which was already in South Vietnam.

Before my experiences with Special Forces ended, I would wear two other flashes. The 5th Group flash (above Center), worn during my time in Vietnam, then the JFK Center's flash (above R) after returning to the states.

Chapter 11

Training is Over

WHEN I DROVE THROUGH the gates and away from Fort Bragg in late December of 1967, I had completed nearly two years of exceptional military training that had grown progressively intense. Now, I was no longer a trainee. Rather, as a military adviser, I would become the trainer. I felt confident, self-assured, and ready to take on the job and begin my next assignment.

In a manila envelope on the passenger's seat next to me were a set of military orders directing me to duty with the 5th Special Forces Group in the Republic of South Vietnam.

The 5th Special Forces Group was activated at Fort Bragg on September 21, 1961. Then, in early 1965, the unit was deployed to South Vietnam and established its Headquarters in Nha Trang. It was there that I would join the unit.

With the early morning sun rising behind me, I turned my metallic "Hunter Green" Pontiac GTO (I loved that car) southwest and started toward my home in Pensacola where I would spend Christmas and celebrate my 22nd birthday. I had a 30-day leave to enjoy before taking a long flight to Seattle, Washington, then the much longer flight to Vietnam.

Before leaving home again, I spent my time hunting, fishing, or simply with my family and friends. Once more, for a few weeks, all I had to do was to enjoy a carefree civilian life. And, I did—for about two or three weeks. After Christmas and my birthday, with all the training I had received, I was more than ready to get on with my military job. Just sitting and waiting for days to pass was making me antsy. So, I told my mother and father that I was going to leave early, packed up, and went to the Pensacola Municipal Airport to catch my flight to Seattle.

When I arrived at the Processing Center in Seattle, I was told that they could get me on an earlier flight than the one for which I had been scheduled, but that might take a day or two to accomplish. They suggested a nearby hotel and told me that they would contact me there when my flight was booked.

It was early evening when I checked in at the hotel, so I asked the desk clerk if she could suggest a nice restaurant. If this was going to be my last state-side dinner, it was going to be a very good one.

"Have you been to Seattle before?" the very pretty young woman asked.

"No, I haven't," I said.

"Then, you might want to consider going to the Space Needle," she said. Then, quickly added, "You'll have a spectacular view of the city and Mount Rainier. I'll be happy to make your reservation."

"That sounds just perfect . . . please make the reservation."

The view from the top of the Space Needle was indeed spectacular. The restaurant revolved and, as it did, the lights of Seattle twinkled in the very crisp late January air. And, even though it was dark, the snowcapped peak of Mount Rainier could easily be seen.

I was seated alone near one of the windows and, besides a beautiful view, the food was delicious, and the service excellent. Because I was alone, the waiter often engaged me in polite conversation. I wasn't in uniform, but my short haircut probably gave me away as a serviceman. Anyway, able to see the snow on Rainier, during one of our brief exchanges, I commented that I had grown up in Florida, but had always wanted to learn to snow ski.

Later, after the waiter walked away, one of the two older women (late 40s, early 50s) sitting at the table next to me turned and introduced herself as Eve Johnson and said, "I heard you mention that you would like to learn to snow ski."

I laughed and said, "Yes, I would, but in a day or two I'm leaving for Vietnam. So, I don't think there will be time."

Eve was pleasantly attractive, very kind, and after I introduced myself as Lieutenant Tom Ross, she smiled and told me that her husband was an Air Force Colonel stationed at nearby McChord Air Force Base. Then, after a bit more small talk, she said, "I thought you might be military and thought I might be able to help you learn to ski."

I laughed politely and continued to listen.

"My daughter works in a ski shop in the Snoqualmie ski area, which isn't very far away, and she would be happy to arrange a lesson for you."

"You would trust me with your daughter?" I asked.

Now, Eve laughed and responded, "Well, you are an officer and a gentleman, aren't you?" And, with that, we were both laughing.

Long story short, the next morning I rented a car and was on my way to the Snoqualmie ski area. Not far into the mountains, my car got stuck in the snow. After finding snow chains in the trunk, I had to figure out how to put on the chains. Luckily there was an instruction sheet with them, so I got them on and continued my trek.

Eventually, I made it to the ski shop, parked, and went in search of Gina Johnson. When I found her, she was dressed like a snow-bunny in fluffy warm-looking clothes and she was very nice looking. I was disappointed that I was from the opposite corner of the country and on my way to the opposite side of the world. Sitting fireside with Gina on cold winter nights would have excited any young male.

After becoming acquainted, Gina began to make a list of the things I would need for my ski lesson. Here, it is probably unnecessary to remind you that I had just flown in from Florida and was on my way to South Vietnam, not the Himalayas. I didn't have one thing with me that was on Gina's list and I think the tab was around $250, not counting a lift ticket and the lesson costs. When I told Gina that I didn't want to buy the snow, I only wanted to ski around on top of it, she laughed, then said "I understand. My Mom told me that you are on your way to Vietnam. So, I'll take care of you . . . come with me."

After walking to a rack that held what appeared to be thin colored rain-suits, Gina said, "You can wear one of these over the clothes you're wearing. Then, all you will need is some gloves and something to keep your head warm. And, I don't think you will have time for a real lesson. So, after you rent your skis and boots, I will arrange for one of our instructors to show you some basics."

That was just perfect for me. There was only one issue. The clothes I had on were slacks, a white shirt and tie, and a blazer. I was wearing the civilian clothes I had worn to dinner the night before. And, the only covering suit they had was clear. So, that meant everyone would be able to see me skiing in a suit. *How dumb is that?* I thought. Then, I decided that there was no one at the lodge besides Gina who knew me. So, if I made a fool of myself, no one would ever know who I was—I was wrong.

After gearing up, a very kind older (60s) ski instructor named Bob took me to a relatively flat area and taught me how to make "controlled turns" and how to stop. After demonstrating some other basics, he said, "Why don't you just stay here near the lodge and practice what I've shown you. I think you'll have fun doing that and it will give you a chance to get a feel for the skis."

"Great . . . thank you. I appreciate your time and help," I said.

Then, Bob suggested, "If you catch that rope over there, it will pull you to the top of what we call "The Bunny Slope. That's where we start all beginners, so don't be embarrassed if there are a lot of kids around you."

After thanking Bob and trying to tip him, he declined the tip and said, "Have fun and . . . take care of yourself in Nam." Then, he skied away. It seemed obvious that Gina had told him where I was headed.

How difficult can this be? I thought, having water skied for years. I was about to learn. I began gliding toward the tow rope. So far, so good. When I reached the rope, I was perpendicular to it. I expected the rope to just pull me around and up the hill—wrong.

I was abruptly dragged sideways and very quickly found myself lying in the snow and on my back. When I looked up at the sky, a little head popped into view. A pretty little blonde girl with pigtails and bright blue eyes was looking down at me. She was probably about six years old. "You okay mister?" she asked.

"Yes, I'm just fine. Thank you for checking on me."

As I made my way to a vertical position, the little blonde tugged at my arm, trying to help me steady myself. "Thank you very much for your help," I said.

"It's okay, I've been skiing for years. It's hard at first, but you'll get it." Then, she took her ski poles, pushed herself off, and zipped away like a pro.

During my challenge of the Bunny Slope and a slightly higher hill, I found myself down and in the snow many times. Snow skiing was very different from water skiing. I had just gotten to my feet after one fall when an announcement began to boom over a loudspeaker, "Attention skiers. Attention skiers. We have a visitor here today. He is from Florida and has never snow skied before. His name is Lieutenant Tom Ross and he is on his way to Vietnam. If you see him down, give him a hand. He will be easy to spot, he's the only one out there wearing a tie and blazer." My anonymity was blown.

Only a little embarrassed by the announcement, I laughed out loud when I heard it. Then, almost immediately, I was offered near limitless help and more cups of hot chocolate than I could ever drink. That day at Snoqualmie was a very special one.

The reason I am sharing this brief chapter with you is to make the point that most of those who went to Vietnam were young and they had no combat experience. Nor had they ever seen the things they would see there. They weren't born as soldiers. They were sons and daughters, brothers and sisters, even mothers and fathers—and more.

Before they went, those who served in Vietnam weren't different from anyone else. They were from different ethnic backgrounds, they were us. And, like us, they had dreams and plans for life beyond their service. And, like me, most of them enjoyed life. And, also like me, most would enter the war fresh from a very peaceful life recently spent with family and friends. The war was a very quick and abrupt change for almost everyone.

My training was over. In only a little more than forty-eight hours, I would be standing in a very different environment where there would be no snow—about to begin the challenge of my life.

Beginning the Long Trip to South Vietnam

As the Northwest Airlines jet lifted off and gained altitude, I turned and looked out my window. Mount Rainier was drifting off behind us. I smiled as I thought about my day in the snow. There would be no snow ahead of me.

Chapter 12

No Ticket Home

SHADING MY EYES FROM the sun, I turned when the whop, whop, whop sound of a landing helicopter caught my attention. Then, carrying my duffel bag to the Ops building, I dropped it and stepped into a small piece of shade afforded by the building's overhang. I took my beret off and dropped it on top of the bag. Then, following the chopper with my eyes, I watched it until touch down and continued to watch as more shuttled troops unloaded their gear.

One of the Army specialists in Cam Ran Bay who was involved in troop movement told me earlier that morning that hundreds of new troops and replacements were scheduled to be transported all over the country that day. He said there had been a lot of recent enemy activity and he had been directed to route as many troops as possible to their assigned service destinations as quickly as possible.

They all look so young, I thought. But then—we were all young.

It was getting hotter and I was growing weary of waiting. Turning to look for my ride to 5th Group Headquarters, a jeep was coming in my direction along the edge of the runway.

Maybe it's mine, I hoped.

As I leaned over and picked up my beret, I realized something very important. There was a reason that when I arrived in Nha Trang, only about twenty-five minutes earlier, the questions *Have I made the right decision?* and *Am I really where I want to be?* seemed to answer themselves. Questions like those were very likely common, logical, and perfectly natural rhetorical considerations. Especially, when one is on the brink of entering a war. But even though they had flashed through consciousness, I had no questions and no doubts regarding the decisions and choices I had made about coming to Vietnam. It was with absolute certainty that I was exactly where I wanted—and needed to be. With that realization, a calm and confident feeling settled over me. If I were going to war, I felt that I couldn't have been better prepared to enter it than at that moment.

Personal changes since joining the military had been both physical and mental. My body was leaner and harder and I was more mature. My personality hadn't been sucked out of my body and I hadn't been turned into a zombie or made robotic. My warm and easy sense of humor still existed. But the metamorphosis from college student to combat soldier felt complete.

So, now, with two years of exceptional military training behind me and about to enter a war I had watched only on television, I was ready to begin doing the job I had been trained and had come to do.

Then, for a moment, I remembered the three young Marines whose courageous actions had prompted the action that brought me to this point in my life. I hoped that the wounded Marine had survived his injuries and that all three were now safely back in the USA. It was also my hope that, if I found myself in a desperate situation similar to the one that they experienced, I would react and behave as courageously as they had.

Of course, I couldn't know it at that moment, but my service would introduce me to other extraordinary men and women whose selfless deeds and courage would be remembered for a lifetime.

After repositioning my beret on my head, I picked up my duffle bag and turned to the sound of an approaching jeep. I was ready to go.

I'm not sure what I would have done had my questions been more than rhetorical and I concluded my decision to volunteer for service in Vietnam had been a huge mistake. It was obviously far too late to ask for—a ticket home.

Driving Through Nha Trang — Street Scenes

These are a few of the things you will read about in the next chapter.

Local residents, street vendors, and shopkeepers were still cleaning up from TET and trying to return to normal as best they could.

As you can see in the picture above, a Laurel and Hardy movie was playing at this theater. All of these pictures show that the streets were deceptively calm for most of the ride. Then—Bang, bang, bang! Boom!

Chapter 13

You're in it Now LT

A JEEP ROARED UP and stopped beside me. A young Special Forces soldier was at the wheel. He had the face of a high school student, but was wearing a .45-caliber sidearm and had an M-16 lying across his lap. He eyed my name tag, offered a crisp salute, then queried, "Lieutenant Ross?"

"Yes," I said, returning his salute.

"I'm Spec 4 Daily. I've been sent by 5th Group to take you back to collect your orders and draw equipment. Welcome to Nam, sir."

"Thank you Daily," I responded, amused by his welcome to war.

I threw my duffel bag in the back of the jeep, mounted the passenger seat, and Daily quickly sped away toward 5th Group Headquarters.

As we drove along the busy runway, aircraft roared overhead, and I again surveyed my environs. Passing a line of obviously departing soldiers, I noticed a hand-scrawled sign on the pack of one. It read, "FOLLOW ME BACK TO THE USA." Daily and I made eye contact and we both smiled—this soldier was clearly ready to go home.

Farther down the runway, we passed an Army aviation headquarters building with the unit's crest prominently displayed. "Intruders" was emblazoned diagonally across the red-and-white-on-blue painted crest. Across the bottom of the crest was the unit's motto, "Hell from Above."

"Sound like guys to have as friends," I commented, regarding the crest.

"Absolutely. That's the 281st AHC (Assault Helicopter Company), some of the most fearless men in Nam. They fly the Delta missions."

"Impressive. Everyone in SF knows about Delta's missions and reputation," I said, having learned about Delta back at Fort Bragg.

"Right, but the 281st doesn't just fly for Delta, sir. They fly for you too."

Confused, I asked, "What do you mean?"

"They also fly for Detachment A-502. The Ops (Operations) officer who sent me, said that's where you're headed. I'm taking you there after you pick up your orders and gear."

With that, Daily turned, drove through the gate, and off the base.

At that moment, like so many other things, I had no real understanding of the 281st's role in the war—or any thought that men of this unit would one day risk their lives to save mine. But what I did know was that helicopters were the workhorses of the Vietnam War. They were the primary means of delivering troops and supplies to the battlefield. The derring-do of U.S. helicopter pilots and crews was already well documented—even legendary. They were professional airmen from whom you could expect selfless and courageous actions on a routine basis.

During the year ahead, I would be amazed and proud to discover that a person's job description was no indicator of anyone's level of personal courage. Especially, for those holding what seemed to be routine and often mundane non-combat positions.

As we drove along a base perimeter road, I quizzed Daily. "So, what do you know about 502?"

"Well, I know it's the largest A-Team ever formed. Rather than the standard 12 men, 502 has over 50."

"You're kidding."

"No, sir. They've got a really big job. 5th Group has given them the responsibility for the defense of Nha Trang City and the Northern approach to Cam Rahn Bay."

"You're right. That sounds like a huge job."

As we entered the city, Daily told me that our ride to 5th Group Headquarters was taking longer than usual. The reason was obvious. Barricades had been erected and placed in strategic locations to restrict rapid movement through the city. We were driving past heavily combat-scarred shops and buildings of Nha Trang's once charming inner city. Residents and shopkeepers were busy trying to restore a small measure of normalcy by clearing debris and repairing the damage.

"Looks like it was a hell of a battle," I commented on what I was seeing.

"TET, sir! We had a hell of a battle here the other night. They say at least two battalions hit us. The Cong were running around everywhere, so our guys put these things in the road in case they tried to roll in with heavier stuff."

The "Cong" Daily referred to were Viet Cong, South Vietnamese who sympathized with our North Vietnamese enemies. They fought against the South and its allies, which, of course, included the United States.

"Looks like they did enough damage with what they had," I muttered, noting the damage caused by the recent battle.

"Yes, sir. They did—and they came out of the damn woodwork like roaches. They were everywhere!"

I had arrived in Vietnam in the middle of the 1968 Tet Offensive, a major surprise attack mounted by almost seventy thousand North Vietnamese and Viet Cong soldiers. The attack, launched during Tet, the lunar New Year, violated a holiday truce and occurred virtually simultaneously all over the country. In a single night, the war moved from the jungle and rural villages to the heart of over a hundred Vietnamese cities and towns, some previously thought to be impregnable. Nha Trang had been one of the first coastal cities hit as its inhabitants prepared to celebrate the New Year, the Year of the Monkey.

According to superstition, the monkey is considered a harbinger of bad luck. Certainly, in this case, it was. During the Tet Offensive, South Vietnam and its allies lost thousands of troops, hundreds of American soldiers among them. However, the Viet Cong and North Vietnamese who launched the attack lost thousands more.

While dissension had been growing regarding the war in Vietnam, the Tet Offensive would dramatically change public opinion in the United States and around the world. Events surrounding this offensive would cause antiwar resistance to intensify significantly. On that note, my tour of duty began.

As we wound our way through the narrow streets, I began to be concerned about our safety and eyed the M-16 lying across Daily's lap. Not having been issued a weapon yet—I was unarmed.

"Are we okay riding through here?" I asked.

"Yes, sir," he said. "We should be fine. Not much has happened during the past couple of days, but they're still active and probe us at night. So, they're still around."

Daily's words proved prophetic. We rounded the next corner and "Pow! Pow! Pow!" The street ahead erupted with explosive gunfire. Red and green tracers blazed back and forth across the road.

The enemy soldiers were the source of the green tracers and they were far outnumbered by the red ones being fired by the friendly ARVN troops. That was the first and only time I ever saw green tracers. And, for the few minutes they ricocheted around me, that was enough.

Daily jammed on the brakes, the M-16 flew off his lap, tires screeched, gravel flew and we skidded to an abrupt sideways stop. A cloud of dust boiled up and quickly enveloped our jeep.

In front of us, a 2 1/2-ton troop transport truck blocked the road. From behind a low wall, South Vietnamese soldiers were shooting into an abandoned building where enemy soldiers were hiding. The enemy fiercely returned fire.

Suddenly, the windshield of our jeep was shattered by enemy gunfire, glass chards flew everywhere. Daily grabbed his M-16 off the floorboard and rolled out onto the street. I quickly followed and moved around to the protected side of the jeep with Daily. I peeked over the back of the jeep and watched a furious exchange of gunfire.

"This is crazy!" I said. "I haven't been here for fifteen minutes, and I'm not ready to be shot!"

Daily, clutching his M-16 was crouched behind the front tire of the jeep and shouted to me, "You're in the middle of it now, LT!"

LT was an abbreviation for lieutenant and was pronounced just as it appears, ell tee. This was a common way that enlisted men addressed lieutenants.

"Yeah, and I'm unarmed!" I answered—feeling very helpless.

Daily responded immediately. He reached down, drew his .45 pistol, and tossed it to me.

I nodded thanks and again peeked over the jeep. Through gun smoke and settling dust, I was shocked by what I saw. At the rear corner of the truck, an attractive American brunette in her mid-20s was standing at the center of the shoot-out. She was wearing green Army fatigues and was holding a long lens camera.

"What is she doing out there?" I said, astounded by the sight.

Daily peeked over the hood of the jeep.

"I don't know who she is, but I've seen her around. I think she's a reporter or something like that.

Bullets ripped the road from the truck to the jeep.

She's gonna get herself killed out there, I thought.

As I watched, the brunette leaned out and snapped pictures, documenting the action. As she moved around, presumably to get a better angle on her subject, I was completely awestruck by her tenacity.

Concerned that we were exposed to fire from the upper windows of the building, I shouted to Daily, "Let's get off the street!"

"I'm with you, sir."

"Okay, let's go."

We jumped up and ran toward the doorway of a nearby building about half the distance to where the brunette was busy, still snapping pictures. I wasn't sure what I could do for her, but I felt better just being closer to her.

Inside an alcove, Daily and I stood shoulder to shoulder with our backs pressed against the wall. Gunfire continued to crack and echo along the street.

After the South Vietnamese troops fired M-79 grenades into the building, the gunfire stopped and yelling came from inside the abandoned structure. Shortly, three bloodied men with their hands raised high in the air appeared in the upper windows. When ordered out, they emerged tentatively from the building. The men, who were either VC (Viet Cong) or NVA (North Vietnamese Army), seemed extremely concerned about the reception they would receive once outside. Their reluctance to come out was not without sound reason. The South Vietnamese soldiers began imposing street justice, jumping on them, and beating them violently.

With things seemingly under control again, Daily and I remounted the jeep and pulled out. I had Daily stop near the brunette. She was still taking pictures of the action. As she moved to another position she looked up and we made eye contact. *Pleasantly attractive . . . and bold!* I thought.

"You want a ride outta here?" I asked.

"What?! No, I'm working! I'm a war correspondent. This is my job," she snapped, obviously annoyed by my question.

"Okay, then we'll be on our way. Take care of yourself," I said.

Over her shoulder, as she walked away, "Always do."
She hadn't gone far when she stopped and turned to face me.

"Thanks for stopping," she said and showed me a warm smile. Then, she quickly turned and hurried away to document the capture. I turned and looked at Daily, a huge grin covered his face.

"You've been here less than fifteen minutes and caught a girlfriend LT," he teased.

"I don't think so. Let's go. She doesn't need us."

"Maybe not, but she sure is easy to look at," Daily observed.

When Daily pulled away, I savored a parting view of the attractive bold brunette in the side mirror. I would love to have stayed.

As we continued to make our way through the city, it occurred to me that both Daily and I had reacted to the young female journalist in a typically male fashion. We had observed and commented on her physical appearance rather than the more serious consideration of what she was doing, which was covering a war, a serious and clearly dangerous job. While I had noted the boldness in her effort to document the capture of the enemy soldiers, there was more to consider in assessing her actions. She was the only woman on the street and she was unarmed. While, other than me for a few minutes—and not by choice, every male on the street was armed, some heavily.

Many, many lessons were to be learned in Vietnam, a war brought into American living rooms by journalists similar to the one I had just encountered. My arrival in Nha Trang constituted the first day of class; my first instructor had been the female journalist, whose lesson covered well the courage of women. That day, I learned a woman can be every bit as brave as any man I ever met. And, before I returned home, others would reinforce her lesson.

TET Damage in Nha Trang City

This is a building very similar to the one where Daily and I encountered the shootout. The interior damage was severe and combat damage scarred the facade.

This appears to be one of the local government buildings. They were primary targets.

Chapter 14

Uncommon Warriors

THE REST OF THE ride to 5th Group Headquarters was uneventful. When we finally arrived at the compound, I went in and reported for duty. After my paperwork was checked and verified, the clerk directed me to the supply area to draw my equipment. He said he would have my assignment confirmed by the time I finished collecting my gear over at Supply.

"Here ya go, sir. It's a brand-new piece," the supply sergeant said as he placed the familiar, sleek black M-16 rifle on the counter.

When I picked it up, it looked the same as the one I had been assigned in the States, but with one important difference—the one in the States had been used for training. I rolled the weapon around in my hands and pulled the bolt back to make sure the firing chamber was empty. *Training is over*, I thought.

The M-16 had always reminded me more of a space gun than a military rifle. Its design, the use of synthetic material rather than wood for its housing and stock, and its lightweight almost made it look and feel like a toy.

As I held my new weapon, for a moment I could see the old .22-caliber rifle my grandfather had given me when he first taught me to shoot. I could hear still his admonition after handing it to me. "Now that I've taught you to shoot and have given you this rifle," he said, "please don't ever disappoint me by wasting a life—every life has value."

When released, the bolt slapped forward, I hoped my grandfather would understand and approve the purpose for which it would be used.

My arrival in Vietnam in 1968 came with a clear purpose: Use the weapons of war to help the people of South Vietnam in their effort to stave off Communism and survive as a free country.

Looking back with all we know now; some may perceive that perception as naïve. But at that time, I was certain we were defending freedom and protecting the rights of others. Preventing a weak country from being taken over by the Communists and fighting against the spread of its influence seemed a just and noble purpose. As a child, both at home and in school, I had been taught that Communism represented a great evil. Only six years had passed since the Cuban missile crisis, a potential doomsday confrontation with the Soviet Union. I can remember missile launchers being placed around Pensacola on beaches that were normally used for sunbathing. And, neighbors were talking about building fallout shelters. "Duck and Cover" was taught in schools as preparedness for the potential detonation of a nuclear bomb.

The "Domino Theory" was often espoused. The Domino Theory suggested that if Vietnam fell to Communism, all of the countries surrounding it would fall as well.

The Chinese and Russians, our Cold War enemies, were supporting the North Vietnamese. If we didn't defend South Vietnam and its people, who else could or would confront such formidable powers? Both Russia and China were openly committed to the spread of Communism. In the United States, the word "communism" was equated with loss of freedom, just as the word "cancer" was equated with loss of life. It all seemed to make sense to me.

Picking up the ammunition magazines that went with my M-16, I continued through the supply area. After gathering the rest of my gear, it was time to pick up my orders and see if Daily had been correct about my assignment.

"A-502, sir," the personnel specialist said as he handed me the envelope containing my orders. Daily had been well informed.

"Where is 502?" I asked.

"Out in the valley. 502 is responsible for our defense."

As I turned to leave, he added, "Take care of us, sir."

"No problem . . . I'll keep an eye on you," I said confidently, even though I had no idea where I was going or exactly what I would be doing.

With orders in one hand, my M-16 in the other, and a pack over my shoulder, I left to find Daily.

Outside, in the compound, I used the envelope containing my orders to shade my eyes from the bright sunlight. Searching the compound for Daily, I noticed his jeep in the pickup area not far away.

I was pleasantly surprised to see a good friend and fellow officer, 1st Lieutenant Bill Phalen, already waiting in the jeep. He was alone in the vehicle, sitting on the passenger's side.

"It's going to be tough to drive from that side, isn't it?" I asked.

Bill laughed when he saw me and said, "What the hell are you doing here?"

"This jeep is taking me to my unit. So, are you my driver?" I asked.

Completely ignoring my effort to ruffle him, he asked, "Where have they got you going?"

"A-502. Where are they sending you?"

"502!"

"You're kidding! You mean we're going to be together? Do they know what they're doing?" I asked.

Bill and I had gone through Special Forces training together and had both been assigned to the 3rd SFG at Fort Bragg during and after that training. It was nice to be so far from home and recognize a very familiar and friendly face. I threw my gear in the back of the jeep, and we waited for Daily.

"How long have you been here?" I asked.

"I got in yesterday. It looks as if we just missed some big fireworks."

"Yes, that's what I hear."

"Someone told me last night that when the VC and NVA hit, every unit in Nha Trang got in on the action. Even the Headquarters clerks and mechanics were involved."

"Yes, that's what I hear . . . and, I hear it was bad?" I said.

"Yeah, really bad," Bill said. Then, recounting events of the past few days, Bill shared with me what he had been told about the Tet attack.

"Evidently, what happened was totally unexpected. A large combined force of VC and NVA infiltrated into the city and they struck from inside. Then, another fairly large unit attacked, coming in along Highway 1. That's the main drag. They hit early in the morning, and the battle lasted for a couple of days. The fighting was house-to-house at one point," Bill said.

"Yeah, well, that part of it may not be over yet," I told him. "I watched them drag three guys out of an abandoned building on my way over from the airstrip this morning."

"Really?"

"Yes. I thought I was going to be shot before I reported for duty. It was crazy," I commented.

"No, you haven't heard the crazy part yet," Bill said. "One of the officers in Operations told me that during one battle, a truck came roaring back for ammunition. When the truck slid into the headquarters compound, the driver jumped out and yelled that they needed more ammunition and reinforcements. Everyone within the sound of the driver's voice ran for his M-

16, but by that time most of the combat-experienced people were already gone and involved in the fight. So, this is where the crazy part begins."

"Okay, go ahead," I said, waiting for the punch line.

"Well, since there were virtually no field types left to respond, when they heard both the commotion and call for reinforcements, clerk typists and mechanics from the motor pool grabbed their weapons and ran for the truck. Hell, even the damn cooks who were in the middle of cooking and getting ready for breakfast ran and jumped on the truck!"

"Why am I not surprised?"

"I know. But, still, can you believe it? Clerk typists, mechanics, and cooks . . . I guess you do what you have to do," Bill said.

Bill's observation of doing what you have to do is expected of military men and women. But, as my tour of duty unfolded, I would watch as they often risked their lives doing what they felt they needed to do.

During a visit to headquarters a few days later, lunch in the mess hall gave me the opportunity to speak to one of the cooks who had been involved in the opening Tet skirmishes. He described how he and his makeshift reinforcement unit fought their way—block-by-block and house-to-house—through the city streets, which were illuminated only by the light of artillery flares.

"They were shooting at us from every direction, sir. Rounds were ricocheting off of everything, and we never knew where the next burst of fire would come from. On top of that, with the echoing gunfire, we weren't always sure where they were. Hell, I just kept waiting to get hit," he said. "It was bad! Really bad! All I could think about was getting home to my wife and baby," he added. The cook's voice betrayed the emotion stirred by the telling of his story.

"Why were you out there?" I asked.

"I was on the late shift or early shift, depending on your point of view.

Anyway, when I heard them yelling for reinforcements, I knew our guys needed help and I just took off. I'm not sure I can explain it. I just knew I needed to be out there. Nuts, huh?"

Amazing, I thought.

"Damn!" he exclaimed. "You know, I think I wore my apron the whole time. What kind of soldier is that?" he asked.

"The best," I said. "The very best."

After the cook, I encountered a clerk in the S2 (Intelligence) Office who, as a result of Tet, was now a combat veteran.

When I asked about his involvement in the recent action, the clerk's story was similar to that of the cook's. He was quick to respond—a courageous participant, even though combat was the last thing he expected.

"It was some bad shit, sir," the young clerk typist said. "I heard them calling for reinforcements when the truck came in for more supplies. But, hell, I'm just an ordinary analyst and typist, not an A-Team member. That's not what I signed up for, sir. I'm not a chicken or anything. I wanted to be in the Special Forces," he said.

"I understand perfectly," I said, wanting him to know I didn't think he was cowardly in any way.

"But, you know, when I heard all that yelling for help, I couldn't stay here. I had to go. I was really afraid I might die, but I just had to go. Ya know, sir?"

"I do," was my reply to what I found to be a remarkable character.

"I can't wait to write to my father. He was in World War II, and the last thing he said to me before I left home was—" then he made a strange facial expression and, imitating his father's voice, continued— "'What the hell is a man with a typewriter going to do?'"

I couldn't help laughing at the impression of his father. He laughed as well, then proudly added, "But, you know, sir . . . we saved the city."

"Yes, you did. You surely did," I said, amazed and touched by his tale—amazed by the incredible courage he and his fellow clerks, mechanics, and cooks had displayed, touched that they did it in the face of admitted fear.

Reflecting on the actions of the headquarters support personnel, I could only hope to match their deeds and their courage when the time came for me to act. While they had all received Special Forces training and were well qualified, they had never really expected to see the heat of house-to-house street fighting. Yet, when the call for help came, these men threw down their domestic accouterments, pencils, wrenches, and spatulas to take up the weapons of war. They may have been "ordinary" clerks, mechanics, and cooks but, on that day, they became—uncommon warriors with extraordinary courage.

Next Stop — Trai Trung Dung

Home of Special Forces Detachment A-502's main camp—Trai Trung Dung, was located in Dien Khanh Village, Khanh Hoa Province, South Vietnam.

A-502 was based inside the walls of an old Vietnamese fort known to locals as "The Citadel." Occupying only a portion of the massive structure, 502 and its Vietnamese units were primarily responsible for defense of the Southern wall.

The East Gate of "The Citadel"

The eastern entrance looked like it could be part of a Hollywood movie set.

"The Citadel" — Old Vietnamese Fort

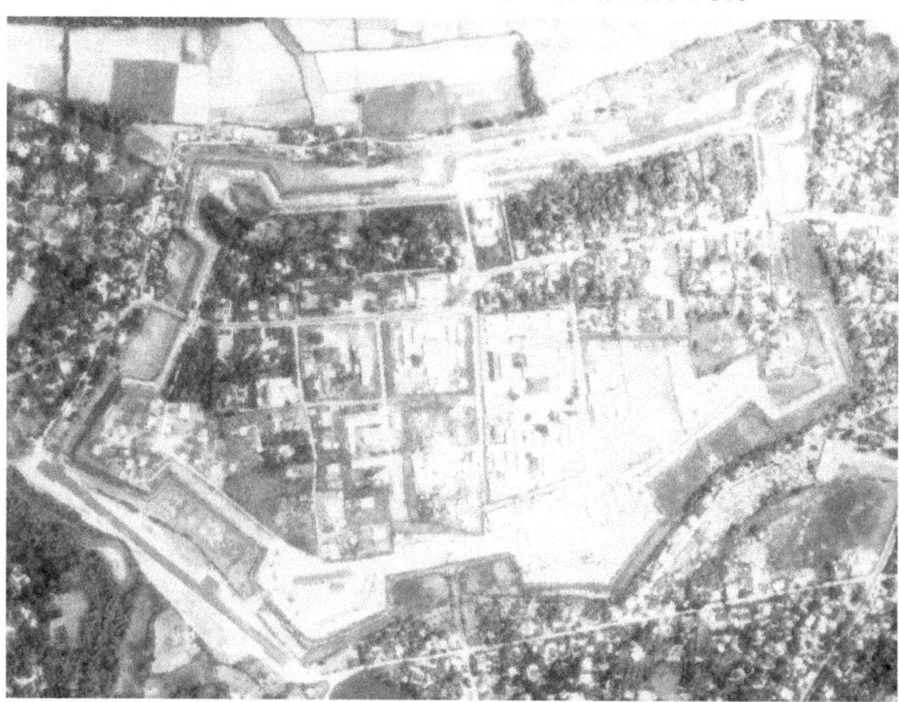

The Citadel was once home to the French Foreign Legion. Picture by the CIA.

CHAPTER 15

Trai Trung Dung, The Team, and Ngoc

WAITING IS PART OF MILITARY service. However, the military doesn't consider these times wasted and might simply apply a dictionary definition to them. Waiting*: periods to remain stationary in readiness or expectation of pending events.* Regardless of how they are defined, in Vietnam long periods of boredom or quiet could suddenly and abruptly be punctuated by the heart-stopping eruption of gunfire or the ear-splitting explosions of incoming artillery, mortars, or RPGs (rocket-propelled grenades).

Bill Phalen and I had no immediate concern about incoming munitions, but we were well into a stationary period as we sat in a jeep in front of the 5th Group Headquarters. We were anxious to get to our new camp, SF Detachment A-502, and were waiting for Daily, the driver who would take us there. As we sat, I looked out across the sandy flats just west of group headquarters that were dotted with mint-green foliage, then beyond up into the mountains that rose with authority from the flat valley floor. The only thing that betrayed the deceptive tranquility of the postcard setting was the barbed wire through which the view was observed.

While working in a job and an environment where you could be killed at almost any moment, one tried not to consider the disconcerting prospect of that reality. However, there were occasions when I felt the icy chill of that

Possibility. And, the feeling was not pleasant. As unsettling as my personal experiences were, I know that my fellow service members also had to deal with the prospect of dying in combat—often on a daily basis.

Having experienced that feeling myself gave me tremendous respect for the courage and fortitude of those who had to deal with it daily. As unlikely as it seemed at the time, one of my experiences with the specter of death would occur in the mountains that were the impressive backdrop to the vista before me. My friend, Bill, would also encounter and dance with the specter in the very same mountain complex. His would be a horrific life-or-death dance.

While we continued to wait for Daily, I pulled my orders out of a large manila envelope. According to those orders, I had been assigned to A-502 as its S2 and S3 (Intelligence and Operations) officer. That was a bit strange, since a Special Forces "A" team, such as 502, normally had only twelve men with no slot for either an S2 or S3 officer. The next-larger team, a "B" team, did have those slots, and both positions were normally staffed by captains, a rank above me.

Because my assignment at 502 was an unusual one, exactly how it was going to work was unclear. *502 must be modified in some way,* I thought. Then, recalling what an SF training sergeant had once told me, "Anything can happen next and you better be ready for it" —I was prepared to do whatever would be asked of me.

Musing over the strange assignment, I muttered out loud, "This is really bizarre."

"What?" Bill asked.

"I've been assigned as S2 and S3 of an 'A' team."

"That may not be so strange. I've heard 502 has a large AO (Area of Operation). Someone told me they have almost fifty men and several outposts."

"Yes, I've heard it is an expanded team with important responsibilities. I suppose we'll find out soon enough," I said.

At about that time, Daily approached with another soldier who was to ride "shotgun" as armed protection, just as occurred on stagecoaches in years gone by. Typically, during stagecoach days, the shotgun rider carried a double-barreled shotgun, thus the nickname. However, our shotgun carried an M-16 with several pouches full of ammunition. Daily got into the driver's seat, the shotgun climbed into the back with me, and we were quickly on our way out the main gate.

Passing outward-bound through the 5th Group gate meant that Bill and I were leaving personal security and relative safety behind. But since the headquarters had been established in Nha Trang in February 1963, we weren't the first; many men had passed through the gate ahead of us.

As dry, choking dust swirled behind the jeep, neither Bill nor I had a clue about what to expect regarding our new jobs. One of the few things the clerk at headquarters had shared with me about my assignment was that I would be replacing an officer who had been wounded during the Tet attack. So, we would clearly be going to a location that had been involved in the recent action.

Any remaining doubt about my presence in Southeast Asia vanished on the road to A-502. Less than a mile from the 5th Group gate, we passed a beautifully constructed Buddhist temple, colorfully painted in bright yellow and red with black Chinese characters adorning its columned facade. Two white ascending dragons faced each other and formed a large arch over the temple gates. Unquestionably, the distinctive architecture was Asian.

As we continued, we once again encountered the recently erected barricades that were designed to slow enemy movement into Nha Trang.

Upon entering the city, Vietnamese lettering appeared on buildings and signs everywhere. Small cars, open three-wheeled motorized taxis, motor scooters, bicycles, and human-powered cycle rickshaws (also known as "Cyclos") crowded the busy narrow streets. The steam and the aroma of what I now recognized as Asian cuisine rose from the cooking pots of street vendors and restaurants as we made our way through the city. I was surprised to see that business and life seemed to be going on with what appeared to be a great degree of normalcy, despite the recent battles.

On the north side of the city, a huge white Buddha sat upon a tasseled pillow atop a decorated pedestal at the pinnacle of a small hill. Even Buddha seemed unscathed by what had happened during the past few days. From a distance, neither the statue nor its ornate pedestal showed signs of the war-related damage that appeared in other parts of the city—I suppose Buddha was honored and respected by both the North and South Vietnamese. Wearing a thin smile, Buddha continued to watch over Nha Trang from his commanding position, just as he had for years.

Occasionally, Bill and I turned and continued to admire the gigantic icon of Buddhism even after we had driven far beyond it. While it grew smaller in the distance, before this night was over, we would have a much closer view of the dramatic statue and the hill on which it sat. Our purpose there would become the same as Buddha's.

Continuing west beyond the city, we drove into the rural farming area where the cars and taxis of the city were replaced by slow-moving carts drawn by huge, dark-gray water buffaloes. While they were large and lumbering, the animals were relatively docile and were almost always led by young Vietnamese boys who carried a stick to guide the slow-moving beasts. The Americans often referred to the boys, who seemed to like the nickname, as "cowboys."

Small, picturesque hamlets appeared here and there while the fronds of tall thin palm trees in and around each hamlet waved gently in warm easterly breezes off the South China Sea. Rice paddies that appeared to extend to the base of distant mountains lined both sides of the road and shimmered like a vast inland sea. It was still difficult to associate the unexpectedly striking beauty of this Southeast Asian country with the controversial war that seemed to be tearing it apart. But war it was and, as we passed by one particular hamlet, that fact became all too evident. Even though we were moving fairly quickly in order not to provide an easy target for VC or NVA soldiers who might still be hiding in the area, a nauseating stench blew through the jeep.

"My God! What is that smell?" I asked.

Daily responded immediately, "There was a big battle here the day before yesterday. Your team was involved in it and had to call in air support. They dropped napalm all along here, and enemy soldiers trying to get away from it jumped into the drainage ditches, but that didn't help. They were smoked [killed]. They've been burying them, but I'm not sure that all of the bodies have been hauled out yet."

The beautiful Vietnamese countryside we were driving through held the disgusting evidence of war. That realization came with the foul stench of death.

During the long ride to A-502, Daily would occasionally talk over his shoulder, offering information he felt we might find interesting. He told us that he made this trip many times before and had become somewhat of a historian on the area. As with his account of the hamlet battle, he was quite willing to share his knowledge and began telling us about Trai Trung Dung (Camp Trung Dung), where A-502 was located.

"Trung Dung is situated inside an old Vietnamese fort," Daily said, "complete with a moat. According to the locals, the fort was built under the Nguyen Anh Dynasty around 1793. It was later occupied by the French when they were here in South Vietnam. The fort was strategically located north of Cam Ranh Bay and west of Nha Trang, near the village of Dien Khanh. That's where we're headed, Dien Khanh, in Khan Hoa Province."

Gesturing as he spoke over the sound of the jeep's engine, Daily pointed and continued with his history lesson. "From that key location, the fort's occupants could help defend the seaport cities by patrolling that pass over there that runs to the south toward Cam Ranh Bay and the one we're in, the major pass to the east. It runs back to Nha Trang."

Daily also shared with us the fort's more recent history, saying that the Seabees, a Navy engineering unit, had built and occupied the camp prior to the A-Team moving in. 502 inherited the facilities when the Seabees moved to work at a new location. He said he thought we would find our accommodations to be above average for an A-team encampment.

After winding our way out through the Nha Trang Valley with its rich history dating back more than four thousand years, we finally arrived at Dien Khanh Village, then the fort and camp Trung Dung.

The fort, known to locals as the Citadel, was situated on the western edge of the village of Dien Khanh and was the second-oldest such structure in Vietnam. As we approached and then passed through the thick massive walls of the eastern gate, the old fort looked more like a Hollywood set than a modern military installation.

After passing through the security gate at Trai Trung Dung, Daily drove us to the A-502 team house. Three men were standing out front and they watched as we approached and arrived. Over the team house doorway was a rectangular green sign with large orange letters painted on it that read "A-502," our address for the next twelve months.

"Welcome to your new home," Daily said as he pulled up and stopped.

Bill and I unloaded our gear and I thanked Daily for his chauffeur services.

"Thanks for the rides, Daily. The first one was explosive and the second one was very educational. Thank you for both."

Daily laughed, saluted, put the jeep in gear, and headed back to 5th Group.

As Daily and his shotgun departed, the three men who had watched us arrive walked over to greet us. As they approached, Bill and I both recognized one of the men immediately, Major Lee. Lee had served as our "Student Leader" during one of our Special Forces classes back at Fort Bragg.

I saluted and greeted him before he reached us, "Major Lee . . . it's very good to see a familiar face so far away from home."

"It's good to see you too, Lieutenant Ross. Welcome to A-502. And, it's good to see you too, Lieutenant Phalen. Welcome."

Will Lee was tall with chiseled features, looking like someone whose image could be used on a Special Forces recruiting poster. When I last saw Lee, he was a Captain back at Bragg where he had a reputation for being a stern, but experienced, and extremely professional officer. It was good to see he had been promoted and would be my CO.

Major Lee was an interesting man whose life story, like his appearance, seemed straight out of Central Casting in Hollywood. He was orphaned at an early age and dropped out of high school when he was sixteen years old. Forging his birth certificate, Lee enlisted in the Marine Corps and was eventually sent to Korea where he saw heavy combat duty. His involvement in numerous combat actions resulted in his being wounded on three separate occasions. He had a drawer full of Purple Heart medals.

After Korea, Lee switched military branches and joined the U.S. Army, where he obtained an appointment to officer's candidate school, ultimately earning a commission as a 2nd Lieutenant. Then, leaving active military duty to attend college, he graduated with a degree in civil engineering. When the Vietnam War began to escalate, this high school dropout, now an educated, combat-experienced Army officer, responded to his patriotic urges. After applying for and receiving Special Forces training at Fort Bragg, where I met him, he was sent to Vietnam. Will Lee was a pragmatic man who had met life on its terms and had succeeded under extremely difficult circumstances. I was glad to see him. Serving under his command would be a good experience.

Major Lee, gesturing to the man on his left, said, "I'd like you both to meet Lieutenant Bill Lane, he'll be taking over soon as my XO (Executive Officer). Right now, 1st Lieutenant Bob Sweeney is my Exec. You'll meet him inside."

We exchanged handshakes and pleasantries. Bill Lane was warm and articulate, with a slight New York accent that seemed particularly distinct to me as a southerner. After spending time with him, it was easy to discern that Bill was an intelligent man who had set high standards for himself. Even dressed in a camouflaged military uniform, Lane had panache. As he turned back to face Major Lee, I noticed a flash just below his waist. The bright silver flash had come from his sidearm—a chrome-plated sawed-off shotgun. *I want one of those*, I thought.

Even though he had been in Vietnam for only a very short time, Lane had become combat initiated. Tet had made thousands of Americans combat-experienced overnight.

On the night of the nationwide Tet Offensive, Nha Trang was the first city attacked. Both the NVA and VC brought the war out of remote areas and into the cities of Vietnam. They swarmed out of the darkness, attacking Nha Trang City and the surrounding villages.

Bill's initiation began when he became involved in a battle at the hamlet that we passed through on the way to Trung Dung. He was trying to reinforce Lieutenant Sweeney, who I was yet to meet.

Bob Sweeney had led a CIDG reaction force to reinforce one of the team's night ambushes. The unit was engaged with the enemy in a fierce firefight that was the beginning of the Tet Offensive. There, Sweeney and his CIDG reaction force came under intense fire. Forced to get out of the open, they took cover behind the three-foot-tall walls of a graveyard.

During the daylong battle, Bob and his unit were continuously exposed to heavy enemy fire. Repeatedly, Sweeney along with two A-502 American sergeants, a Vietnamese sergeant, and the CIDG unit tried to break out of the graveyard and their precarious situation. They repeatedly attacked the enemy-held village but, try as they may, they were driven back each time. They were clearly outnumbered and fighting powerful dug-in NVA/VC forces. Even an air-strike failed to dislodge the enemy.

In the late afternoon, Bill Lane entered the battle when he arrived with additional CIDG reinforcements and badly needed ammunition. The wounded, and a Vietnamese sergeant who was killed during the battle, were immediately evacuated back to Trung Dung.

After fighting from behind headstones for hours and deciding that he and his men were not going to become permanent residents of the graveyard, Lane called for air support. A converted C-47 initially responded. The modified aircraft called "Spooky," belched a hailstorm of blazing munitions from sets of Gatling-style miniguns. Later, a pair of F-105s dropped the earth-scorching, battle-ending napalm from which enemy soldiers had tried to escape by diving into ditches. Those were the ones Spec 4 Daily had told me and Bill Phalen and me about on our ride to A-502. The decaying bodies were the source of the foul smell we drove through.

Lane stayed in a blocking position all night trying to stop the NVA/VC from escaping into the nearby mountains. Sweeney took the two A-502 American sergeants and CIDG troops into Nha Trang where they mounted a counter-attack on Buddha Hill. They fought an uphill battle all day to recapture the prominent terrain feature that was occupied by NVA and VC troops. Victorious, they established a perimeter and secured the hill.

CIDG troops would still be securing Buddha Hill when I would have the opportunity to see it up close.

Major Lee then turned to the Vietnamese Special Forces officer standing on his right side, "And . . . this is Major Ngoc Nguyen. He is the man we work for."

Major Ngoc laughed as he extended his hand to me and responded to

Lee's remark, "No, no . . . not work for. Advise . . . A-502 advises me. Welcome to South Vietnam and Trai Trung Dung."

When I first met Ngoc Nguyen, I could easily have mistaken him to be an accountant. He was mild in tone, gentle in manner, and warm in personality. Other than his combat attire, there was no suggestion of the combat-seasoned soldier who had led a fierce counter-attack on the North Vietnamese Army and Viet Cong during the past few days.

During the enemy's Tet offensive, Major Ngoc commanded all of the responding CIDG (Civilian Irregular Defense Group) units in western Nha Trang. And, he led an impressive counterattack with one of his combat recon (reconnaissance) platoons in the assault of an enemy bunker complex. During the battle, he killed four enemy soldiers. Silencing the bunker cleared the way for friendly units in the area to be reinforced.

Then, while directing an organized withdrawal, Ngoc observed and killed two snipers who were firing on withdrawing troops. During the continuing battle, Ngoc boldly exposed himself to enemy fire while rescuing wounded soldiers and resupplying ammunition to his troops.

Finally, when the enemy began to withdraw, Ngoc organized a heliborne pursuit team and led the chase to find them. After the enemy unit was located, he landed and led his men on another assault. When a machinegun opened up on his force, Ngoc personally attacked the position and killed three more enemy soldiers. A short time later, he spotted the position of yet another enemy sniper who was firing on American advisers. Ngoc quickly killed the sniper, saving several American lives.

As a result of his leadership and courageous actions during the battle that killed a total of 87 enemy soldiers, Major Ngoc was awarded the Silver Star by the United States government.

The Silver Star Medal, unofficially the "Silver Star," is the United States Armed Forces' third-highest personal decoration for valor in combat.

The Silver Star Medal is typically awarded to members of the United States Armed Forces for gallantry in action against an enemy of the United States.

Ngoc was awarded the medal for saving American lives, a unique and distinctive honor that was well deserved, certainly not something you expect from an accountant—which he was obviously not.

When Major Lee finished the introductions, he explained to Major Ngoc the roles Bill and I would play as A-502 advisers. He explained that Bill would be commanding 502's Blue Bandit team, while I would be serving a dual role. Elaborating, he said, "Lieutenant Ross will be our Operations and Intelligence Officer. Give him a day or two to come up to speed, but anything you need from A-502 going forward, he's your man."

Ngoc looked at me and smiled, "Good . . . very good. Glad to have you with us."

When I responded, "Thank you, sir," Major Ngoc warmly corrected me and asked that I call him *Thieu ta* (pronounced "Too ta"), Vietnamese for Major. Then, he smiled and explained that his first name was pronounced just as "knock" in English. "You know, like...Knock, knock. Who's there?" he said.

When I started to laugh, Ngoc grinned. I was immediately taken by this man's gentle appearance and warm relaxed manner.

He then said, "I will call you *Trung uy* (pronounced "Trung wee"), Vietnamese for 1st Lieutenant. Okay?"

"Thieu ta, you can call me anything you like. I've been called much worse," I said.

Ngoc burst into laughter and Lee, Lane, and Phalen all chuckled at Ngoc's amusement.

Major Ngoc was still laughing when Major Lee asked me about our ride out from Group Headquarters, "I heard you talking to your driver. Have problems getting here?"

"Only a little," I said. "The driver and I found ourselves in the middle of a shoot-out on our way from Nha Trang Air Base to 5th Group."

"Where?" Lane asked.

"In town, just before we reached Group Headquarters."

"Damn! They're still coming out of their holes!" Lane exclaimed.

"I'm just glad to have lived through my first day," I said.

Lee, Lane, and Phalen laughed, but Ngoc seemed to have other plans for me when he smiled, waved his finger, and said, "Day not over yet, Trung uy."

"No? You have plans for me, Thieu ta?"

Ngoc looked to Lee and asked, "Major Lee, can you assign Trung uy Ross to Buddha with me tonight? We have information VC and NVA may try to retake the hill."

"Good idea," Lee said. "We'll send Lieutenant Phalen as well, you can break them both in tonight."

"Excellent!" Ngoc responded. "Now, I must make plans. I will see both of you tonight."

Like Ngoc, formalities at Trung-Dung were relaxed, so he only waved a salute as he departed.

After we returned Thieu ta's salute, Lane invited us into the team house, "Come inside. I'll introduce you to Bob Sweeney, our XO, then show you where you'll bunk."

Inside the team house, Lane introduced us to the team's Executive Officer, Bob Sweeney, who was tall and lean with strong angular facial features. His welcome to the team was warm, but cautionary, "Welcome to A-502. You've arrived after a couple of very active days and I suspect there are more to come. So, we're glad to have you."

Before Bob left the team, he was extremely helpful and very considerate as I settled into my job and developed the positions I would hold. 502 had both an Intelligence and Operations sergeant but had never had an officer leading either of those functions. So, in his role as the team's XO, Lieutenant Sweeney oversaw both areas. As a result, he had become very familiar with the enemy composition in the area, as well as their commonly used infiltration routes.

Having served as an Intelligence Officer for the 3rd Special Forces Group back at Ft. Bragg, I knew the job intimately. But every area and every assignment will have its unique intelligence information. So, having someone like Bob Sweeney to provide me with a solid base of meaningful information made my transition to the team's S2 almost instantaneous.

Bob was also extremely helpful with my role as the Operations Officer. It was Bob who first outlined 502's operational role and key unit contacts for me. He was experienced and, as I have described, had been heavily involved in the Tet action.

Notwithstanding the courage he had already demonstrated, I found Lieutenant Bob Sweeney to be an intelligent, sensitive man with his own unexpected sense of panache. He had chosen "Moon River" as his callsign and that was, of course, the title of a Henry Mancini musical piece used as the theme for the Audrey Hepburn movie, "Breakfast at Tiffany's."

There was and would be a great deal of irony in serving in a war with a man who used Moon River as his callsign. Much of my heritage is Italian and my family was always proud of the claim that we were related to the famous composer. But, beyond that, I would one day serve as a senior executive with Tiffany & Company, where I would have the opportunity to meet Audrey Hepburn and share breakfast at Tiffany's with her. She was a very special lady and I will never forget our all-too-brief encounter.

The man with the far-from-war callsign invited me to use him as a source of information for anything I wanted or needed to know. Lieutenant Bob Sweeney made learning and doing my dual jobs much easier than might have otherwise been the case. If I never told him that—I should have.

After showing us our quarters, Lieutenant Lane gave us some time to unpack our gear and get settled, then took us on a tour of the camp. He took his time showing us around the interior of the historic fort, which had also been occupied by units of the French Foreign Legion when they were in Vietnam. It was shaped like an irregular hexagon with arrowhead-type points at each corner. The expanse of the Dien Khanh Citadel was astounding, it covered an area of approximately thirty-six thousand square meters. Built in Vauban military-style architecture, which was popular in Western Europe during the seventeenth and eighteenth centuries, the walls of the Citadel were approximately eleven feet high and massively thick. The outside of the wall was vertical with the interior portion terraced into two levels. This dual-level formed a fighting platform for men and equipment.

Cannons had originally been mounted on each of the Citadel's corners or arrowheads. Lane showed us one of those cannons, which now decorated the center square in the assembly area of the camp's compound. The cannon had been salvaged from the moat that ran around the fort. The moat was approximately four to five meters deep and about ten meters wide.

Our tour of the Citadel was quite interesting. The more I saw of the old fort, the more it looked like the set of an old Humphrey Bogart or Cary Grant movie. You could almost hear the marching footsteps and clattering equipment of French Foreign Legion troops as they marched through the compound to man their posts. While my impression of their presence was imagined, some of the Vietnamese soldiers claimed to have seen the ghosts of Legion troops, seemingly continuing their long-past responsibilities to guard the fort.

One night, months later, as I sat atop the Citadel wall watching the flickering candles in the village across the moat, a Vietnamese soldier who was on guard duty approached me from the near-utter darkness. Despite our broken use of each other's native language, we were able to communicate reasonably well. After some ice-breaking exchanges, the soldier said that when he first saw me, he thought I might be a French legionnaire. When I asked what he meant, he said that when he had been on guard duty before, he had seen French soldiers on guard duty as well. However, as he drew close to them—they disappeared. Whether a supernatural phenomenon or a result of too much Ba Mui Ba, a favored Vietnamese beer, or simply a ghost story designed to pass time while on guard duty, the tale was an amusing one that made my assignment to A-502 more interesting and memorable.

In addition to its present-day housing of A-502, the fort was also home to several South Vietnamese military units as well as a small village that provided accommodations for the locals who were needed to service the walled behemoth.

As we made our way back to and through the A-502 compound, we were introduced to several of our new teammates. They were short and tall, black, white, and Hispanic, with a rich blend of heritage and unique backgrounds. We were an All-American team.

The team had many members, but a standout on the roster was the top sergeant, Jose (Joe) Vasquez, who was responsible for the NCOs. Sergeant Vasquez was a tall man of medium build with high cheekbones, an olive complexion, and jet-black hair. While his ancestry was Portuguese, in appearance he had the strong looks and bold features of an American Indian. As might have been the case with an American Indian chief, he commanded his men with a firm but caring hand. And, like many Americans whose heritage was foreign, Sergeant Joe Vasquez was extremely patriotic and passionate about his service. He was an easy man to like and respect.

Military courtesy requires that noncommissioned officers and enlisted men salute commissioned officers upon meeting. While there was a swipe at an implied salute by each of the men we encountered, there were also the immediate offers of a handshake and varied verbal welcomes to the team. I was impressed by the warmth and firm grip of each encounter and realized that a silent but very strong bond immediately formed with each man. Special Forces and other special operations soldiers often advise or work in small teams of two or three. In a very real way, each man's survival depends on the other. Regardless of the team's direction of movement, every man is expected to protect his teammate's vulnerable backside, often referred to by clock position as his "six." Each man trusts that the other will protect him with his life. That unique commitment and sense of brotherhood could be felt in the handshake of each team member.

The men of A-502 were exceptional and, by military standards, so were the accommodations. The buildings were wooden, with tin roofs. The outside walls were sandbagged for protection against attack, and the main living area in the team house even had air conditioning—far beyond my most optimistic expectations. One day, after commenting about the quality of the team's accommodations, one of the sergeants quickly responded, "Sir, any grunt can sleep on the ground, but a professional will make the best of a bad situation."

While the team had been creative in upgrading the quality of its living conditions, 5th Group Headquarters had been equally creative in its design of A-502's mission, a huge one with unique responsibilities.

The detachment was originally authorized as a standard twelve-man SF A-Team in March 1964. Later, in October of that year, team members were assigned to the unit. Then, in December 1964, Detachment A-502 was made operational, with a stated mission of providing security for the 5th Special Forces Group Headquarters and the Nha Trang Air Base. As a result, the team was located and quartered with a unit of the South Vietnamese LLDB (Luc Luong Dac Biet—Vietnamese Special Forces), which was strategically located within A-502's TAOR (Tactical Area of Responsibility).

In 1965, 5th Group Headquarters determined the need for two A-Teams in the Nha Trang area, but each with different responsibilities. This resulted in the establishment of Detachment A-503, which would assume the original responsibilities of A-502. Because of their familiarity with the mission, key members of A-502 were assigned to the new team. The XO of A-502 became the CO and Team Leader of the new A-503 team.

Released from its original assignment, A-502 was given an even greater mission; responsibility for the security of the entire Nha Trang area. Overnight, the team's AO and responsibilities became significantly greater. With the acceptance of its new mission, A-502 would also begin to create its history as the largest-ever Special Forces A-Team.

As we stood at the heart of Trai Trung Dung, Bill Phalen and I had just become a part of A-502 and its history. We were beginning tours of duty that would expose us and our teammates to both the worst and, oddly enough—the best of the human experience.

Trung Dung's Center Quadrangle

This elaborately designed garden, with Trung Dung's "T" and "D", planted initials, formed an attractive frame for the Vietnamese flag pole and flag. But more than that, the flowers provided a momentary distraction from all the other trappings of war—like the underground bunker in the background. The green mound hid a secure place where team members could go if the camp were overrun by the enemy.

A-502's Main Compound

Our main compound is inside the pointed portion of the fort below the white dashed line in the picture above. You can see the gardened flag pole frame and flag in the center of the compound. Our area extended to the left to the runway.

This is the east-to-west view and you can see across the compound to the runway.

PHOTOGRAPHS

Republic of South Vietnam — 1968

ADVANCES IN COMMUNICATIONS TECHNOLOGY brought television pictures of the Vietnam War into America's living rooms. Advances in photographic technology miniaturized cameras to pocket size. As a result of this technology, I began carrying a small camera with me on parachute training jumps at Fort Bragg.

My first effort at airborne photography was an attempt to capture the opening of my own parachute. Unfortunately, I made this attempt during a training jump from a Lockheed C-141 Starlifter, a huge Air Force jet powered by four Pratt & Whitney TF33-P-7 turbofan engines.

Because the C-141 was a jet, its airspeed at jump time was necessarily faster than that of the propeller-driven jump aircraft we were used to using. As a result, the sudden and abrupt jerk caused by the rapid opening of my parachute ripped the camera from my hands. I am confident that a hunter or naturalist will one day find that camera in the North Carolina forest where it fell.

While in Vietnam, as a function of my role as S2 and S3, I often carried a camera in my pocket to document various missions and key terrain features in A-502's area of operation. After Sergeant Gordon Gilmore, a team member, built a darkroom in one corner of the team's motor pool, he taught me to develop my film and print pictures. After that, I began taking more pictures and many of those photographs appear on pages throughout the book. Others were taken and contributed by my friend, 1st Lieutenant Bill Phalen, and others who wanted to help me tell the stories told here.

After learning the skill, I taught Phalen what I had learned from Sergeant Gilmore and, in the process, I created a monster—Bill took and developed hundreds of pictures while he was in Vietnam. And, that's a good thing because nothing helps tell a story like a picture.

SFOB (Special Forces Operational Base)

5th Special Forces Group Headquarters—Nha Trang, South Vietnam

Buddha and "Buddha Hill"

My first view of Buddha on my way from 5th Group Headquarters to A-502

Compound Center — Trai Trung Dung

Home of Special Forces Detachment A-502's Base Camp.
The old cannon was discovered in the moat that surrounded the fort.

A-502 Team House

This is where Daily dropped me off the day I arrived at A-502 and where I met Thieu ta. The team house is on the left and the "Hospital" is on the right.

S2 & S3 Offices — Opposite the Cannon

The S2 Office, with Sergeant Paul Koch as staff, was on the left side and the S3 Office, with Sergeant Roy King as staff, was on the right side. When I wasn't in the field, I worked back and forth between both places.

Fort Perimeter Moat

This is part of the moat that surrounded the fort. In days of old, attackers would have to swim or use boats to cross the moat, neither a wise option.

Emergency Bunker

If the camp were overrun by enemy units, team members could move to the bunker and continue to direct support units from underground. The bunker had maps, radios, and supplies needed for the emergency command center.

"Fire Arrow"

If the fort wall were breached, the Fire Arrow on top of the bunker could be turned from inside to indicate the direction of an enemy attack to Air Force FACs flying overhead. As you can see, the arrow had lights for a night attack.

My Corner of the Team House

Everyone did what they could to make their private area seem just a little less military. The cards were on the wall over my bed so that I could see them.

What you can't see is the shelf with hand grenades, smoke grenades, and flares.

Fighting Positions on the Fort Wall

These fighting positions were constructed around the top of the fort wall.

Doing What We Did

A-502 advisers overseeing training for Thieu ta Ngoc's CIDG soldiers.

Wall Top Bunker

This bunker was at the top of one of the fort's star points, so it had a wide field of view and could fire down two sides of the wall.

Gun Jeep

This was one of two custom-made gun jeeps owned by A-502.

More of the People & Things You Will Read About

Major Ngoc Nguyen

Vietnamese Camp CO

1st Lieutenant Bill Lane

A-502 XO — Incoming

Major Will Lee

A-502 Team CO

1st Lieutenant Bob Sweeney

A-502 XO

Sergeant Paul Koch

S2 (Intelligence) Sergeant

Sergeant Roy King

S3 (Operations) Sergeant

Major Ngoc & Lt Colonel Chang

Lt. Col. Chang, Korean "White Horse" CO

Sergeant Jose Vasquez

A-502 Team Sergeant

Friends

Me and my shadow, Ahat, Montagnard radioman, and trusted bodyguard.

In Combat Gear and Ready for any Mission

Vietnamese Camp Commander, Major Nguyen Quang Ngoc was a fearless warrior, dedicated to the freedom of his country.

Major Dubovick

A-502 CO after Major Lee left the team.

Military Counterparts

ROK (Korean) Captain Lee and my friend, 1st Lieutenant Bill Phalen.

CIDG Troops in Formation

Some of Thieu ta Ngoc's troops in formation. These were the men we helped train and those we advised in the field. And, when we went to the field with them, there were typically only two of us (American advisers) with them.

CHAPTER 16

Ghosts and Guardians on Buddha Hill

WITH OUR ORIENTATION AND TOUR of the old Vietnamese fort and A-502's position within it complete, Lieutenant Lane began walking us back toward the team house. Still amazed by the quality of living conditions the team had established for itself, I chuckled to myself as we passed small landscaped areas planted with brightly colored flowers. *Could be my grandmother's garden*, I thought. As I would learn later, Major Ngoc had the flowers planted for his family as well as other officials and dignitaries who occasionally visited Trung Dung. The small patches of floral color seemed to bring some measure of civility to the otherwise austere looking military base camp.

First surprised by the unexpected beauty of a country at war, I was now equally amazed by the appearance and facilities of the camp where I would serve my tour of duty. I had expected to sleep on the ground in the jungle or, at best, on the ground in a tent or bunker in the jungle—and I would indeed do those things many times before returning home.

Upon reaching and reentering the team house, we were once again greeted by cool, refreshing air-conditioning. But we wouldn't enjoy it for long. Phalen and I immediately began preparing for our night on Buddha Hill.

As soon as we were geared up and ready to go, Lane quickly exchanged cordiality for a franker conversation. He told us that we were going to gain experience very quickly and shared 5th Group's serious concerns about the recently initiated Tet offensive. The enemy's actions had been unexpected, and no one was quite sure what they might do next. So, to provide additional early warning and protection for Nha Trang installations, our team had been assigned the task of advising Vietnamese security units at several key locations in our AO. That night, my friend Phalen and I would be meeting Major Ngoc at one of those sites.

During his briefing, Lane described the strategic value of Buddha Hill. "As you will discover, the hill overlooks the entire city of Nha Trang and the surrounding area," he said. "You can see everything from up there." He also told us that Major Ngoc could be right about the enemy returning to the hill. He said our night could indeed become very active because the enemy also understood the strategic nature of the hill. They had briefly occupied the hilltop as their command-and-control center during the recent attack, before being forced off by counter-attacks.

Then, Lane mantled me with a responsibility that I was readily prepared to accept, but I hadn't expected so quickly—I wasn't simply going to be an observer on the hill that night. "Tom, this is a map of Nha Trang and these are the call signs of all of our support units," he said, as he handed me a folded map and paper. "I have included notes about those you are likely to need tonight and have marked their locations on your map."

Then, he continued, "Officially, you will be on the hill as Major Ngoc's Senior American adviser. Your job will be to support him and his troops by directing allied support in the event those bastards do make another attempt to move into the city. But, since you are brand new and don't know the area yet, you will have two of our team sergeants up there with you. They have both been there the past couple of nights and can provide backup if you need them. Just stick with Major Ngoc, he will tell you what he needs. And, I will be available via the radio here if you need anything. Major Ngoc has asked Major Lee to organize quick-response reinforcement teams that can react to action anywhere in our AO. So, you will have plenty of support available if you need it."

He finished by giving me a military identity, "Our callsign here is Bunkhouse, as our S2, yours is Bunkhouse Zero Two."

I took what Lane had said confidently and without any show of the apprehension I felt. After all, I was a "Green Beret"—a "fighting soldier from the sky" (words from the "Ballad of the Green Berets" by Barry Sadler). How could I react any other way?

Back at Fort Bragg, pre-mission training and preparation had been taught as key to the success of any mission. *This could become interesting,* I thought. I had barely been in Nha Trang for six hours and knew little more about the city than what I had seen or been told by Daily, my driver. Just three evenings earlier, I had been enjoying a thick, juicy steak in the Sky City Restaurant at the top of the Space Needle in Seattle, Washington.

When I looked out over Seattle my last night in the United States, lights twinkled and sparkled in the cold crisp winter air. Now, only days later, my location and the landscape had changed dramatically. This night, I would be looking out over the lights of a city in South Vietnam.

Nearly everyone who went to Vietnam would experience a similar and abrupt change in their surroundings. For some, the transition either to or from the war zone could prove difficult, or at least challenging. At that moment, I felt ready for whatever might come—time would tell if that were true.

Lieutenant Lane's next remarks were consoling when he finished his briefing by saying that it wasn't routine for 5th Group to send anyone to the field, especially a potential combat situation, on the day they arrived. It felt better just knowing that my apprehension wasn't illogical.

Normally, there was a one-to three-week orientation period that familiarized each Special Forces member with the country and his pending assignment. This was followed by a two-to three-day field exercise. Understandably, because of the Tet Offensive, emergency conditions existed, and selected positions were being re-staffed or filled immediately. Phalen and I were two of those who bypassed orientation. Unusual, maybe—but, fine with me. Despite some concerns, I had been training for over a year and was ready to get on with my job.

In an A-502 jeep driven by one of our team's radiomen, we made our way up toward the hilltop. Along the way, we passed some of Major Ngoc's troops digging in. When we reached the summit, I was astounded by what I saw. A huge white statue of Buddha rose dramatically before me and a brilliant blue Asian sky served as a fitting backdrop for the iconic symbol of Buddhism.

Major Ngoc was standing at Buddha's base, surrounded by several of his lieutenants and sergeants. Two American sergeants from A-502 were also with him. Ngoc was giving deployment instructions for the night.

The driver stopped, let us out, then parked next to Ngoc's jeep and quickly began making radio checks. Phalen and I no longer looked like polished garrison troops. We were dressed in tiger fatigues and we carried full combat gear. In my left hand, I carried my M-16 and wore my web harness with extra ammunition, grenades, and a medical pouch attached. For balance, I had a .45-caliber pistol strapped around my waist that hung on my right side. Unlike earlier in the day, I was now prepared to meet the enemy.

And, I was now connected with a vast array of American support units. One of A-502's Vietnamese interpreters was serving as my interpreter and radioman. The list of unit designations and callsigns was in my shirt pocket.

Prepared to Meet the Enemy

After I had changed clothes and prepared my web gear, I carried it and my M-16 into the common area of the team house. Lieutenant Lane was sitting in a chair waiting for me. He asked when I had last fired my M-16 and .45 pistol. When I told him that it had been at least a month or more, He told me that I needed to go out to a corner of the fort and fire a few rounds out of both. He told me, and it made sense, that I needed to be very familiar and comfortable with both of them this night.

Lane then explained that, normally, refresher training would have taken place at 5th Group when I first arrived. But because of TET, I had been sent directly to the team. He said, "Anything that happens tonight won't be training." So, I took my friend, Phalen, and we both did some target practice. Because Bill had his camera with him, you can see how I was dressed that night.

Welcome to Southeast Asia — Buddha Hill

Buddha and his dragons are some of the first things I saw when arriving on the hill. Later, these Asian icons took on a very different appearance.

Major Ngoc's briefing was breaking up as Phalen and I approached. We both saluted and I greeted Ngoc as he had asked, "Good evening, Thieu ta."

Ngoc returned our salutes and my greeting, "Chao, Trung uy. Lieutenant Phalen . . . good to see you again. Welcome to Buddha Hill."

"Thank you," we said in unison, sounding like magpies.

"I just finished my operations briefing for tonight. My officers and sergeants with your sergeants will now make sure all of our soldiers and equipment are in position as I have instructed."

One of the American sergeants and a Vietnamese sergeant were still standing nearby, so Ngoc called them over. They saluted, then Ngoc introduced both, "This is your Sergeant Freedman and my Trung si (Sergeant in Vietnamese) Hoang. Sergeant Freedman is your Bac si (doctor) and Trung si Hoang is, like you say...my right arm."

The American sergeant quickly offered, "I'm Sergeant Larry Freedman, one of the team medics, sir. They radioed that you were coming. Welcome to the team."

"Thank you. I'm glad to be here," I said. Freedman smiled as if anyone was truly glad to be in Vietnam.

Ngoc continued, "Sergeant Freedman will work with Trung si Hoang tonight, Lieutenant Phalen will work with my Lieutenant Be and Trung uy Ross, you will be with me."

Ngoc then asked Sergeant Freedman if he would find Lieutenant Be and introduce Lieutenant Phalen to him. "He knows they will be working together tonight," he said.

"Yes, Sir. I'll track him down," Freedman responded.

Phalen and Sergeant Freedman saluted and left in search of Lieutenant Be.

"Come with me Trung uy, I will show you why we are here."
Major Ngoc led me to the nearby overlook and, with a wide sweep of his arm, gestured across the expansive valley floor. Below, was the lush,

beautiful seaside city of Nha Trang.

"As you see, we have total view of Nha Trang City." Then, pointing, he continued, "There, Nha Trang Air Base. There, 5th Group Headquarters. Over there, Vietnamese High Command Headquarters. From here, easy to observe and fire onto many key locations. That is why the NVA would like to have this position again."

"Yes, I understand," I replied.

"Come. Now, I show you how our troops and weapons are deployed."

As Ngoc and I walked away from the overlook, I realized that I was now truly a part of the Vietnam War. While I was confident in my skills, no one truly knows how they will react the first time in battle. I prayed that I would behave as trained and wouldn't embarrass myself—or my country.

Making our way around the top of the hill, Major Ngoc would occasionally stop and point out troop locations, key weapons positions, and explain his plans to defend the hill if it were attacked. At one point, we encountered Trung si Hoang and Sergeant Freedman, who now had his face painted with camouflage. They had just finished checking their positions and their men and were sitting on sandbags eating dinner from beautifully painted bowls. Both were using chopsticks, a skill I would soon acquire.

Major Ngoc called Trung si Hoang over and began speaking to him in Vietnamese, so I took the opportunity to walk over and visit with Sergeant Freedman.

"Smells like dinnertime," I said.

"Yes, sir. Do you like Asian food?" Freedman asked.

"Yes . . . I do."

"Then, you will love Vietnamese food," he said.

"How did you come by what you're eating? Did you order 'Take-out?'" I asked.

He laughed and explained the source, "Ha . . . it's a great story, sir. Over the past few days, some of the villagers have wandered up here and we've gotten to know a few of them. Well, last night, one family watched as we ate our C-Rations." He laughed again and said, "They made horrible faces as we ate out of the tins. Then, they left. A little later, they came back with covered bowls of food for us. It was really very good."

"That was a kind gesture," I said.

"Yes, sir . . . and, they just brought what we have now. They told Trung si Hoang that they wanted their American guardians to have something better to eat than whatever was in our cans."

With that, Freedman and I both laughed. Then, he became thoughtful, "You know ell-tee (again, familiar military slang for Lieutenant), it's made me and the other American advisers who have been up here feel good to believe we might be thought of as guardians."

"I'm sure it has," I said. "Makes me feel good just to hear that."

Just then, Ngoc called, "Trung uy, come. We continue."

The more we walked and talked, the more acquainted and comfortable we became with each other.

Interested in why I was there, Ngoc asked, "So, what has brought you to Vietnam, Trung uy?"

"Well, Thieu ta . . . that is a very easy question for me to answer," I said. Then, I explained, "For a couple of years now, I've been watching news of this war on TV. I have watched as other young men and women served and decided it was now my time to do something meaningful with my life. So . . . here I am."

Ngoc chuckled, smiled, then spoke warmly, "I am grateful you are here Trung uy . . . and, I hope your time here proves meaningful to you."

The more we talked, the more Major Ngoc seemed a kind, sincere, considerate man to me. It wasn't at all necessary on his part, but it pleased me that at one point, as a courtesy, he asked my thoughts about his deployment and defensive plans. Ngoc very clearly knew exactly what he was doing—he had been fighting the VC and NVA for years. *I can learn from this man. And, if I do learn, maybe I can survive my time in his country,* I thought. Ngoc was ten years my senior—I was twenty-two years old.

As we continued around the hill, I sometimes glanced back at Buddha. When actually on the hill with it, the huge statue seemed even more impressive. In a sitting position, Buddha was at least fifty feet tall. Possibly the only thing more dramatic than Buddha himself was the view he commanded. The glittering South China Sea and the city of Nha Trang, which was spread across the valley floor, seemed to present themselves as reverent offerings to Buddha's imposing presence.

By the time Major Ngoc and I completed our circle survey of the hilltop, the sun was nearly set. With the lights that normally illuminated the statue turned off, light from the village and city around its base provided a soft golden illumination for Buddha.

Then, as darkness settled over the city, the hill took on a near-surreal appearance. The sky, a rich mixture of deep blues and vivid purples highlighted by faint yellows, oranges, and reds, now served as the statue's background. Even Buddha himself was reflecting the beautiful colors of the Southeast Asian night sky. To find such beauty amid such oppressive danger still seemed strange to me. But, then, many things seemed strange to me and distinctly foreign. Brightly painted dragons that cascaded down both sides of the steps leading up to Buddha seemed to slither into the darkness as night cloaked the hill and the valley below us.

When Ngoc and I returned to the overlook, it was completely dark. The once bright white Buddha, facing east, had softened dramatically and was reflecting the faint glow of a waning Gibbus moon that rose from the sea. The night was still, except for soft Vietnamese music from a villager's radio and the ubiquitous barking dog. The only things clearly visible from the hilltop were the flickering lights from the city and the candlelight that made its way through the foliage between the hilltop and the village around the base of the hill. Candles and small cooking fires also flickered here and there across the expansive valley floor. Such was the setting for my first combat assignment in Vietnam.

Pointing to a location on the overlook, "This will be our headquarters for the night," Major Ngoc advised. "From here, we can watch many key approaches to the Hill."

With that, we took our positions and sat on sandbags behind a low sandbag wall that had been prepared by Ngoc's troops. Vietnamese soldiers were dug-in below and on both sides of the overlook, their weapons locked and loaded. Ngoc's radioman and mine stood a short distance away. Everyone was ready for whatever the night might bring.

"Now, Trung uy . . . the watching and waiting begin," Ngoc said.

A short while later, as we sat in the darkness and waited for an attack, Ngoc offered some chilling information. "If they hit here again tonight, the enemy soldiers could be half crazy," he said. "After the attack the other night, we discovered that many of the soldiers were high on opium. Some of the bodies we found the next morning had notes pinned to them. They read—*We volunteered to die.*"

"They sound like Japanese kamikaze pilots, only on the ground," I said.

"Yes, that is true . . . they were fanatics. I am sure others as crazy are still out there."

"How do you fight an enemy that has volunteered to die," I asked rhetorically.

"You must kill them before they kill you," Ngoc said very matter-of-factly. And, he knew what he was talking about.

In the past few days, Major Ngoc with his soldiers and the A-502 advisers had dispatched a great many of the VC and NVA.

As we waited and I pondered the possibility of fighting a drug-crazed enemy, Vietnamese families in villages around the hill were preparing their evening meals. The smell of Asian dinners, like the one Freedman was enjoying, swirled in the humid night air and mixed with a warm salty sea breeze that blew in off the South China Sea. Along with the now-familiar aroma of Vietnamese food, the gentle sea breezes also carried the chatter of Asian conversation from the village below. Over the indiscernible voices, the melodious gong of heavy bronze bells echoed back and forth across the glittering valley floor. The view before us was amazingly beautiful—like a place a young man would want to take a young woman to park. The exotically romantic setting and my combat mission were difficult for me to reconcile.

Looking out over the valley, I commented to Major Ngoc, "You know Thieu ta, with this beauty, it's hard for me to believe there is a war in this valley." Then, reminiscing, I continued, "I was once in California. There is a road named Mulholland Drive. And, from an overlook like this one, you can see the San Fernando Valley. At night, it is beautiful, just like Nha Trang."

"Yes, but no war in that valley Trung uy."

Barely a moment had passed when we saw tracers spray like a fan on the other side of the valley. Seconds later, the sound of erupting gunfire reached the overlook. Then, illumination flares streaked skyward and burst, lighting the faraway battlefield.

Dogs began barking and Ngoc's radio started to squawk. Ngoc motioned for his radioman, then listened to several frantic radio transmissions, shouted in Vietnamese.

During a pause in communications, Ngoc looked at me, gestured toward the action, then told me what was happening, "One of our units has ambushed an enemy patrol. They report two KIA (Killed in Action) and call for reinforcement." He paused, then asked, "War in this valley still hard to believe?"

"Only a little," I said.

We were listening to Ngoc's radio as well as gunfire and impacting artillery from the battle on the other side of the valley. Suddenly, I noticed movement out of the corner of my eye and instantly spun, swinging my M-16 as I did. When Ngoc and our radiomen saw my action, they reacted.

When we confronted the movement, we found that we had leveled weapons on a Vietnamese woman carrying a small child and pulling another by a shirt.

From the shadows, the woman called out in panicked Vietnamese, "Please help us!" They emerged from the shadows so that we could see their faces, all three appeared frightened. The woman had a small girl in her arms and a young boy at her side.

Ngoc studied the trio for a moment. Then, "I know this family. They are from the village."

Ngoc walked toward the woman while I watched, still uncertain about what was happening. I could hear the conversation in whispered Vietnamese but couldn't understand much of what was being said. After a few moments of continued discussion, the woman gently guided the boy over to Ngoc's side, said something to him, put her hand on Ngoc's arm, and rushed away with the girl.

Ngoc walked back to join me with the boy now at his side. The boy, who appeared to be about nine or ten years old, watched over his shoulder as his mother disappeared into the darkness—tears rolled down his cheeks.

"His father was killed by VC first night of Tet," Ngoc explained. "His mother has heard that the VC might return tonight and is afraid they take the boy to fight with them."

"This happens?" I asked.

"Yes, often. That's why his mother asks that he stay with us for the night." Ngoc paused, smiled, then said, "Now, we more than soldiers, Trung uy. We have become babysitters."

I smiled and looked at the small boy, who was staring right at me. I was very likely the first "round-eye" (American) he had seen up close. The boy was shaking, apparently scared to death. I dropped to one knee before him and smiled gently, warmly. Then, I patted myself on the chest and said, "Trung uy, Ross."

I looked to Ngoc, then back to the boy, and asked, "Thieu ta, will you please translate for me." Then, warmly to the boy, "What is your name?"

After Ngoc translated, we were both pleased when we heard, "Chi."

He was still quivering as I again spoke softly to him, "Chi, at my home in America, I have a little sister like yours."

This time unprompted, Ngoc translated almost simultaneously as I continued slowly and deliberately, "If she were alone and frightened, I would want someone to take care of her."

Then, hoping it sounded respectfully Asian, I said, "You would honor me by letting me take care of you. Would you think about being my little brother for this night? I will stay awake and stand guard over this hill while you sleep."

When Ngoc finished his translation, the boy looked into my eyes and studied my face closely, carefully—his quivering began to subside and he nodded slowly.

Having been taught a few key Vietnamese words and phrases before I left the States, I used one when I responded, "Cảm ơn nhiều" (Thank you very much).

When I stood, Ngoc was looking directly at me and said "You have a kind heart, Trung uy. Still difficult to believe war in this valley?"

"No, not anymore." Then, I looked down at the small frightened boy and asked, "What will we do with him?"

"He can sleep in my jeep," Ngoc said. "My driver will guard him."

When Ngoc showed me a big grin, I said, "What?"

He chuckled and said, "Come, bring your little brother. We put him to bed."

I put my hand on the boy's shoulder and we followed Ngoc towards his jeep, parked at Buddha's base.

Shortly, Major Ngoc and I were back on our sandbags, weapons across our laps, sitting quietly for hours—fighting boredom and the urge to sleep. As time passed, gunfire, tracers, flares, and the boom of RPGs (Rocket Propelled Grenades), mortars, and artillery had become all too familiar to me. Out in the darkness, Ngoc and I had watched and were still watching battles occurring across the valley floor.

With the darkness restricting my vision, my other senses grew sharper, as did my dependence on them for information that might protect me. I could hear the occasional rattle of equipment and the snapping of twigs, along with a plethora of other unidentified sounds. The most recognizable sound was the crack of gunfire as it occurred throughout the valley.

Until that night, the only thing the sound of gunfire meant to me was that someone was involved in a training exercise. Before, the worst that was to be feared from the sound of rattling equipment or snapping twigs was the sudden appearance of an "aggressor" from an opposing training unit who might shoot me with a blank cartridge. That night, however, I was only too well aware that if I were shot, it wouldn't be with blanks.

For hours, I sat quietly and looked into the darkness. At one point, I watched a flare fired from Hon Tre Island. Its bright pinkish-orange glow reflected and glittered in the small ripples on the South China Sea. As the flare hit the water and extinguished, even the sea grew dark.

With each new sound of distant gunfire, I became more and more alert to the presence of objects closer to me. The movement of nearby figures occasionally interrupted the flicker of candles and fires in the village. I also became conscious of changes in patterns of the darkness itself, changes that indicated movement.

When illumination flares lit the night, ghostly shadows appeared to march up the hill toward our position.

Is that an approaching VC patrol? I wondered. It was hard to tell. I raised my rifle, snapped off the safety, eased my finger onto the trigger, and waited. My heart pounded with the anticipation of a life-or-death firefight that could erupt any second. The sights of my rifle and my attention were focused on shadows created by the eerie pink glow of the flares that drifted slowly toward the valley floor. After the flares went out, I waited for the enemy soldiers to emerge from the darkness and prayed that I would see them before they saw me. Despite an ocean breeze, the night was hot and perspiration dripped down my forehead. I reached up and wiped away tiny sweat beads so they wouldn't run into my eyes.

When it became apparent that there wasn't going to be an attack, I snapped on my rifle safety and relaxed.

During my early days in Vietnam, I often felt the constricting grip of fear. Every man and woman had to learn to live and deal with it in his or her own way. During the night on Buddha Hill, as I worked to adapt to my new surroundings, I remembered a discussion in one of my college classes about fear. Someone read a passage that had stayed with me; the passage suggested that we experience fear to warn us about the potential of evil or harm. Samuel Johnson wrote that the purpose of fear, "like that of other passions, is not to overbear reason, but to assist it."

Taking the remembered passage and its meaning to heart was how I learned to live and deal with fear. Whenever I began to experience it, I would quickly gather reason and sort through what was and was not real. For me, that process became an indispensable survival tool until experience gave me the confidence to understand fear, live with it—and use it.

Professional soldiers readily admit to experiencing and living with fear. Acknowledging fear is not a sign of weakness; rather it is a sign of intelligence and confidence, and an understanding of the serious nature of their profession. Interestingly enough, what truly scares a professional soldier is another soldier who is unwilling to say he has experienced fear. In my opinion, a soldier has two reasons for denying fear; he is either lying or he is crazy. In either case, the professional soldier has no need for this type of individual.

In my case, the adaptation to daily life in a combat zone affected my entire body. On occasions when the hair on my neck would begin to stand on end, I knew immediately that one of my senses had detected something important that required my attention. Then, I would become keenly observant of my surroundings, knowing that I needed to be completely aware and alert. Simultaneously, I would snap off the safety on my M-16.

At about 3:00 in the morning, I whispered to Major Ngoc, "I've looked into the darkness so long that I'm starting to see things. Sometimes, I can't tell whether they are real or ghosts."

Ngoc whispered, "Yes, I know. Eyes play tricks on brain. I have also seen them." Then, still whispering, "Come, we check perimeter, make sure everyone is awake."

I welcomed the chance to move around, this had been a very long day and I was growing weary. As Ngoc and I walked, I looked out into the darkness and wondered if an enemy attack would actually occur.

"I think maybe the VC and NVA know you and your troops are here, waiting for them," I whispered to Ngoc.

"Yes, that could be. They have agents in the city and prefer sneak attack when no one expects them."

After only a few steps more, RAT, TAT, TAT, TAT! BOOM! The perimeter ahead of us exploded with automatic gunfire and the boom of grenades. Red tracers ripped down the hill. Ngoc and I immediately began running toward the action. Loud gunfire and exploding grenades echoed around the hill as we raced, weapons ready, directly into the conflagration. *The battle has started!* I thought. My heart raced.

As we approached the source of the gunfire, I saw Sergeant Freedman and Trung si Hoang. I yelled to Freedman, "What's happening?!"

He shouted back, "I don't know, sir. But somebody must see something!"

Sergeant Freedman and I went down on a knee behind one of the firing positions with M-16s pointed downhill. I saw nothing. Ear-splitting gunfire and explosions continued.

Ngoc, also down on a knee behind the next firing position, yelled, "Do either of you see anything?!"

"No!" I exclaimed.

Then, Freedman yelled, "Nothing!"

Looking downhill, I could only see outgoing fire. There were no muzzle flashes from enemy weapons. Puzzled, I shouted to Friedman, "Do we have flares?!"

"Yes!"

"Have them fire flares . . . now!" I yelled.

Freedman then shouted to Trung si Hoang, "Trung Si, fire flares!"

Ngoc heard my direction to Sergeant Freedman and immediately understood why it had been given. He beat Trung si Hoang to the order and shouted in Vietnamese, "Fire flares! Fire flares! Quickly!"

In seconds, the air filled with bright orange streaks headed skyward. These were followed by multiple loud pops of bursting flares that hung beneath small white parachutes and illuminated the battlefield bright as day.

Our view of the empty battlefield was an eerie one. Again, ghostly shadows seemed to march across the hill under the glow of floating pinkish-orange flares, trailed by white smoke that rippled like thin ribbons.

Red tracers fired by Major Ngoc's troops crisscrossed the battlefield. Then, when it became clear that no enemy unit was assaulting the hill, Ngoc called out in Vietnamese, "Cease fire! Cease fire!"

After Ngoc's command was echoed by Trung si Hoang and others, the gunfire ceased and the hill fell quiet. Gunsmoke, the only evidence of a battle, wafted across the hillside in clouds. Dying flares flickered and burned out, darkness again enveloped the hill.

With calm restored, I quizzed Major Ngoc, "Any idea what they were shooting at Thieu ta?

"No . . . but I will find out."

A short while later, Ngoc had gathered several of the men involved in the unopposed firefight. From a distance, I watched and listened as he questioned them. While I didn't understand, I could tell by his tone that Ngoc was not happy.

When the questioning ended, Ngoc, clearly aggravated, waved his arm dismissively for the men to return to their positions and he walked back to me to share what he had learned, "Nothing! They know nothing!" He paused, then added, "A sergeant says that one of his men saw movement and yelled . . . 'VC!' Then, everyone started shooting! Crazy!"

Using his words from earlier, I said, "Eyes play tricks on brain . . . right?" I hesitated, then added, "At least, we still hold the hill."

Ngoc smiled but shook his head—still irritated.

The dawn's early light brought definition to murky forms and ghostly figures on the hill. Buddha was again bright white against a beautiful blue morning sky.

Thieu ta Ngoc and I, followed by both of our radiomen, were walking toward his jeep. As we drew close, we could see Chi—sound asleep in the back seat.

"Little brother sleeps well," Ngoc said.

"Yes, I'm glad," I said. "I'm sure the past few days have been very difficult for him and I feel sure all the gunfire last night was terrifying for him."

Just as we reached the jeep, we heard an indistinct Vietnamese voice and turned to the sound. It was Chi's mother. Again, carrying his sister, she had come for her son.

When she reached the jeep and saw Chi asleep, she grabbed his foot and shook it, saying to him in Vietnamese, "Chi, Chi . . . come. Time to feed the chickens and water the goats."

I was standing over him when Chi roused wearily, rubbing his eyes and stretching. He looked up at me, then climbed from the jeep and stood by his mother.

Speaking in Vietnamese, the woman thanked Major Ngoc for protecting her son, "Thank you, Thieu ta." She pointed up at the statue and continued, "Buddha will bless you."

She then took Chi by the hand and hurried away. But, after a few steps, Chi pulled from his mother's grasp, turned to face Major Ngoc and me, and—saluted.

Both Ngoc and I, taken by the unexpected gesture, quickly snapped to attention and returned Chi's salute. Chi grinned and ran to rejoin his mother, who had continued moving. Over his shoulder, as he ran, he shouted something in Vietnamese.

"What did he say," I asked?

Ngoc looked at me, smiled, and responded, "He said . . . Goodbye, big brother."

I was touched by the boy's farewell, ours had been an unusual and unexpected encounter. Very likely, I would never see him again. It may sound saccharine, but it was families like his that I had come to defend. I hadn't been in Nha Trang for 24 hours yet. But, at that moment, I was already very glad I was there.

"Babysitting job done," Ngoc said, as Chi, his mother, and little sister disappeared down over the hill.

Just then, Ngoc's radio began to squawk with his callsign. His radioman passed Ngoc the handset. Ngoc acknowledged, listened, acknowledged again, then passed the handset back.

"That was Sergeant Hoang," he said. "He and Sergeant Freedman have found bodies."

"What?" I said, obviously surprised.

"Yes. Let's go."

On our way to find Sergeants Hoang and Friedman, Ngoc reached into his pocket and produced a Vietnamese military patch. He said, "Here, this is for you. It is a Vietnamese Special Forces patch and will show you are an adviser to us. I hope you will be proud to wear it."

Ngoc's gesture, for me, was one of acceptance and the beginning of a bond between us that would last a lifetime—and beyond.

Thieu ta and I were approaching a treeline, where we could see Trung si Hoang, Sergeant Freedman, and several other South Vietnamese soldiers. Trung si Hoang and Freedman were on the opposite side of some waist-high bushes, looking down. We couldn't see what they saw, but Sergeant Freedman started smiling as I neared.

When Ngoc and I rounded the bushes, we saw the bodies.

"Pigs?! They shot pigs?!" Ngoc exclaimed.

Looking at two large dead pigs, I was equally dumbfounded by the sight.

When Ngoc looked over at me, he appeared perplexed and was shaking his head.

"Well, there is a bright side to this tragedy, Thieu ta," I said. "If you like bacon and eggs for breakfast, you only need the eggs."

Ngoc started to chuckle and, just as he did, a nearby rooster robustly crowed the arrival of morning. So, I quickly added, "And, it sounds like you may not have to go far for the eggs."

Still trying to understand exactly what had happened, Ngoc asked, "You always see opportunity in craziness, Trung uy?"

His puzzlement quickly faded when a Vietnamese farmer burst from the treeline, shouting. Everyone immediately whirled to face him. The farmer was unarmed, so no one fired as he ran to the pigs—waving his arms and yelling in Vietnamese all the way.

Ngoc later translated his words. "You killed my pigs! Are you crazy?!" he screamed. "My pigs no shoot at you!"

If the man hadn't been so angry, the situation would have been very funny, but Ngoc stepped forward and quickly tried to calm the man. He spoke to the old farmer in Vietnamese. I didn't understand what he was saying, but the man soon calmed, took Ngoc's hand, and shook it vigorously. The man displayed a huge smile, obviously, very happy by whatever Ngoc had said to him.

"What did you say?" I asked.

"I told him we would pay for the pigs . . . and would pay top price."

The man was still holding and shaking Ngoc's hand as he excitedly said something else to Ngoc.

Ngoc, Trung si Hoang, and other nearby Vietnamese soldiers, immediately burst into loud laughter.

Again, I asked, "What did he say?"

Ngoc started shaking his head and said, "He asked if we want to shoot more pigs." He paused, then, "Crazy! Let's go Trung uy. Enough for your first day in war."

I was carrying my equipment to the jeep when Sergeant Freedman walked up beside me, "An interesting first night for you, wasn't it, sir." he said.

"That it was," I replied.

Freedman was still clad in his camouflage face paint. Looking at him might have given one the impression that he was a fierce warrior who had been hardened and made insensitive by his training and combat experiences as a career soldier. But, as we looked out over the village at the base of the hill, the war paint seemed more a disguise as his true nature was unmasked. Beginning that morning and continuing through the time we would serve together, it became clear to me that this Special Forces soldier was a very dedicated, warm, and sensitive man.

"You know, sir . . ." he said, "We've been up here several nights now. And, every morning as I stood and watched the sunrise across the hill, I have felt good. I don't know . . . maybe because, as the villagers suggested, we have served as guardians over the city and the families in the village down there." After a brief pause, he added, "The other guys feel the same way and, as I mentioned last night, we like the feeling. This kind of assignment is the best part of what we do."

It had been a very long, exhausting night for me. Knowing that the VC and NVA might renew their recent attacks at any time during the night had kept me from any thought of sleeping all night long. I was mentally drained and physically tired. Even so, the feelings so openly expressed to me by Sergeant Larry Freedman were both unexpected and, quite frankly—inspiring. Freedman's words gave a lift to my morning. I felt good and proud knowing that I was joining a team with men such as these.

I felt better still when my friend Bill Phalen strode up looking as tired and worn as I felt. We loaded our gear into the jeep and headed back to Trung Dung. Looking back as we drove away from the hill, it occurred to me that, indeed—both ghosts and guardians had been present on Buddha Hill that night.

Finally, it seemed safe to assume that I had survived my first day in the Vietnam War—but, I wasn't going to say that out loud again, especially in Thieu ta's presence.

Village and the South China Sea

This was my view of the village from the south side of Buddha Hill and the South China Sea is visible in the distance. It looked like a tropical resort view.

Vietnamese Special Forces LLDB Patch

This is the patch Ngoc presented to me that morning on Buddha Hill after our first mission together. Because it was a Vietnamese insignia, it wasn't sewn onto my uniform. Rather, it was encased in clear plastic and was made with a buttonhole attachment at the top so it would fit on the pocket button of my jungle fatigues. Over fifty years later—I still have it, a memento of immeasurable significance to me.

Chapter 17

Angels in Camouflage

IT WAS A LITTLE past midday. I don't remember whether it was a weekday or the weekend. I had been in-country for almost a month, and the day of the week didn't seem important anymore. I was now accustomed to the unexpected as routine. The war, rather than the time or day of the week, dictated the flow of work.

Paul Koch (pronounced "Cook"), my intelligence sergeant, and I had been working on a report for 5th Group Headquarters for most of the morning. I was sipping on a Coca Cola while he went to retrieve a map from the Operations office. I lived on Coke while in Vietnam. I was just putting the bottle down when Lieutenant Lane walked in.

"Good morning. Where is Sergeant Koch?" he asked.

"Gone to get me a new map."

"Any hot intel?" he then queried.

"Yes, as a matter of fact. We're working on a report for Group that will confirm that 10 to 15 percent of our CIDG soldiers are very likely VC sympathizers who would probably kill you given the opportunity," I said.

"Makes being out with them at night a bitch. Right?" he quipped.

"Yeah, but it keeps me awake," I said.

Lane chuckled.

BOOM! BOOM! BOOM! Not so far away explosions suddenly rocked the building. My Coke fell over and rolled off the desk, shattering on the floor in bubbling brown foam. Lane and I jumped up and immediately rushed out into the compound. Over the fort's southeast wall, we could see black smoke billowing near the base of the Dong Bo Mountains.

Sergeant Koch, a mild-mannered, detail-oriented man who often wore glasses, rushed up, handed me a map, and exclaimed, "What the hell was that!?"

"I don't know, but it wasn't thunder, and it wasn't an impact from the ROK's (pronounced "Rocks") artillery. We would have heard the guns first," I said.

"ROKs" was what we called the Republic of Korea troops, one of our important allies during the Vietnam War. Their ROK 9th "White Horse" Division base was just north of the Song Cai River, which ran along the north side of Dien Khanh village. The Song Cai served as a boundary between our AO and theirs.

Occasionally, the ROKs provided artillery support for our operations. But their camp was northwest of us, and this explosion had seemingly come from the southeast. If the ROKs had been the source of the explosion, we would have heard their guns fire, and then heard the shells when they streaked over the camp. Because we had heard neither, I felt sure it wasn't the Koreans firing.

"The train! I'll bet the bastards ambushed the supply train again," Lane surmised.

In only moments, things became exigently hectic. Two large 2 1/2-ton trucks roared into the compound and Vietnamese soldiers in full combat gear began climbing aboard. A Vietnamese Special Forces soldier ran toward me through the loading troops. He was yelling and his message was urgent, "Trung Uy! NVA have exploded the train that comes from Cam Rahn Bay!"

"I knew it!" Lane exclaimed.

The soldier continued, "Thieu Ta want you come with him to respond."

"Okay! I will get my gear. Tell him I am coming."

The soldier dashed off and I ran to the office. As I reemerged donning my gear, I scanned the compound, looking for my Montagnard radioman and bodyguard, AHAT (pronounced "Ah-ott"). Ahat had the devilish appearance and demeanor of a young teenage boy, but he would protect me with his life. I spotted him, radio pack on his back, carbine in hand, and already running toward me.

"Ahat! We di-di (go fast)!" I shouted.

The trucks, loaded with troops, roared away as Ngoc's jeep skidded up.

"Get in!" Ngoc shouted.

I jumped in the back seat and looked over my shoulder for Ahat. When he saw me looking for him, he grinned widely, as if pleased that he had reached me so quickly. He jumped onto the rear bumper, climbed over the seat, and plopped down next to me. He looked at me—and grinned again. The jeep sped after the trucks.

The Special Forces often used Montagnards as radiomen, bodyguards, and trail watchers because of their loyalty and dependability. The Montagnards, who had also fought with the French when they were in Vietnam, were a tribal people who often lived in remote areas throughout the country. Frequently referred to by Americans simply as "Yards," the Montagnards were looked down upon by the Vietnamese. A minority group, they were considered inferior because of their primitive lifestyle. Vietnamese called them *moi,* which meant savages. In many ways they were very primitive; often they had only their traditional crossbows with which to hunt food and defend themselves.

Obviously, so poorly armed, they were no match for the VC or NVA, who either by force or intimidation would press the Montagnards into servitude. But to the Americans who clothed, fed, and offered medical care to them, the Montagnards were fiercely loyal. After training from SF advisers, they proved to be equally fierce soldiers.

Typically, two or more of our SF team members would go out on a mission serving as advisers to a squad, platoon, or company-size Vietnamese force. As my report to 5th Group would indicate, and as American and Vietnamese officers at Trung Dung agreed, as much as 15 percent of the Vietnamese CIDG troops in camp could be VC sympathizers. So, the Montagnards were used in the dual role of radiomen and bodyguards. During the day and at night they took turns standing watch over their American advisers, if and when they slept.

Despite the primitive nature of the tribesmen, SF advisers and the Montagnards they trained developed many warm relationships as they shared some of their respective cultures with each other. It was not unusual for an SF adviser to be taken as an honorary member of the Rhade or one of the other Montagnard tribes. The induction ceremony could be elaborate, taking as long as two hours, or it could be as simple as giving the honoree a carved metal bracelet, which symbolically bound him to the tribe. Such a bracelet given to me remains one of my proudest possessions.

While they were primitive, the Montagnards seemed to me to be an attractive, gentle people with many fine qualities. They had dark-brown skin, straight black hair, and larger, rounder eyes than the Vietnamese. They looked somewhat Polynesian to me, though with darker skin.

The Montagnards and their consistently demonstrated loyalty to SF soldiers were critically important and meant a great deal to the men of A-502. One day, when desperately needed, team members would be given the opportunity to reciprocate. The team would launch a bold and daring rescue mission into enemy territory in an attempt to free the enslaved inhabitants of a Montagnard mountain village—while risking their own lives in the effort. My next book, Rescue in the Valley of the Tigers, describes that mission in detail.

Ahat, who I used as a radioman and bodyguard whenever possible, was young, about eighteen or nineteen. At twenty-two, I wasn't much older than he was.

I came to treat him as a younger brother and thought of him as a friend. He possessed all the qualities he had been hired for and more. He was loyal and dependable, and he took his role as my protector very seriously.

Because the Vietnamese troops treated the Montagnards as inferiors, no love was lost between the two groups. In addition, because of the ever-present suspicion about VC sympathizers residing among the South Vietnamese troops, Ahat watched the South Vietnamese troops as closely as he watched the jungle for the known enemy whenever we were out on a mission.

On one particular patrol, we had stopped and set up camp for the night. It was almost dark when a Vietnamese soldier with our unit spotted a piece of fruit hanging in a tree—just above my head. He had taken his knife out and was moving toward the tree to harvest the fruit. Ahat saw his knife come out and had no idea of the soldier's intention. When Ahat saw him moving in my direction, he didn't wait to discover the soldier's intentions. He sprang out of the semi-darkness and jammed his carbine up into the soldier's ribcage. After a Vietnamese sergeant convinced him that the soldier wasn't trying to kill me, Ahat stepped aside so he could cut down the fruit. Not surprisingly, the soldier had momentarily lost his appetite and put his knife away.

After that incident, the soldier always stayed far away from me whenever Ahat was around. Ahat would laugh and point when he saw the soldier taking the long way around us.

When we reached the site of the explosion, we could see enemy soldiers fleeing into the Dong Bo Mountains. From the engine to the caboose, all the cars of a munitions train had been derailed into a rice paddy. The heavy engine was sideways, astride twisted blown away tracks. Boxcars and flatcars, loads scattered, were on their sides. Small fires burned and swirling smoke filled the air. Shocked, injured train personnel and guards wandered aimlessly.

The train was carrying several types of ammunition that had been shipped into Cam Ranh Bay for distribution around the country.

Our troops immediately began to deploy. Ngoc and I quickly dismounted the jeep and began walking with weapons ready toward the wreckage to survey the damage.

"See any bad guys?" I asked.

"No, they go back to the mountain. Hidden base camp there."

I took a step, then came to an abrupt stop. "Stop!" I shouted.
Ngoc immediately stopped and looked at me to see why I was alarmed.

I pointed, "Mortar rounds everywhere Thieu ta. And, they've been blown far enough that some may be armed. We need to treat the entire area like a minefield."

Mortar rounds, grenades of different types, and mines had been blown out of the derailed cars and were strewn about. Some rounds can become armed after traveling a certain distance from the firing tube or barrel. Because these had all been blown out of the train with much the same force as if they had been fired from a mortar tube, we had no way to know which, if any, were already armed.

Ngoc understood my concern, "Yes, very dangerous. I go back to jeep and radio for the explosives team. We may have to drain paddy."

While Ngoc went to radio for help, I continued toward the railroad berm and carefully stepped down into the old rice paddy. The murky water was ankle-deep with holes that were shin-deep, a hazard—even without the explosives that were everywhere.

A Vietnamese soldier who saw me stepping gingerly through the area was amused at my cautious movements and started to laugh. He was obviously unaware of the danger involved in handling the explosives that were scattered all around us. Stupidly, he bent down and picked up a large mortar round and held it out in my direction.

"You want, Trung Uy?"

"No, I don't want. You keep it. You go boom!"

Without warning, he began running toward me with the round. I believed he was just clowning around, trying to scare me, because he was laughing as he ran. However, his demeanor changed quickly when Ahat and I leveled our rifles at him. His laughter stopped abruptly, and he froze in his tracks.

I asked my Vietnamese interpreter, who was also standing nearby, to explain the potential danger of the mortar round to the soldier.

"Tell him it could explode at any second," I said.

The words had barely passed the interpreter's lips when the soldier, now very frightened himself, turned and threw the round toward an open part of the rice paddy in which we were standing.

Instantly, I yelled warning in Vietnamese, "Xuong, Xuong! (Get down!)" and dove for the ground.

Everyone, close enough to realize the danger of the situation, immediately followed me down, all trying to get as low as possible before the anticipated explosion. But because we were in a rice paddy, we all hit water and mud rather than dirt.

Holding my breath, with my face in the mud at the bottom of a Southeast Asian rice paddy, I very slowly counted to five to be sure the round had more than enough time to impact and explode. Luckily for everyone, nothing happened. The round simply splashed and buried into the paddy mud.

When we stood, we were dripping wet and muddy, with pieces of rice plants hanging all over us. The sight of soldiers covered with mud and weeds was ridiculous. Someone started to laugh and the laughter became contagious.

As the laughter subsided, I was struck by both the absurdity and the more serious aspect of the incident. There I was, halfway around the world from my home, standing in water and muck almost up to my knees, and my life could have been lost because of a senseless accident, an accident caused by one of the very people I had come so far to help.

SF advisers had to deal with similar incidents far too frequently. We laughed about it at that time, but other events weren't funny at all—some ending in tragedy.

I was still shaking off rice fronds when Thieu ta Ngoc sloshed up beside me. He was clearly confused by the scene and asked, "Trung Uy . . . what has happened? Explosion?"

Annoyed and a bit exasperated, I answered, "No, Thieu ta. No explosion." Then, I asked my interpreter to explain what had happened.

After learning what had occurred, Ngoc became angry and yelled at the soldier, reprimanding him. The soldier, humiliated by the public scolding, was dismissed and left to rejoin his unit.

Now, wiping at the mud on my face and pulling pieces of rice plant off my M-16, Thieu Ta decided to have some fun at my expense. He was smiling widely when he said, "You know how funny you look, right?"

Shaking water out of my rifle, "Yes, Thieu ta, I know."

Regarding the mud on my face, he continued, "Look like you try to harvest rice with your mouth."

I wiped at the mud, then started to laugh. Ngoc and others who understood what had been said started to laugh as well.

Suddenly, SPLASH-ZING! SPLASH-ZING! SPLASH-ZING! Something had just torn into the water around us. Almost immediately, we heard the report of distant gunfire. The fire was sporadic, but it only takes one bullet in the right place to kill you. The fun was over, I yelled, "Incoming! Take cover!"

Ngoc echoed (in Vietnamese), "Incoming! Get down!"

We were standing in an open paddy, so everyone began to run, sloshing for cover behind either one of the overturned boxcars or the railroad berm. Rounds ripped the water around us as we ran.

When a Vietnamese soldier was hit and went down, one of Ngoc's sergeants pulled him up and helped him to cover behind a boxcar. At the same time, Ngoc's troops who had already reached the berm were returning fire, trying to provide cover for those of us caught in the open.

Ngoc and I, with Ahat close behind, jumped out of the paddy, ran through the underbrush, and slammed into the base of the berm. A hailstorm of bullets tore along the berm just above our heads, some twanging when they hit the rails. Others flashed sparks when they struck small rocks in the railroad bed.

"Sounds like they're somewhere on the mountain," I said to Ngoc.

"Yes, hilltop. I saw flashes when we running."

Incoming and return fire cracked and echoed around us.

"Looks like they may have us pinned down," I said.

"Yes, and mortars at Trung-Dung too far away. We will need artillery," Ngoc said.

I pulled out the new map Sergeant Koch had just given me and studied it. Then, pointing on the map, "I think we are here and they are there."

"Yes, I agree," Ngoc said.

"Okay, let me see if I can get us some help."

Ahat was hugging the berm about six yards away when I called to him, "Ahat!"

When he looked at me, I motioned him over. He quickly jumped up, ran over, and dropped down next to me.

Ahat was very concerned by our situation and asked, "What we do, Trung uy?"

Trying to reassure him, and maybe myself, I told him, "We're gonna blow their butts off that hill."

Ahat smiled as he gave me the radio handset off his web harness. I adjusted the radio frequency and made my call.

Bullets again tore along the tracks with something added. BOOM! BOOM! The NVA were now firing B-40 rockets at us.

We had responded to the ambush of the train so quickly that the NVA hadn't had a chance to carry much, if anything, away from the site. Apparently, when they saw us coming into the area they had returned to the safety of the mountains. Some of them had taken up positions on the nearby hilltop and were obviously trying to kill a few of us or chase us far enough away from the train so that they could regain access to the spoils.

My first call for artillery support went to the ROKs. Unfortunately, they were already on a fire mission in support of one of their own units and couldn't help. As Ngoc had pointed out, the mortar tubes at the camp were too small and too far away to help. The guns in Nha Trang were my next consideration, but I was concerned that they might be on the wrong side of the mountain to hit the hilltop. We were certainly in a tight spot.

With the NVA still taking potshots at us, we were prevented from moving without exposing ourselves to the possibility of a more intense fire. I decided to call the artillery battery in Nha Trang to see how close they could come. "Trip Hammer, Trip Hammer . . . this is Bunkhouse Zero Two, Zero Two. Over."

After a brief pause, they responded, "This is Trip Hammer. Go ahead, Zero Two."

"Trip Hammer, this is Bunkhouse Zero Two. We are pinned down west of your location by an enemy unit sniping at us from a hilltop. I have a fire mission. Over."

"Roger, Zero Two. Give me your fire mission. Over."

"Trip Hammer, Zero Two. Give me one smoke round at coordinates 9535-5125. Will adjust. Over."

"Roger, Zero Two. Understand, one smoke round at 9535-5125. Over."

"Trip Hammer, Zero Two. Confirmed. Fire when ready. Over."

"Roger, Zero Two. Stand by. Trip Hammer, out."

Ngoc had been thinking, "Trung uy, I know this artillery. They are on other side of mountain. May not be able to hit hilltop."

"Yes, I know," I agreed.

We heard a distant BOOM! The artillery round was on its way. Ngoc and I quickly crawled up the side of the berm and peered over the rails to see where the round would hit.

BOOM! The round exploded on the mountainside, missing the hilltop. White smoke billowed from the thick dark green trees and jungle foliage.

"Damn!" I said.

"Yes, no surprise," Ngoc said.

We slid down the berm and I again took the radio handset. "Trip Hammer, Zero Two. Over."

"This is Trip Hammer. Go, Two."

"Trip Hammer, that round was about 300 yards long. Over."

"Roger, Two. Afraid of that. We can't hit your target from here. Over."

"Roger. Understand, thanks for trying. Zero Two, out."

BOOM! We recoiled at the earsplitting sound of a B-40 rocket exploding on top of the berm. Debris rained down on us and dust swirled.

"You know what we have to do?" Ngoc said.

My ears were still ringing and I was annoyed by the harassing gunfire and bombardment when I responded, "Yes, get the hell out of here! Their aim is getting better."

"Yes, they kill us if we stay here. We need to go over tracks and try to reach tree-line. If we can get there, better than here," Ngoc said.

We weren't about to leave the train and its cargo to the NVA. But Ngoc was correct, our only immediate alternative was to assault across the tracks and through the wreckage to the other side of the railroad bed. Once there, we would be hidden and could pursue the enemy or set up defensive positions and wait for reinforcements to arrive. At least, on the other side of the tracks, we had options. Where we were, we amounted to little more than ducks in a carnival shooting gallery.

As I looked around, I could see that we were in a large area of open paddies. Any approaching reinforcements would also be easy targets for the enemy, who from their hilltop perch had a bird's-eye view of the entire valley floor. We needed to assault over the berm and we needed to do it soon.

Ngoc and I had moved down the berm to determine the best path for our assault when Ahat called to me. He waved the radio handset over his head and yelled, "Zero Two! Zero Two!" That was his way of letting me know someone was calling me on the radio.

I motioned for him to stay where he was and I made my way back to where he had taken cover with the radio. An occasional bullet ricocheted around us and we could hear a rocket boom not far away.

Taking the handset, "This is Zero Two, go ahead. Over."

"Zero Two, Trip Hammer. We could have some good news for you. Over."

"We could use some good news. Over."

"5th Group's FDC (Fire Direction Center) has been monitoring our transmissions. They have a flight of two Air Force F-4 Phantoms available. Do you want them? Over."

That was just one of many, many times that I was very proud to be an American soldier with other Americans backing me up. "Yes, I want them! How do I contact them? Over."

"We're giving them your frequency and call sign on another radio right now. They will be contacting you shortly. Their call sign is Red Dog. Over."

"Got it. Thanks for the help. Zero Two, out." I passed the handset back to Ahat and told Ngoc, "Help is on the way."

Ngoc smiled and showed me a thumbs-up.

After some time had passed, we began scanning the cloudy sky for our incoming air support from our tenuous position along the railroad berm. Shortly, the two F-4s checked in.

"Bunkhouse Zero Two, Bunkhouse Zero Two . . . this is Red Dog Leader, Red Dog Leader. Over."

I was ready, "Roger, Red Dog Leader, this is Bunkhouse Zero Two. Go ahead. Over."

"Ahh, Roger, Zero Two. Understand you have a problem. How can we be of assistance? Over."

"Red Dog Leader, this is Zero Two. We have incoming fire from VC located on a small hilltop just south of our position. We'd like to discourage them. Over."

"Roger. Understand. We can do that."

"Good. Do you have my location, Leader? Over."

"Roger, Zero Two. Fire Control passed it to us. We should be over your location shortly. We are going to have to punch through the cloud cover somewhere. We'll check in with you when we think we're over you. You'll need to direct us from that point. Over."

"Roger, Red Dog. Will do. Zero Two, standing by. Out."

Only a couple of minutes had passed when we began to hear the sound of jet engines in the distance. They were coming toward us from the east but were still somewhere above the clouds.

This was my first experience directing an airstrike, and I wanted to avoid friendly casualties on the ground or in the air. The hilltop where the VC were located was flanked and backed by higher mountains. I was concerned about the two incoming pilots and how they might approach our target, deliver ordinance, and regain altitude before smashing into one of the taller mountains.

We were still receiving incoming fire from the hilltop when Ngoc said, "They are getting close."

Just then, the radio came to life. "Bunkhouse Zero Two, this is Red Dog Leader. Over."

"Roger, Red Dog. Go!"

"Ahhh, Roger, Zero Two. We should be over your position just about . . ." There was a long pause and then, "now! Over."

BOOM! BOOM! Simultaneously, there was a screaming roar of jet engines as the two camouflaged jets burst through the clouds almost directly overhead. They were on an east-to-west heading, which would take them up the valley toward our camp. The two camouflaged Phantoms were a glorious sight—powerful and menacing.

All along the railroad berm, Ngoc's troops began cheering. Ahat was nearly glowing. "We gonna live," he said, showing me one of his big grins.

Advising them of their location, "Leader, Zero Two. You came through right on top of us. Over."

"Roger, Zero Two. You say our target is to the south? Over."

"Roger, Leader."

"Ahhhh . . . Okay Zero Two, we're gonna make a turn to the north and pass back over you, headed toward your target. I'd like you to pop some smoke and direct us from your position. Over."

"Roger, Leader."

After tossing a smoke canister up on the railroad bed, I prepared to give directions to the hilltop. Then, I remembered the magazine of all tracer rounds I had been carrying around for about two weeks. I had loaded the tracers one day before a night ambush. My plan was to use it to mark a potential target for air support we were to have available that night. But since it hadn't been used, the magazine was still in one of my ammo pouches. Marked with red tape, it stood out clearly when I opened the pouch.

After pulling the regular magazine out, I shoved the one with tracers up into my rifle, climbed to the top of the berm, and waited for the F-4s to return.

When the jets began their turn to the south, I called Red Dog.

"Red Dog, Zero Two. We've got smoke out and are prepared to mark the direction to your target. Over."

"Roger, Zero Two. We have yellow smoke. Over."

"Roger, Red Dog. That's us. Over."

"How are you marking our target? Over."

"Your target will be clear. It will be the hilltop at the end of our pointer. Over."

"Roger. Understand . . . at the end of your pointer?"

"Roger, Red Dog. And, watch the mountains on the south side of your target."

"Roger. Thank you. Get ready to mark. We are inbound."

Just before the two jets passed over my head, I pointed my M-16 at the hilltop and squeezed the trigger. It looked like a long red neon pointer. I held the trigger down until every round was gone.

"That's clear enough. We have your target, Zero Two," Red Dog said as they screamed directly overhead.

Immediately, their M61 Vulcan rotary cannon began to roar. As they did, dust, dirt, bark, and branches on the hilltop were blown into the air. They were right on target.

We could hear gunfire coming from the hilltop, but nothing seemed to be hitting anywhere around us.

"VC firing at the F-4s," Ngoc said.

After making separate passes on the target, each jet appeared to narrowly miss hitting the top of the mountain on the far side of the hill. Even Ngoc was concerned, "Very close, Trung Uy," he said as we watched the jets clear the mountain range.

This is crazy, I thought. *One of those guys is going to get killed trying to help us.* The mission needed to be ended.

"Red Dog Leader, this is Zero Two. Abort your mission! We don't want one of you piling into a mountain. We're getting ready to move across the tracks. Over."

Ngoc was listening and gave the signal for his troops to get ready to go.

"No, stay where you are, Zero Two. We're okay and only getting started. We just needed to get the lay of the land. Over."

"Roger, it's your call. Over."

"Roger. Thank you. Keep your heads down," was Red Dog's response as they again screamed back overhead, en route to another pass.

What followed was an extraordinary display of aviation skill and commitment to men on the ground who depended on them. The two jets made pass after pass, firing their cannons and dropping bombs. Each time, they came in low and pulled up steeply just in time to miss the mountaintops beyond the target. Watching the two pilots work was nothing short of electrifying. Their flying reminded me of the air shows put on by the Blue Angels back home in Pensacola, only in this context the show was considerably more exciting—the Blue Angels didn't drop bombs.

The bombs being dropped had fins on them that popped open as they cleared the plane's wing. The fins created drag and slowed their forward movement so they appeared to drop almost straight down. The accuracy with which the two pilots hit the hilltop time and time again made me believe they could drop their bombs down into a narrow well if that was their mission.

With apparent disregard for the danger he and his wingman faced with every pass, Red Dog Leader asked about our status as they began another one of their runs toward the hilltop.

Even before making their final pass, gunfire from the hilltop had ceased and we were able to move up onto the railroad tracks to secure the area. Ngoc and I were looking inside a damaged train car when Red Dog called again.

"Bunkhouse Zero Two, this is Red Dog Leader. Over."

As I took the radio handset, I looked around above the horizon to see where they were. Ngoc saw them. "There," he said, pointing. The two jets were coming out of a slow turn to our north and were headed straight for us again.

"Roger, Leader. Go ahead. Over."

"Roger, Zero Two. Ahh, I think we've eliminated your problem, and I'll bet they've been appropriately discouraged. But we're making one more pass just for a look-see. Over."

"Roger, Leader. We have no incoming, and we're up on the tracks now. Over."

Ngoc and I had moved some distance along the tracks to check all the cars. The two jets were almost directly over us when they made their final pass at a very low altitude.

"Roger, Zero Two. I've got ya. I assume that was you and your radioman on the tracks. Over."

"Roger, that was us."

"Good to see ya! We rarely ever see the people we're flying for."

"Roger, understand. Well, we were very glad to see you. You two saved lives down here. We're glad you were around. Zero Two, out."

The two jets, one behind the other, passed low over the hilltop that was now smoking and virtually bald. Each pulled up steeply as he had on earlier runs, then rolled out to the west.

They had made their attack runs individually but were now reunited and circled together from the west, headed back to the east, the direction from which they had originally come. Close together, the pair was flying down the valley. They were truly stirring to watch.

It is easy to admit that I felt a great swell of pride as I stood there and watched the two American jets approach our position. *Something is missing,* I thought, as they flew low through the valley toward us. *Where's the American flag, rippling behind them? Where's the symphony orchestra echoing through the valley with them? Where's "The Star-Spangled Banner"?*

Yes, romantic and theatrical I know. But, having survived another day in Vietnam—that's exactly what I thought and exactly how I felt.

Clearly, there was great admiration and appreciation for the two pilots and the two WSOs (Weapons Systems Officers) who flew with them. They had all unhesitatingly flown on our behalf. We had all watched as they carried out their mission, exposing themselves to ground fire and the possibility of a fiery crash into the mountains, not just once or twice, but time and time again. Still watching them, I considered the reality that it would be only a matter of time, maybe only hours, before the two crews were again called upon to exercise their courage and skill on behalf of another unit in trouble.

As they drew near, I squeezed the button on my radio handset.

"Red Dog, Zero Two, over."

"Leader. Go ahead, Zero Two."

When Red Dog Leader responded, the very low passing jets were just north of us. Ngoc and I, with troops all along the berm, were waving our appreciation.

The Phantoms seemed almost at eye level and, as they passed by us, we could see hands raised inside their cockpits.

"Take care of yourselves," I said.

"Roger, will do. You may need us again."

There was a short pause.

"Zero Two, Red Dog flight is headed home. Out."

With that as their last transmission, the two jets pulled up and disappeared back into the clouds almost as quickly as they had appeared.

Now able to safely transport our wounded and refocus on the aftermath of the train derailment, Ngoc and I turned and started back down the tracks. But, Ahat remained fixed, looking up into the clouds. "Trung uy," he said over his shoulder, ". . . look like big angels."

Ngoc and I laughed, but that wouldn't be the last time those supporting us from the air would be thought of as angels.

During my short time in Vietnam, I had already experienced bad days—days void of civility or warmth. And, I was sure there would be more to come. But this day had included courage, selflessness, and caring. I felt good and savored the feeling.

As Ngoc and I continued down the tracks, he quipped, "Big mess to clean up, Trung uy." I chuckled, but my thoughts were still with the two Air Force pilots. I wondered what they would think if they knew that they had been thought of as— angels.

On the next two pages, you will see one of Ahat's "Big Angeles" and—the train wreck. So, can see some of what Thieu ta Ngoc and I saw that day.

The F-4s that flew for us that day were part of the 12th Tactical Fighter Wing in Cam Rahn Bay. The 12th TFW was deployed from MacDill Air Force Base, Florida, and assigned to Cam Rahn Bay in November, 1965. The unit was the first F-4 Phantom II wing permanently assigned to Southeast

Asia.

The following operational squadrons flew for the 12th TFW:
557th TFS (Tactical Fighter Squadron), 558th TFS, 43rd TFS,
559th TFS, and the 391st TFS.

It was two planes and their two-man crews from one of the units just listed that came to our rescue. I choose to recognize and thank all of them.

"Red Dog" type Aircraft

The two U.S. Air Force Phantoms got Thieu ta, me, and our troops out of a very tight spot that day at the railroad berm. Ahat was certain they had saved our lives, and that may have been true. But what was certain, was the fact that Air Force pilots were responsible for saving countless other lives of American, Vietnamese, other allied troops, our Special Ops advisers, and more. So, Ahat may not have been so far off in his assessment of the two jets as angels, after all—they had descended from the heavens.

12th Tactical Fighter Wing Crest

Ambushed Train Wreck

This is the site of the train ambush and just part of the mess Thieu ta and I decided to let someone else clean up. The engine, on its side, was to the right and other cars were scattered to the left. You can see that the paddies were significantly drained and you can also see cases of supplies still on the ground to the right of the bottom boxcar.

Righting the Wrong

This picture and the one above were taken and contributed by Norm Kaufman, a 281st pilot who was flying by the train wreck a couple of days after the ambush. This picture was taken from the opposite side of the train tracks from the one at the top of the page.

In this picture, you can see the engine at an angle down over the side of the railroad berm and the crane in the center is righting a flatcar that has lost its entire load.

CHAPTER 18

In the Hands of the Unseen

NOT FAR FROM THE LOCATION of the supply train ambush, there was a village we suspected to be a safe haven for NVA soldiers who lived in the Dong Bo Mountains. In fact, we suspected that those who had attacked the train might have used the village as a staging area for the ambush. During an after-action discussion of the train derailment, Ngoc and I agreed that we should set up an ambush at a point between the village and the mountains. Our strategy was that a successful ambush might discourage the NVA and VC from using the village as a site from which to launch future attacks or deeper penetrations that would bring them closer to Trung Dung.

My friend, 1st Lieutenant Bill Phalen, was scheduled for ambush duty the night of the village mission. Sequence for ambush duty was typically determined by a rotation schedule, and it was Bill's turn. He would serve as the senior U.S. Adviser to his Vietnamese counterpart and a platoon-size unit (twenty-five to thirty-five men) from CIDG Company 555. A CIDG company was made up of Vietnamese who served as part-time soldiers. They could be farmers or they might work any variety of daytime jobs in nearby villages when the unit wasn't scheduled for a mission. Bill's primary mission, and that of the entire A-502 team as American Advisers, was to turn these civilians into a well-trained, well-equipped fighting force. And, as we knew, VC/NVA sympathizers would infiltrate the group for intelligence purposes.

For me, a bothersome aspect of Company 555 was that the unit's Vietnamese commander had been a Viet Cong soldier who decided to change alliances. The role reversal always bothered me, but Bill and Ahn, the ex-VC company commander seemed to have forged a very strong relationship. Even though Bill would always take at least one other American adviser with him when the patrol went out, I was always concerned about his safety.

As mentioned earlier, Bill and I met at Fort Bragg. We went through Special Forces training together and were now serving together. Bill was a low-key person who had been an enlisted man in the Army before requesting OCS where he was commissioned a 2nd Lieutenant. He then earned his green beret and SF assignment. So, he knew the service and wasn't easily ruffled.

Bill and his wife, Lisa, had been very kind to me when we were stationed at Fort Bragg. They lived off-post and, on several occasions, had invited me to dinner at their home. Lisa was a wonderful cook, so I always looked forward to those evenings. Other times, the three of us just went out for dinner after a long, hard day of training. Those times were a welcomed diversion from the rigors of intense training. We had become close and I enjoyed the time shared with them. So, when Bill's call for help came the night of the ambush, I would unleash a hellish artillery barrage in an aggressive and desperate attempt to save his life. While using every artillery direction skill taught to me since entering the service, ultimately, it would be unseen artillerymen who would have to help me deliver the firepower that would either save—or kill my friend.

I had been asleep for about two or three hours on the night I will never forget when one of our radiomen, SPC 4 (Specialist Fourth Class) James Miller, burst into my room.

"Lieutenant Ross! Wake up! Wake up! Lieutenant Phalen is in contact!"

For non-military readers, that meant that Bill's unit had triggered their ambush and at that moment they were probably in a blazing gunfight with the enemy.

Instantly awakened by Miller's loud intrusion, I responded, "Let's go!" exploding from my bed.

On my feet, but still not fully awake, I bounced off the walls of the hallway on my way to the radio room.

"Where is he?" I asked, trying to focus my eyes on the map in the bright light of the radio room.

I knew where the original ambush site was located, but I wasn't sure whether or not they had moved from that position.

Miller put his finger on the map.

"He's right there, sir."

I picked up the radio handset and immediately tried to reach Bill to determine his status.

"Blue Bandit Zero Six, Blue Bandit Zero Six, this is Bunkhouse Zero Two, Zero Two. Over."

When the radio remained silent and there was no response, I tried again.

"Blue Bandit Zero Six, Blue Bandit Zero Six, this is Bunkhouse Zero Two, Zero Two. Over."

Miller and I just looked at each other while the radio remained silent.

"You know," I said, "they're not that far away. Go to the door and see what you can hear."

Unless there was heavy rain, we could almost always hear the intensity of a firefight from camp.

Miller came running back to the radio room.

"It sounds like a hell of a fight out there, sir."

"Okay, get the rest of the team up and make sure the Vietnamese know what's happening and are getting reinforcements ready to roll."

I tried again to make radio contact with my friend, whom I knew might have already been down and hurt—or worse. Knowing the fighting must be fierce and loud, my call was louder this time. "Blue Bandit Zero Six, Blue Bandit Zero Six, this is Bunkhouse Zero Two, Zero Two. Over!"

Finally, the first response came. Initially, there was no voice, just the sound of gunfire. Someone had squeezed the button on the handset but hadn't said or wasn't able to say—anything.

The possibilities of what might be going on out there raced through my mind. *Is he hurt and unable to talk? Has an enemy soldier picked up the radio?*

Then came the familiar sound of Bill's voice. Instantly upon hearing it, I knew his situation was extremely serious. Over the sound of hammering gunfire, his voice was unemotional but matter-of-factly urgent.

"Tom, we're not going to make it outta here!"

As he spoke, the speakers pounded with the background sound of exploding rockets and grenades. The ear-piercing clatter of gunfire filled any void between the sound of rockets and grenades.

Bill was a skilled, confident military man, but when his response came in the clear, using my name and no call signs, I knew he was in serious trouble. I was sure he believed what he had just said to me—he expected to be killed.

"Bill, reinforcements are on the way," I tried to reassure my friend.

"They won't make it, Tom. We've ambushed a whole damn company [perhaps 75 to 150 men], and they are going to roll right over us. In fifteen minutes, there won't be anyone left to reinforce."

With Bill advising a unit of no more than 35 men and the enemy company having 75 to 150 or more, Bill's unit was vastly outnumbered.

"All right, all right!" I said. "Have you moved since you set up?"

"No, we're still here. But, they're all over the place and might be trying to surround us."

"Okay, stay near your radio and listen for me to call back."

I drew an X over Bill's position, then drew lines on three sides around him, essentially drawing a box around his position with one side open. Then, I asked Miller to plot the three-line positions. Artillery would be fired along these three sets of coordinates. Hopefully, a wall of fire would separate Bill from his enemy.

"Give them to me in this order," I said, pointing to the sequence we would use.

While Miller was writing down the line positions, I picked up one of the other radio handsets and set the frequency to the Korean artillery battery.

"White Horse, White Horse, this is Bunkhouse, Bunkhouse. Over."

The response of the Korean voice was quick and professional. "Roger, Bunkhouse, this is White Horse. Over."

We had often entertained Colonel Chang, the commander of the ROK unit to our north, at Trung Dung. For that reason, we enjoyed an excellent relationship with several of his officers. I was sure they would help unless they were already firing a mission for one of their own units.

"White Horse, we have a fire mission. We have a unit in contact and need your assistance. Over."

"Roger, Bunkhouse. We will help. At what coordinates do you want us to fire? Over?"

"Wait one, White Horse."

I asked for the first set of coordinates, checked the map quickly to confirm them, and squeezed the handset.

"White Horse, Bunkhouse. Use these coordinates," I said, and immediately gave them to him. "Wait for my command to fire. Then, fire all rounds HE (high explosive). Over."

"Roger, Bunkhouse. You don't want smoke first? Over?"

"No, we have no time. Over."

"Roger, we are ready. We wait for your command. Over."

"Roger, White Horse. Bunkhouse—out."

Normally, smoke rounds are fired first as marking rounds, to ensure that the high-explosive rounds don't kill friendly troops in case the coordinates were calculated or reported incorrectly. However, as I had told the Korean radioman, we had no time to take that precaution. Bill and his unit might all be killed even before we fired.

Miller changed the frequency on a third radio as I took the handset and called Trip Hammer, the artillery battery in Nha Trang. As soon as they answered, I repeated the same instructions given to the ROKs, using the second set of coordinates. Again, I was challenged when the high-explosives portion of the fire mission was given.

"Bunkhouse, this is Trip Hammer. Confirm . . . no marking round."

"Trip Hammer, this is Bunkhouse. No smoke, HE first rounds. Wait for my command to fire. Out."

"Roger, understood. Trip Hammer is standing by. Out."

Then, quickly changing the frequency to reach the big guns in Ninh Hoa, several kilometers/miles away, fire mission directions were given using the third and final set of coordinates.

As with the other two artillery units, they questioned the request for HE rounds first. The HE confirmation with these guns was critical and more important. They were firing 175-mm shells from miles away, and any one of them could kill or injure many of our own troops if they went off target.

The direction to Ninh Hoa was confirmed and in fewer than five minutes all guns were now ready to fire.

I called Bill to tell him what was about to happen. Because time was extremely short, much of our communication was abbreviated.

"Blue Bandit Zero Six, Blue Bandit Zero Six, Bunkhouse. Over."

"Go, Two."

Heavy gunfire and explosions could again be heard in the background when Bill responded.

"Bill, we've built a wall of artillery around you and are ready to fire. Over."

"Roger, Fire!" he yelled.

"Bill, there's no smoke."

"Roger, understand, no smoke. Fire!!"

"Roger. Bill, after impact, run north and into the village. Give me a mark every hundred meters, and we'll follow you. Get down! Over!"

"Roger, understand! We're down! Fire the damn things!"

At that point, I had a handset in each hand. I quickly dropped the one Bill was on and picked up another one, on which one artillery battery was waiting. All sets of guns were waiting, and two handsets were now open.

As I moved them close to my mouth, I looked at the X over Bill's position on the map and into both handsets gave the command to fire simultaneously.

"This is Bunkhouse. Fire! Fire! Fire!"

Then, quickly, Miller rolled the frequency dial around to the third set of guns, and the "Fire! Fire! Fire!" command was given once more.

Again, focused on the map and the X that indicated my friend's location, I could do nothing more for him—other than pray. I had made marks on a map with a grease pencil and reported them to the artillery batteries just as I had been trained to do. The effort to save Bill and his unit now fell to men at those various batteries. They had taken the coordinates they had been given and translated them into firing settings for their artillery pieces.

The "Fire!" command had barely passed my lips when we heard multiple distant booms. All three artillery batteries were pouring ordinance into the inky-black night sky. All we could do was wait and hope to hear Bill's "Mark" after he began to move.

When the artillery rounds began to impact, we could feel tremors in the radio room. As the big ones impacted, they boomed like thunder. I prayed they had been on target.

While the first rounds were still impacting, each of the artillery batteries was called and given directions for shifting their next volley of rounds. When we received Bill's "Mark", they would shift fire to cover his disengagement and withdrawal as he and his unit made their way to a nearby village that happened to be home for some of our soldiers.

While we waited to hear from Bill, one of our teammates ran in and told me the trucks with reinforcements were on their way. Several of our American advisers were with them. Those of us gathered around the radio wanted to believe they were going to make it in time to help.

Time seemed challenged to pass as we waited for Bill to call with the signal indicating he was still alive, had been able to disengage, and move a hundred meters north. I began to wonder if the call would even come.

Maybe I've killed him, I thought. *How ironic and terrible it would be if he has been killed by a friend, rather than by the enemy.*

As the sound of impacting artillery rounds continued to thunder in the distance, Miller, who I'm sure didn't want to make anyone feel worse, voiced his concern.

"Sir, that's an awful lot of ordinance hitting the ground out there. I hope he's still there."

Miller had simply verbalized what we were all thinking.

Then, visualizing my friend out in the dark in a fight for his life, and even though he couldn't hear me, I began to encourage him.

"Come on, Bill . . . come on. Call! I know you're out there somewhere. Call me!"

I rubbed my forehead, looked at my watch, folded my arms, and leaned back against the radio room wall.

Then, finally—the call came!

"Bunkhouse, this is Blue Bandit! MARK! MARK! MARK!"

Without a moment's delay, the order was given to the three sets of guns that were providing Bill's lifesaving wall of protection.

"Shift and fire!" to the ROKs.

"Shift and fire!" to the Nha Trang guns.

"Shift and fire!" to the guns at Ninh Hoa.

Then, without knowing anything about the emergency situation to which they had been asked to respond, and without being able to see their target, the gunners at three artillery batteries once again lit the black Vietnamese sky with huge bright orange muzzle flashes. More high-explosive rounds were on their way to shield Bill and his men from enemy pursuit.

After giving my command to the guns, I again urged Bill and his unit on. "Run, damn it, run!"

The contributions of the men who manned the artillery batteries in Vietnam have sometimes been taken for granted or simply overlooked. The men who pulled the lanyard dispatching what could be lifesaving artillery rounds often spent long and boring hours or even days at remote firebases waiting for a fire mission. When ground troops received support from jets dropping bombs and firing 20-mm cannons or helicopters launching rockets and firing .50-caliber machine guns, you could almost always hear and see your support. Often, though, artillery rounds fired by unseen hands would arrive from so far away that you couldn't hear them being fired. Nor would you see the faces of those who had fired them illuminated in the dark by the muzzle flash of their artillery pieces.

Men who served in the artillery had a tremendous responsibility. After days of inactivity, a call for help transmitted through the crackling static of a radio receiver could require them to respond within seconds. When they ran to man their guns, it could be mid-afternoon or the middle of the night, under a hot, scorching sun or in cold, drenching rain. Their mission was to send life-protecting artillery fire on its way to a distant target that they would probably never see. They might never know the outcome of the battle, or whether their efforts had helped at all.

The men of the forward firebases, on the other hand, might have welcomed more frequent breaks in the action. Those artillery units were in highly active parts of the country and were given equally active missions. They were charged with disrupting enemy movement and supporting field units on combat patrol, those that were out constantly seeking enemy contact. When they did make contact, the artillery battery would either aid in the attack or assist in defending the field unit.

Action at the forward firebases could be fierce and last for days. The artillery units often came under attack themselves during both day and night, even while they were firing in support of the field units who were counting on them to deliver. And they did deliver, continuing to do so unless or until an enemy hit silenced their own guns. These men who stood in support of others were extremely brave and dedicated.

I once visited a field artillery unit that had been set up near Trung Dung. It was early in my tour and the purpose of my visit was to become accustomed to the sound of loud explosions. My thinking was that if I became accustomed to it, the sound of explosions would be less distracting in the field if we ever came under attack. I felt that if I could maintain my composure and focus in such a situation, then I would surely have a better chance to do my job when the time came—and, maybe, survive the experience.

I'll never forget the look on the young artillery sergeant's face when I told him why I had come to his camp.

"You want to do what, sir?"

"I really want to go up next to the guns while they're firing."

Then, I explained the reason for my strange request.

"Well, sir . . . you're welcome to go help yourself to all the sound you want. But, here, take these earplugs. You'll need 'em."

"No, that's the point," I said. "I want to be exposed to the shock and raw sound."

"Okay, sir. Go ahead," he said, shaking his head as I walked toward the guns.

It was very dry that day. Every time the guns were fired, the earth shook and dust rose from the ground, boiling in the shockwaves that surrounded each gun. The first few times, I flinched as if hit when they fired. By later in the day, I had become accustomed to the sound.

At the time, the logic of the artillery exercise made sense to me, but it probably wasn't the smartest thing I've ever done. To this day, I experience ringing in my ears and often punctuate conversations with my wife, Amy, by asking "What did you say?" She has long since grown weary of that too-often-asked question.

Despite my hearing loss, the experience served me well later in my tour of duty. It also allowed me to meet a great group of men, young artillerymen who were still improving their skills as well as older seasoned men who were teaching them their art. They all seemed to love the idea that when a unit needed help, they could reach out to a distant battlefield and provide their explosive ordinance. Their intervention often meant the difference between life and death for the combat unit they were supporting. Their responses were always urgently quick and focused even though, as I've said, they might never see the battlefield or know the outcome. For that reason, I always made the effort to visit each of our supporting artillery batteries to thank them and tell them exactly what they had done and how they had helped.

My visits to the various batteries weren't altogether without other motives. While there, I would make it a point to go around and introduce myself to the radiomen who would receive a fire mission call as well as the men who manned and fired the artillery pieces. When I introduced myself, they could see my rank insignia and name on my uniform. So, other than for military protocol, there was no need to say, "I'm Lieutenant Ross." Rather than following protocol, I would say, "My name is Tom and my call sign is Bunkhouse Zero Two. If you ever receive a call from Bunkhouse Zero Two, I hope you will move just a little bit quicker." That introduction always drew a few chuckles. I would then spend a few minutes telling them where I was from in the States and what I did at A-502. I wanted to create a relationship so that, if/when I did have to call in a fire mission, they would be able to put a face with the person who needed their help. It wouldn't simply be a unit; it would be Bunkhouse Zero Two—it would be Tom.

In reality, those who served in the artillery, moved with energetic swiftness for every call because they knew an American life or other lives were at risk.

While we knew that he was still in danger, we were encouraged that Bill's unit had moved the first hundred meters successfully. We were hopeful that they would make the next hundred. With artillerymen now firing a second volley of rounds, I plotted and called the battery with the next set of shift directions.

Then, once again, we waited for Blue Bandit's next call.

While we were waiting for the next "Mark!", Lieutenant Colonel Allan Baer, an Air Force FAC (Forward Air Controller) had gotten his 0-1 Bird Dog observation plane airborne. He had heard what was happening from his headquarters at the Nha Trang Air Base and was headed our way. He checked in with an offer to help, one I quickly accepted.

Colonel Baer had more or less adopted or been adopted by, A-502 after Major Lee convinced 5th Group that a runway would give us greater mobility. Our resulting runway was built by the Navy's Seabees with the assistance of the 864th Engineer Battalion. While it was only about twelve hundred feet long, it gave us the ability to stage and launch missions quickly—an advantage I would one day need. Major Lee and Major Ngoc named the airstrip "Baer Field" in honor of the colonel who was the first pilot to land on it.

Colonel Baer, Captain William "Billy" Boyd, and another FAC flew many missions for A-502, both before and during my time in Vietnam. Just before I left the country, the word was circulated that the third FAC pilot had been reported MIA (Missing in Action) after failing to return from a mission far west of the camp.

The FAC's primary mission was to direct artillery fire or close air support, which is fire provided by other more heavily armed aircraft, from a key vantage point above the action. They also flew observation missions to seek out and report any detected enemy ground activities. That job was often more dangerous because it required flying low and slow which, of course, presented a tantalizing target of opportunity to the enemy, which perhaps is what had happened to the missing pilot. I never learned of his fate, but I always hoped he had somehow survived. And, if he had been captured, when American prisoners of war were released after the war, I hoped that he was among them.

Having a FAC available in support of a mission was always helpful because he could fly directly over any ground activity and see where the artillery rounds or bombs were impacting in relation to both enemy and friendly positions. After observing the impact, he could then adjust fire as necessary. However, at night, as in this case, even the FAC was likely to have difficulty determining who was where, especially with both friendly and enemy units on the move.

While Colonel Baer might not be able to see much by the light of hand-fired illumination flares, just knowing he was up there was enough to give all of us in and around the radio room a measure of comfort.

"Bunkhouse Zero Two, this is Walt Three Zero. Over."

With Bill due to signal at any second, I wanted to keep the frequency clear. My response to Walt Three Zero was brief. "Roger, Walt Three Zero. This is Zero Two. Try to determine Blue Bandit's location and stand by. Out."

When the word "over" is used on the radio, a response is expected. When the word "out" is used, it means the transmission is complete and no response is required. It was a good thing our communication was short because just as the button on the handset was released, Bill's signal came.

"Bunkhouse, this is Blue Bandit! MARK! MARK! MARK!"

Once more, the guns were called with the direction to "Shift and fire!" As before, battery gunners sent rounds of various sizes streaking on their way to a point between Bill and anyone foolish enough to still be pursuing him.

For the first time since the situation had begun, everyone began to relax a bit.

They're going to make it, I thought. Miller and others who had gathered around the radio room were also confident that Bill and his unit had successfully disengaged.

Comments like, "They're good!" and "Yes!" could be heard from more than one person. I hoped they were right.

After the third set of artillery fire hit the ground, Colonel Baer called to report. Knowing the situation, his transmission was concise.

"Zero Two, Walt Three Zero. Assuming they're on the north side of your fire, I have your men, over."

"Great! Please stick with them. We may need you. Out."

"Roger. Will do—out."

Then, as twice before, a new set of shift directions were given to the guns and, one more time, we waited to hear from our teammate who was quite literally running for his life.

Finally, after his last "Mark!" and after the last volley of rounds hit the ground, Bill radioed that he and his unit had made it into the village.

"Bunkhouse, this is Blue Bandit. We are in the village."

When that call came, cheers of "All right!" "Yes!" and "Okay!" once again burst from the small brotherhood of American advisers collected around the radio room. Smiles of relief and back-slapping went around the room.

Bill and his unit had reached cover from which they could more effectively defend against the much larger unit they had ambushed. Now they waited, and we waited, to see if the battle would continue.

After a few minutes, Bill called to say that there was no sign of the enemy, any pursuit had ended. He said they were moving through the village to the north side, where they would set up defensive positions and wait for reinforcements.

Momentarily, the reinforcing unit called in on Bill's frequency to say they were offloading from trucks and would soon be approaching the village from the north. I called Bill to make sure he had heard the transmission, so he and his men wouldn't open fire on the reinforcements.

With the battle over and the artillery now silent, the night was once again quiet. *Finally, I can relax*, I thought—I was wrong.

As time passed, it seemed obvious that the enemy unit had been forced to break contact. The artillery batteries had effectively discouraged the NVA from continuing the battle and required them to deal with their own survival. They had apparently taken their casualties and headed back into the Dong Bo Mountains.

However, the night was far from over. Responding to the impact of the final set of artillery rounds, Colonel Baer called in with a message that ensured there would be no more sleep for me that night.

"Zero Two, Walt Three Zero. Over."

"Roger, Walt Three Zero. Go ahead."

"Zero Two, I think one of those last rounds hit inside the village."

"No! Are you sure?" I asked, my stomach turning as I considered the possibility.

I couldn't believe what I had just heard. But the fire had been moved so quickly—*Maybe I made a mistake,* I thought.

Because I knew there were families with children living in the village, I began to ache with the fear of what I might have done. The accidental killing of adult villagers caught in the middle of this war was upsetting enough, but the thought of children being hurt or killed flushed me with nausea.

"Zero Two, this is Walt Three Zero. Yeah, I'm afraid so. I was in a turn and didn't have a real good angle on it, but it looked to me like it hit inside the village. And, I've got smoke rising from just inside the village perimeter on the south side. Over."

"Roger, Three Zero. I knew we were getting close, but I thought sure my last plot was far enough away to miss the village."

Colonel Baer sensed the distress in my voice. "Ah . . . Zero Two. Nearly all the flares have gone out. It's very dark out here now. Your unit is in the village and they're okay. I could be wrong about the artillery. I'll come back out at first light and take a closer look. Over."

He was trying to make me feel better about the situation until we could be certain and I knew that. At that point, there was little either of us could do.

"Roger, Walt. Thank you much, I would appreciate that. I'm going to see what our ground unit can find out, but I'll be right here with the radio at first light. Over."

"Roger. See you in the morning, Zero Two. Walt Three Zero — out."

Putting the handset down, I told Miller he could find me outside. I asked him to let me know when Bill and the reinforcements linked up. However, my joy over Bill's escape was now tempered by the anguish of the terrible mistake I had apparently made. My friend and his unit were safe, but if my direction of the artillery had accidentally killed innocent children in the process of saving him, my sorrow would be crushing.

Outside, I walked a small, slow loop around the compound, then stopped, leaned up against a fence post, and looked out across the dark night sky. Off in the distance, the last flickering of a dying flare was barely visible. As I watched it drift down over the village, I wondered about the families below it and hoped that they were all safe. In my mind, I pictured the faces of some of the children with whom I had only a passing, but warm relationship.

From time to time, I would borrow one of the motorcycles in camp and ride out through some of the villages near the camp. It was a way for me to relax and at the same time familiarize myself with the area around the camp. While out on some of those rides, I had encountered children in or near their villages. After they had seen me a few times, they would return my wave as I passed by. After that, I would occasionally stop and pass out goodies my mother had sent to me. Those were the faces I now pictured in my mind's eye.

This isn't what I came here for, I thought.

Children weren't supposed to be involved in a war, but sometimes it happened. I was now learning in a very personal way that children are unfortunately and sadly all too often involved as innocent and direct victims of war.

For a while, I struggled in an unsuccessful attempt to rationalize what might have happened. *This is a war—these things happen—my friend is safe,* I considered. But, none of it worked. It didn't make any difference to me why or how the village had been shelled. If it had been hit, I knew I was responsible. If the worst had happened, I would carry the thought of that horrific and sickening tragedy with me for the rest of my life.

The euphoria I felt only a few moments before when Bill and his men reached safety was gone—replaced with feelings I'd never experienced before and don't care to experience ever again.

This turn of events was unexpected and caught me completely by surprise, the kind of mistake I never expected to make. I honestly loved being a Special Forces officer and tried not just to be good, but to be exceptional at my job. No one could have been tougher on me than I was on myself for having made such a horrifically stupid mistake.

During the entire episode, I had known exactly where the village was located, since that was where Bill was headed. I had watched the movement of fire as it neared the village to be sure it wasn't hit.

I know it wasn't hit, I thought. *But, then, what was the smoke Walt Three Zero had seen?*

"Lieutenant Ross, the reinforcements have linked up with Lieutenant Phalen." In the quiet of the night, Miller's voice boomed from the doorway, refocusing my attention on the here and now.

"What?"

"The reinforcements have linked up with Lieutenant Phalen."

"Great. Thank you, Miller."

"Yes, sir. Everything turned out fine."

I didn't say anything else but followed him back into the team house. Returning to the map in the radio room, I retraced one last time all that had happened. Across the clear Plexiglas that covered the map, coordinate numbers given to the artillery batteries were written in grease pencil.

All of the numbers looked good, and I had checked each set myself before calling them into the guns.

Could I have repeated the last set of coordinates wrong when I called them in? I wondered. I didn't know. Whatever had happened, it was too late to do anything differently now. In a couple of hours, daylight would break over the village and I would know with certainty.

The "Unseen"

Above and below are a few of "the unseen" artillerymen who fired from long distances and dispatched life-saving munitions on their way to faraway battlefields. It was men like these who saved my friend Bill Phalen.

These pictures were taken by me and this is the battery where I went to become accustomed to the—Boom!

Chapter 19

Tortured Hours

RADIO ROOM SHIFTS WERE changing and Miller was going to bed. So, I asked Staff Sergeant Jean Lavaud, his replacement, to let me know when Walt Three Zero checked in, then walked down the hallway to my room.

Back in my bunk, I closed my eyes and tried to sleep, but there wasn't a chance that would happen. I knew I would be haunted by thoughts of those who may have been killed or injured until I heard Colonel Baer's morning report. Rolling over to face the wall next to my bunk, I stared at the strange shapes formed by the camp lights shining through my bamboo curtains. With nothing to do but wait until daylight, my mind flooded troubling images.

It was only a couple of hours, but during what seemed like a very long night, the images that filled my head were often muddled and disjointed, a jumbled collection of life experiences. Because the possibility of having shelled the village was tormenting, my mind searched for good thoughts of better times. For a while, that tactic helped distract me from the horrendous situation I now faced. Sadly, good thoughts never lasted very long, always replaced with images of a smoking crater inside the village and bodies of dead villagers. And, scattered among them were the tiny bodies of children I knew.

Just before dawn, I sat up on the edge of my bed. As morning approached, my fears remained unabated. Closing my eyes, I could see the village children lined up like pickets on a fence. They were waving and smiling as I passed.

The luminous dial on my watch indicated that first light was imminent. Still sitting on my bunk, I decided to get up and wait out what was left of the night.

Sergeant Lavaud, was still on duty in the radio room when I walked in to look at the map one more time as if that were going to change anything.

"Good morning," I said.

"Good morning, sir. That was one hell of a battle last night, wasn't it?"

"Yes, it was. Have you heard anything from Walt Three Zero yet?"

"No, sir, not yet."

"Okay, I'm going outside. Come get me when he calls."

"Will do, sir."

Outside, I found the post that had supported me in my distress during the early morning hours. Leaning against it once more, I watched and waited for the first glimmer of sunrise.

On the eastern horizon, sky met ground with a faint, thin, gold glow. As the light along the horizon widened and grew brighter, I wondered how bright the morning would be for me. With my friend's life spared, I felt the morning should be a glorious one. Instead, the day dawned with me leaning against a post, anxiously waiting to find out how much damage I had done.

My God, how will I ever explain this to my family and friends back home? I pondered with serious concern. I was deeply troubled over the possibility of actually having to tell them I had been involved in killing innocent people.

What will I say? What will I tell them? And, Dear God, how can I tell my mother I killed children. I didn't know, but just the thought was horrifying and physically sickening. If true, the incident would haunt me—forever.

Finally, Sergeant Lavaud opened the screen-door and called out to me. "Lieutenant Ross, Walt Three Zero just called to say he was airborne."

I immediately went to the radio room where it had all started the night before and made a call to Colonel Baer.

"Walt Three Zero, this is Bunkhouse Zero Two. Over."

"Roger, Zero Two. This is Walt Three Zero. How are you this morning?"

"Tired. Where are you?" I did not attempt to hide my anxiousness.

Sensing the importance of his report, Colonel Baer gave me his location and began to narrate his flight for me.

"I'm close, Zero Two. I'm only about five klicks (kilometers) east of the village now. I'll tell you what I see."

"Roger, thank you, Three Zero."

There was a short pause as he approached the ambush site and then turned north toward the village. "Well, I'm headed toward the village and can see where the artillery rounds impacted first. I'll follow them in."

There was another pause that seemed endless. Then, he continued, "Zero Two, I'm coming up on the village now. We'll know in a minute."

Then, he started to count slowly, "One . . . two . . . three . . . four." He was counting the impact craters created by the artillery rounds. There was another long pause that made brief seconds seem like long minutes. My insides turned, churned, and twisted in anticipation of his pending observation.

Then, finally, the torture of waiting for a report—ended. "Zero Two, Walt Three Zero reports NO (he emphasized) . . . I repeat, NO friendly damage. Over."

You could tell in his voice that Colonel Baer was as glad to make his report as I was to hear it.

While that moment may have been as close as I ever came to tears while in Vietnam, my response was brief and unemotional. "Roger, Walt Three Zero . . . understand, no damage."

I put the handset down and didn't move for a minute so I could let Colonel Baer's report echo around inside my head. Then, I turned my head slowly and smiled at Lavaud, who was sitting at his station next to the radios. He met my smile with one of his own and two thumbs up.

My outward response to Walt Three Zero's report was subdued, but my inner response was far more dramatic. I felt my spirit soar, as though it had burst out through the top of my head and up through the ceiling of the radio room. A feeling of incredible relief poured over my body like a hot refreshing shower, a feeling of genuine redemption, and peacefulness.

After a minute or two, I reached out, picked up the handset, and called, "Walt Three Zero, this is Bunkhouse Zero Two. Over."

"Roger, Zero Two. Go ahead."

"Roger, Three Zero. Thank you for your report and thank you for getting up and out so early to make it. Over."

"No problem, Zero Two. I was sure you wouldn't sleep last night."

"Well, you're right about that. Not a wink."

"Ahhh, Zero Two, wait one . . ." he paused. Then, "Okay, now I know what I saw last night. Yea, that's it! Zero Two, there's a flare chute hung up in the trees, right smack in the center of a housing cluster. It must have started a fire down there."

"Roger, Three Zero. I was sure you had seen something. Over."

"Roger, Zero Two. I'm sorry I called it wrong last night."

"Forget it. You were reporting what you saw. Believe me, I'm glad you were wrong. You made it right this morning. Over."

"That's a roger, Zero Two. I'm glad I could. Walt Three Zero is returning to base. Out."

I placed the handset down on the countertop and pushed it over to Lavaud. "Sergeant Lavaud, I'm going outside to enjoy the sunrise."

"Enjoy it, sir. I hope it's a nice one."

"Sergeant, I can guarantee it. Even if it were pouring rain it would be beautiful to me."

Just about the time I stepped outside, the trucks began to arrive bringing back to camp the reinforcements and the ambush team. I walked along the column as it rolled in, looking for Bill inside the front and back of each truck. Finally, near the back of the column, there he was, sitting in the passenger's side of one of the trucks.

We made eye contact as I crossed in front of the truck to his side. I jumped up on the running board of the truck as it rolled to a slow stop.

"Have a rough night, did ya?" I asked with a half-grin on my face.

As my grin grew bigger, he started shaking his head and hesitated only momentarily before responding. "Yes, I damn sure did! And, I don't ever want another one like it, thank you very much!"

With that, he pushed me off the side of the truck as he opened his door. Then, bouncing down from the truck, he looked me eye to eye. "I thought it was all over," he said.

"I know you did . . . and it is now," I said, a little softer, and added, "It's good to see you."

"It's good to see you too," he responded as he put his hand out and we shook hands. A great deal was communicated in that handshake. Nothing more was said or needed to be said.

The terrible experience Bill had been through showed on his face. I suggested that he go clean up and get some sleep. He nodded his head in agreement, picked up his gear, and headed for the team house. Turning, I continued down the column past the last of the trucks.

With my friend back in camp and the village intact, I could now savor the new morning and the glistening sunrise. There was no doubt in my mind that the joy found in this day was owed to artillerymen whose faces might never be seen, but whose presence was known and felt in the power and protection they had dispatched with surgical precision. Deeply grateful to them for the difference they made in the events of the past few hours, I took a deep breath to fill my lungs with the fresh morning air, took one last look at the sun as it continued to rise over the east wall, then went to give Thieu ta a report.

Friends — Teammates

My friend, Bill Phalen, and me, both very glad the night ended as it did.

LTC Allan R. Bear (FAC)

Colonel Bear was a man who knew his job and did it well and—he cared.

Village — In Harm's Way

This is a village like the one I thought had been hit with artillery. This may even be the village. One of our team advisers (radioman, Jean Lavaud) gave me this picture. The beauty of the setting made the war seem so unfortunate.

Chapter 20

A Foolish Ride

MORNING HAD DAWNED WITH a special brightness. My friend had survived an extremely close brush with death. Bill was like a cat with nine lives. The enemy hadn't killed him and I hadn't killed him with the artillery fired to save him. And, more relieving than I can explain with mere words, I hadn't killed families in a nearby friendly village with an errant artillery round. The round that could have been deadly had, in reality, missed the village by a very safe distance. For me, this was a day on which there was much to celebrate.

I was on the way to give Thieu ta an After-Action report when he saw me coming and met me at the bottom of the steps leading up to his quarters. He was in full combat gear.

"Good morning, Trung uy."

"Good morning, Thieu ta."

"Big battle last night."

"Yes, a very big battle."

Before I could give him my report, he had one of his own. "Trung uy, one of my officers that went with the reinforcements last night just called from the ambush site. You fired artillery last night, right?"

"Yes, I did."

"Well, my officer tells me that they have found many enemy bodies at that location. I have called for a chopper to go to that place. Get your equipment and come with me."

Within moments, we were aboard one of the old Sikorsky H34 helicopters flown by the South Vietnamese Army.

Upon landing in the area of the original ambush site, we found fifteen or twenty bodies of dead NVA and Viet Cong soldiers killed during the fierce battle of the night before, some killed by our ambush team and some by artillery. The encounter with Phalen's ambush team had been a costly one for the enemy. It was a gruesome sight.

After returning to Trung Dung, I was too wired to sleep after the activities of the night before and those I had just completed. The day was bright and beautiful, so I borrowed a motorcycle belonging to one of my teammates and headed out for a ride around the nearby village of Dien Khanh. This was something I had done many times before and truly enjoyed.

Before long, I found myself racing along rice paddy dikes and open Vietnamese countrysides. The beauty of the day and an attempt to step away from the war for just a short time had lured me to a place I should never have gone.

In what seemed like no time, I was riding on a trail to one of the villages near the base of the Dong Bo Mountains. I had never ridden that far from camp before, but the motorcycle and day made me feel as if I were back on my old dirt bike riding through the piney woods of Northwest Florida.

Typically, I rode wearing sunglasses, an old jungle hat, and civilian clothes to appear more like one of the local villagers so a VC wouldn't be tempted to take a pot shot at an American. But that day, I planned to stay around Dien Khanh. So, with my sunglasses on, I left camp wearing my green beret with the well-known 5th Special Forces Group flash and my shiny 1st Lieutenant's silver bar pinned over it, an olive-green T-shirt, a pair of camouflaged cut-off shorts, jungle boots, and a .45-caliber pistol strapped to my side—a real military fashion statement.

Before realizing it, my exuberance over Phalen's safe return to camp and limitless joy over not hitting the village with artillery had somehow allowed me to be beckoned beyond the limits of safety. The wind and sun felt good on my face as I raced along the trails and rice paddy dikes. The blue of the sky was reflected in the water filling the rice paddies.

Feeling as though I had indeed left the war back at Trung Dung, I enjoyed the tranquil beauty and pastoral serenity of the Asian countryside. Time and location seemed unimportant, but it soon became evident that I had ridden much too fast and had definitely gone much too far from camp.

As I came to a sharp turn in the trail, I downshifted and slowed just enough to navigate the curve and once again began to accelerate. Upon rounding the turn, I was surprised by what at first appeared to be a group of Vietnamese farmers. They were all squatted in a circle and a couple of them had sticks in their hands. I waved as I approached from the distance, hoping not to scare them and to let them know I saw them on the side of the trail. As I rode closer, they stood up. Clearly, something was strange about the situation. The men were all similarly dressed in greenish faded khaki clothing that I had recently seen—on the bodies of dead NVA soldiers.

The hair on the back of my neck immediately stood upright, telling me all was not right. Just then, I noticed what appeared to be the muzzles of weapons lined up on a log near the men who were now standing at the edge of the trail. Because the weapons were on the far side of the log, and because I was moving by so quickly, I had only a glance. But they looked remarkably like AK-47s—the enemy's weapon of choice. Exactly what type of weapons they were, seemed of little consequence at that moment.

It is at times like this that you realize how magnificent our brains are and how quickly they can process information—quicker than any computer I've ever used. I immediately knew I had ridden into an extremely dangerous situation and could either stop and turn around or ride past the danger.

In a split second, I considered my options. If I tried to stop, turn around, and go back the way I came, the men would have more than enough time to reach their weapons and probably kill me before I got out of sight. If I continued towards them, they would clearly see my beret, recognize my shiny American lieutenant's insignia, jump for their weapons, and maybe kill me before I got out of sight. I don't know how or why, but a third possibility suddenly occurred to me.

Because of the quickness of our encounter and my speed, neither the group nor I could do much except to acknowledge each other's presence. Hoping to surprise and distract them, I showed them a huge smile and waved again as I rode past them within an arm's length of the small assembly. None of them returned my smile, but two gave me a half-wave, perhaps a reflex response. Another man kicked sand across whatever they had scratched in the dirt. It seemed obvious he didn't want me to see whatever it was that they had drawn. After passing the men, I accelerated even more and waited to hear the crack of gunfire. Luckily, I was able to disappear around the next turn in the trail. Without ever looking back, I left the area as quickly as I could.

As I rode a paddy dike headed back to Trung Dung, there was little doubt in my mind that the men were NVA from the Dong Bo Mountains. They were either on a daylight recon patrol or a group separated from the unit of the night before. In either case, I had been—very lucky.

I had momentarily allowed myself to become disconnected from the war and had gone where I shouldn't have been, an error in judgment that could have cost me my life. While we knew that NVA and VC routinely infiltrated the city of Nha Trang, the village of Dien Khanh, and the other outlying villages, such action typically occurred at night. I didn't expect to see the enemy on such a bright sunny day. And, from their reaction, I feel quite certain that they certainly didn't expect to see me in what amounted to their backyard.

When I returned to camp, I went to see Giao (pronounced "yow"), a Vietnamese sergeant who always seemed to have a sixth sense about where to set up ambushes. I mentioned the incident to him and asked if he would check out the location. Sergeant Giao was thought of as fearless by both his Vietnamese troops and all of our American team members. When he led his combat recon platoon out on patrol or night ambush, his unit rarely returned without enemy bodies. He knew the entire Nha Trang Valley as well as team members knew their own hometowns. I also suspected that he had his own well-developed network of informants. His choices of ambush sites were too productive just to be lucky guesses.

When I told Giao about my experience he said, "Yeah, sure. I check it out, Trung Uy." Then, frowning, "That not a good place for you to be. You need stay away from there," he cautioned.

Less than a week later, after an ambush near the site of my bike ride, Giao and his unit returned with the bodies of four VC. Were they four of the men I encountered? One more thing I will never know.

I also mentioned the incident to Thieu ta, who only offered his opinion of my mental health, "You crazy, Trung uy!"

Weeks passed before I said anything about the incident on the trail to anyone else. I didn't want Major Lee or my teammates to find out because of my concern that they might think I was just dog stupid. Although, a dog would surely have had the good sense to avoid an area where he knew wolves prowled. Ironically enough, after sharing a few bottles of beer with him one Saturday afternoon, Major Lee would be the only other person in Vietnam to whom I ever told the story. His response, "Goddamn it, Ross! Don't do that again! I don't want to have to write a letter to your family telling them you're dead!"

While he was appropriately firm, Lee didn't really seem angry. In fact, he seemed amused by the tale—maybe because of the beer. Whatever the case, he never mentioned the incident again and neither did I. While I continued to take motorcycle rides, I never rode that far away again.

Tropical, Beautiful, and Very Dangerous

If the above were a "live" shot and the camera panned down, you might see me in a comfortable beach chair holding a cool tropical drink with a beautiful woman in a chair next to me. But, no, this is just some of the unexpectedly beautiful, but very dangerous terrain within A-502's AO. (Pictures - J. Lavaud)

Hidden Perils

There were many dangers in the unexpectedly beautiful Vietnamese landscape.

CHAPTER 21

The Beast

NOT EVERYTHING THAT HAPPENED in Vietnam was bad. There were many opportunities to laugh and to find inspiration in the American spirit, even though we were all very far away from home.

Over a period of a couple weeks, I noticed that Sergeants Mitchell Stewart and Louis Trujillo, two of A-502's team members, would disappear from the camp for hours. I also noticed that sometimes when they returned, they were covered with dust or mud, depending on the weather. Their appearance caused me to believe that they had been on an extended journey. If they had been involved in a military operation, I would have known about it. Even though their behavior was peculiar, I didn't say anything about it to anyone because they were both very good men. However, despite their excellent military records, I did keep an eye on them because I knew—they were up to something.

Finally, after one of their particularly extended outings, my curiosity got the best of me. I caught up with them as they were walking to our motor pool. "Where have you two been?" I asked.

Then, tauntingly, I let them know that I knew something was going on. "I know you two are up to something. I just don't know what it is yet."

Looking at each other, both men grinned widely. My suppositions were obviously correct, but the duo was only willing to offer a perfectly meaningless explanation. "We've been scouting, sir," Sergeant Stewart said.

"You're gonna like it, sir," Sergeant Trujillo added. "It's a surprise for the team."

"You don't want to know more than that, sir," Sergeant Stewart quipped.

That usually meant either that it was NCO business, something commissioned officers shouldn't be concerned with, or that it was something that could get someone, possibly even everyone—into trouble. Either way, I respected their suggestion that I not become involved. But I couldn't resist asking, as I turned to walk away, "We're not going to have to come somewhere to get you two outta jail, are we?"

They both laughed and, almost simultaneously, said, "We hope not!"

After that day, I didn't pay much attention to their forays to who-knows-where, until one day when they pulled into camp with what I came to call "the Beast." They dragged it in behind a truck and claimed it was an old armored fighting vehicle that had once belonged to the French.

"What are you going to do with that thing?" I asked.

"We're going to fix it up so it can fight again," Sergeant Stewart said. "We have some special, some very special equipment to put on it. That's where we've been going and what we've been working on."

As they began to work on their project the next day, everyone in the camp immediately became interested. Both Americans and Vietnamese would stop to watch as the two sergeants worked on the Beast, which more closely resembled a rusted-out war relic than anything that would ever see battle again. It was in desperate need of serious repairs, from its tires to its hatch.

As days rolled by, the two men worked on the Beast in their spare time at all hours of the day and night. Often, late at night, it was not unusual to see the flashing blue glow of a torch coming from inside the belly of the Beast or to see sparks flying from welding work on its thick outer hide.

I remember the great excitement on the day they finally got it to run. With Sergeant Trujillo at the controls in the driver's position and Sergeant

Stewart on the ground in front of him, Trujillo turned the ignition switch. The deep churning sound of the starter could be heard from within this huge mechanical monstrosity as it struggled to live. Then, after several seconds of trying, the Beast came to life! Belching thick black smoke, followed by a loud "Boom!" its heart began to beat as the diesel engine roared.

After Stewart and Trujillo got the Beast's engine running, they turned their attention to fine-tuning it and replacing or repairing damaged or missing pieces and parts. Their resourcefulness was truly amazing. If they couldn't find or repair an important part, they would simply make a new one. Though the focus of their pride was much larger than a watch, their work was as precise as that of a master Swiss watchmaker.

When all the mechanical malfunctions on the Beast had been corrected, Stewart and Trujillo set to work on its cosmetic appearance. When they sprayed the inside battleship gray, I suspected that one of their excursions might have taken them to the US Navy facility in Nha Trang. No one had any idea where they had found the paint or the air compressor they were using—and nobody was asking or wanted to know. One thing Special Forces soldiers were always known for was their resourcefulness.

When it came time to paint the outside of the Beast, they demonstrated they were not only excellent craftsmen, but they were also talented artists. Their pallet consisted of two or three shades of green, a reddish-brown, gray, and midnight black. With their array of paint, they began creating an interesting camouflage pattern. When they were finished, the work looked as though it had been done in a California custom body shop. The Beast was beautiful!

Just before what Stewart and Trujillo called the "official unveiling," another flurry of secretive work took place. The two sergeants erected a fabric wall around the vehicle's top turret. When anyone asked, "What are you doing now?" their reply was always an elusive, "Oh, just some finishing touches."

The two sergeants selected the day of an important formal camp formation of both U.S. and Vietnamese troops during which some citations and medals were to be presented as the proper time for their unveiling. When they drove the Beast out into the camp square, it was impressive, shining as if it had just come off of a General Motor's assembly line in Detroit, Michigan.

The two men who had given the Beast a second chance to serve were dressed in crisp, freshly starched fatigues. Their green berets were smartly set atop their heads and they had donned a bit of Hollywood glamour by the addition of bold bright red ascots to their uniforms. Sergeant Trujillo was in the driver's position, with only his head and neck protruding from the lower driver's portion of the Beast. And, Sergeant Stewart stood waist-high in the main turret, positioned behind a .50-caliber machine gun. They were both clearly very proud of their creation. Perched on top of their fighting vehicle, they looked a great deal like proud vintage tank men. I am reasonably sure that General George S. Patton, himself a veteran of mobile tank warfare, would have been proud to have men of such ingenuity in one of his columns.

Everything on the Beast looked new, from its headlights to the auxiliary gas cans on the back deck. It even had an imitation leather-grained cover made of vinyl for the machine gun, which pointed forward. A small flap made of the same material covered a strange, small protrusion on the rear side of the turret. When one of the team members asked what the flap covered, Sergeant Stewart said somewhat mysteriously, "We'll show that to you . . . later."

After the formation had been dismissed, the Beast was returned to a restricted area in the motor pool. Then Thieu ta Ngoc, Major Lee, and the American advisers were invited to attend a special demonstration.

Stewart and Trujillo took turns talking about what they had done to the fully restored and improved armored vehicle. When they began describing details of work on the turret, one of the men pointed to the .50-caliber machine gun. He said it had replaced a smaller gun originally installed on the vehicle.

While it was good to have an armored vehicle with a mounted .50-caliber, one might have expected more of a vehicle that resembled a tank and appeared as though it might have had a mounted cannon at one time. But no one would have said or done anything to show disappointment in the Beast. The two sergeants were obviously bursting with pride in their creation. As would soon become apparent, it was a good thing that no disparaging remarks were made.

Demonstrating the ability of the electrically operated turret to rotate as smoothly as the day it was made, Sergeant Stewart quickly spun the .50-caliber to the rear. He then commented, "You may think the fifty is our main gun, and that's exactly what we want everyone to think. But, as you will see, it isn't."

Sergeant Trujillo then unsnapped the small flap covering a small protrusion. When it was lifted, everyone was shocked at the sight. The two resourceful sergeants had removed the damaged cannon the French had originally installed and replaced it with—an electric minigun!

With a function and design based on that of the more famous Gatling gun, the minigun fired 7.62-mm ammunition, and its rotating multiple barrels made it capable of pouring out 6,000 rounds per minute. It could literally cut a tree in half! Problem—the Beast could carry only two minutes' worth of ammo.

With the Beast and its fire-breathing minigun, Stewart and Trujillo had essentially made themselves a rolling two-man army. Everyone attending their demonstration was appropriately impressed. However, they were also very curious as to how they had acquired such a formidable piece of weaponry as the minigun. The reason being, such weapons were very strictly controlled by the Department of the Army.

When asked where and how they had gotten a minigun, the two men would only say they had traded for it, "the same way we got the armored vehicle." Because of the firepower of the minigun and the exceptional mobility the vehicle provided the team, no one was about to press them for a more detailed response.

The only question I never asked them but wondered about is a chicken-or-egg-type query. *Did they find the armored vehicle first and need a gun for it?*

Or did they find the minigun first and need something to put it on? Whichever the case, they had shown impressive creativity and demonstrated typical Special Forces resourcefulness. The Beast would prove invaluable, not only in defending the camp but in serving as a means of rapid reinforcement for many of our ambush locations.

The only opportunity I had to see the men and the Beast in action came on their first emergency response, which occurred late one night, only a couple of weeks after they had made the Beast operational.

Major Lee, 1st Lieutenant Lane, and Sergeant Major Vasquez had been on the outskirts of Nha Trang City working on a construction project at one of our outposts. When work ran longer than expected, it was sometime after dark before the three men were able to start back to camp. Recognizing the potential danger of being on the long, narrow road after dark, they were moving fast on their way back to Trung Dung when the worst happened. An explosive burst of automatic weapons fire erupted as the jeep drove into an ambush.

As soon as their urgent call for support came in, the usual alerts for reinforcements were quickly passed along. No one was ready before Stewart and Trujillo. Within minutes, the Beast was rumbling at the team house door.

I had just taken off my fatigues and was standing clad only in my undershorts and T-shirt when I heard the commotion and learned what had happened. Then, I saw the Beast roar up from its berth in the motor pool. I ran out and yelled for them to wait for me. As fast as I could, I ran back to my room, jammed my feet in my boots, grabbed my web gear and M-16, and ran out the back door.

Climbing up over the side of the Beast, I yelled, "Go!"

With other team members hanging on for dear life, Sergeant Trujillo poured full power to the Beast, which lunged forward as we raced toward and through the camp gates. We then quickly roared through the arch in the Citadel's massive wall and charged down the road toward Nha Trang. In fewer than five minutes, Stewart and Trujillo had a response team well on the way to the location of our ambushed teammates.

As we thundered down the road, Sergeant Stewart rolled the turret around, uncovered the minigun, and prepared it for firing. It took about ten minutes to reach the location where the ambush had taken place. We were alarmed when we found the jeep in which Lee, Lane, and Vasquez had been riding. It was stopped sideways, lights still on, engine still running—abandoned in the middle of the road. The jeep sat as testament to the quickness with which its occupants had fled their vehicle. When we saw several bullet holes across the jeep's windshield, we were sure one or more of the three must have been hit—but where were they?

Those of us riding on the Beast jumped to the ground and fanned out on both sides of the road around the empty jeep. We called out the names of its missing occupants, hoping for a quick response to our calls. Moving along the north side of the road, still, only in under-shorts, T-shirt, and boots, I glanced over at the Beast. The lights of the abandoned jeep illuminated the rumbling behemoth, which sat surrounded in a swirl of its rising exhaust. The sight was a fearsome one. The turret of the silhouetted monster rotated in search of a target or challenge but found neither. If the ambushers were still in the area, they were staying quiet and hidden.

In barely a few seconds, our calls to the missing trio were answered. They had taken cover behind a small village hut on the south side of the road. Remarkably, all three men were uninjured, other than small cuts received from flying glass chards when the windshield was shattered by gunfire.

Would that have been true if Trujillo and Stewart had not arrived so quickly with reinforcements in such an imposing vehicle? Had they not arrived so swiftly, the three men would likely have been pursued and killed by those who ambushed them. Obviously, Lee, Lane, and Vasquez were glad the response to their call for assistance had brought the Beast and its creators.

The two sergeants were feeling pretty good about their response to the emergency, and they had every right to feel as they did. When they rolled around to escort the jeep back to camp, I saw Stewart, who was in the turret, pat the Beast on its side as if it were a loyal mount—just like the Lone Ranger might have patted Silver. When he yelled, "Let's go!" to his "faithful companion" in the driver's position down front, the Beast once again lunged forward and headed back up the road in the direction from which it had come. The only things Trujillo and Stewart were missing at that moment were masks and silver bullets. Knowing them, if they'd had masks, they certainly would have worn them. And, they could have easily made silver bullets.

Clearly, thinking of these men being masked heroes is a bit melodramatic, but one meeting with Sergeants Mitchell Stewart and Louis Trujillo would surely confirm their worthiness. They were good friends and exceptional men. Their indomitable spirit and the pride they took in doing their jobs and doing them well were characteristic not just for these two men, but also for many others I would meet and with whom I would have the good fortune to serve.

"The Beast"

"The Beast" and its Creators

Doctor Frankenstein had his "Monster." Sergeants Mitchell Stewart (L) and Louis Trujillo (R) of Special Forces Detachment A-502 had "The Beast."

Where "The Beast" was Created — A-502 Motorpool

The Beast's "Stinger"

Just like a bee, the Beast had a "stinger" on its backside. That little brown vinyl flap hides a minigun capable of firing—6,000 rounds per minute.

Photo Instructor & Darkroom

Above (L), Specialist Gilmore demonstrates the use of chopsticks for Bill Lane. Gilmore was Australian and had served as a mercenary in another Army. He is the one who taught me to develop and print my own film. Our darkroom was located on an upper floor in the motor pool indicated by white arrow (R).

CHAPTER 22

Are We Who We Were?

IT FELT AS THOUGH A LASER beam had pierced my bamboo blinds and was cutting its way through my eyelids as I tried to sleep. Rolling over in my bed took the beam of sunlight away from my eyes, but not away from the wall. With one eye opened, I lay and watched the thin line of light move, almost imperceptibly, down the wall toward the floor. The sun was getting higher and the hour was growing later. There would be no more sleep, and I had a lot to do that day anyway.

I had been on ambush the night before with a visitor from the British Embassy in Saigon, Lieutenant Colonel Peter Varnwell. 5th Group Headquarters had sent him to 502 as an observer early the day before. He had arrived with instructions that he was to be briefed on past, current, and future operations. Major Lee was also instructed to extend him every courtesy and show him whatever he wanted to see.

The assignment of escorting Colonel Varnwell was passed to me, and I was very pleased to have been given the task. The colonel, who had arrived in tiger fatigues ready for business, was a very pleasant man who spoke with a charming English accent and displayed a lively interest in everything he was shown.

The day began with a tour of Trung Dung and an introduction to several of our team members. The Colonel had many questions for them and listened intently to their responses. Next, we went on an air observation mission so he could see the extent of our area of operation.

After lunch, we went to My Loc (pronounced "Me lock"), our western outpost, a very small camp manned by only three or four U.S. advisers and fewer than a platoon of Vietnamese troops. Referred to as the Rock Pile by team members, My Loc was strategically located on a small hill that wasn't much more than a pile of rocks. However, a commanding view of the western approach to the Nha Trang Valley made My Loc valuable real estate. And, there was nothing between My Loc and the Cambodian border except jungle and lots of the enemy or, at least, that's what we thought.

1st Lieutenant Bob Ochsner, the senior American adviser at My Loc, briefed Colonel Varnwell on the outpost's mission. Bob, who had become a friend, had also served as one of the tactical officers (staff officer) for my Officer Candidate School company at Fort Benning in Georgia. While the assignment in Vietnam was quite different for Bob, his briefing was typically professional as he explained the remote outpost's key role of providing early warning for Trung Dung, Cam Rahn Bay, and Nha Trang.

When we left My Loc, Colonel Varnwell observed that the men who manned this outpost were "extremely vulnerable and dangerously in the middle of nowhere." His observation was recognizably accurate. My Loc was miles west of Trung Dung; beyond it was virtually nothing but abandoned, uninhabited villages, flatland, and jungle. The only activity beyond My Loc was the enemy. They used the area as an infiltration route and could easily approach undetected to within meters of the tiny outpost. Then, with similar ease, they could overrun the hill or shell it with mortars, which they did from time to time. I often wondered how Bob and his men were able to sleep. The truth was that they didn't sleep much, and when they did it was on a rotation basis. The rest of their time was spent reinforcing the hill's fighting positions to give themselves the best chance of surviving a major attack.

Within days of our visit, the small team at My Loc would become engaged in a heavy firefight, not to defend themselves, but to assist and protect others.

By late afternoon, Colonel Varnwell and I had developed a cordial relationship. Enjoying his many stimulating questions, it was with some disappointment that I anticipated his departure. While we had been told that he would be with us for only the day, on the way back from My Loc he asked if he could stay the night. He said that he would very much like to go on one of the ambushes we had described to him.

I was concerned about his safety, but we had been told to show him every courtesy. While going on an ambush didn't seem to be much of a courtesy, I told him that if that were his desire, we would certainly accommodate him.

After an early dinner, the colonel was outfitted for the ambush. Just before we left for the site, he produced a large red handkerchief that he tied around his neck. He said he didn't want us to lose him—or shoot him!

Our ambush was uneventful, but one of the other units near the base of the Dong Bo Mountains made contact with an enemy unit that was also very near the site of my earlier motorcycle incident. A firefight ensued, and the battle filled the radio with chatter and the night sky with illumination flares. We prepared to move and reinforce the unit. Colonel Varnwell was eager to get into the fray, but just as we started to move out, our American adviser called to say that the enemy had disengaged and had retreated across the railroad tracks back into the mountains. Even though we hadn't been involved in any action that night, enough had happened to hold the colonel's interest.

On the walk back to camp from the ambush site, Colonel Varnwell's questioning became more personal and more intellectually probing. He wanted to know about some of my personal opinions and concerns about the Vietnam War. By the time of his visit, I had been in-country for about eight months, more than long enough to change old opinions and form new ones. I certainly didn't have the same optimistic outlook with which I had arrived. While wanting to be honest with my new acquaintance, I was reasonably candid but still guarded with my responses.

As we made our way back to Trung Dung, one of the first things I shared with Varnwell was my opinion that we (the American fighting men) were in an untenable situation.

"What do you mean?" he asked.

I explained by saying that because this war had become so extremely controversial, it was causing pain in the smallest, most patriotic hometowns in the United States. With some sadness, I told the colonel a distressing story that my mother had shared with me in a recent letter. During a trip to her local grocery store, my mother encountered a friend who told her about her son's return from Vietnam. The young soldier arrived on the West Coast and was walking through the airport on his way to a connecting flight. About midway through the terminal, an antiwar activist walked up to him and spit on his uniform.

"It's no secret. We're losing the support of the American public," I said, "and this war will be very difficult, if not impossible, to win without them."

My expression of doubt was also one of frustration. So many negative things had happened since arriving in Vietnam, beginning with Tet. Noting the significant events that concerned me, I shared them with Colonel Varnwell.

"Certainly, these things must be evident to you, even in England. Reporters in the U.S. now discuss them openly on television network news reports," I said.

The Tet Offensive, simply by its occurrence, had demonstrated to the world that the VC and NVA weren't as beaten as we all had been led to believe. They obviously had the men, equipment, and ability to launch well-planned surprise attacks all over South Vietnam, virtually simultaneously. That realization had fueled and significantly increased antiwar sentiment in the United States. This war, everyone now realized, could drag on indefinitely.

Tet was only the first in several negative historical events to cause great pain in our country in 1968. In April, Dr. Martin Luther King Jr., a remarkable man, was killed by an assassin's bullet. Only months before, Dr. King and I made eye contact when I passed within a few feet of him in

Atlanta's Hartsfield Airport. I was just beginning the first leg of my trip to Vietnam. The recognition commanded by Dr. King's mere presence as he walked through the terminal was impressive. When we received news of the tragedy, there was little doubt in my mind that his death would be a significant loss, not just for the black community who had placed so much hope in his efforts, but for our entire country. I was a little surprised by my own feelings of loss, perhaps because I had seen him and witnessed his effect on those around him.

Another assassin struck in June, killing Robert Kennedy in a hotel kitchen. News of his assassination was met at Trung Dung with near disbelief, a second Kennedy assassinated. I can remember one of our team members saying, "What in the hell is going on back home?"

Finally, there was the rioting that took place at the Democratic Convention in Chicago. We had an old television in the team house, and we were watching a reasonably clear black-and-white picture broadcast by the Armed Forces Network. I watched coverage of the convention in open disbelief as pictures of young Americans waving enemy flags appeared on the television screen.

"Our country is in a tragic state of affairs," I told Colonel Varnwell. "We are tearing ourselves apart as a republic."

"How do you and the other men deal with that issue?" he asked. "It must affect your morale," Varnwell probed.

"I'm sure it does, but these men are well-trained professionals and deal with everything by simply doing their jobs as well as they can every day. I have come to know them very well, and what I can tell you with complete confidence is that they will fight until the day they are called home, regardless of their personal feelings about the politics of this war."

To lighten conversion and partially in jest, I asked Varnwell if the British were planning to become involved and help us with the war. In a dry British accent, he assured me that the possibility was "quite unlikely. I'm here simply as an observer," he said. I wasn't so sure.

Because of the nature of his many questions, it occurred to me that maybe the colonel had been sent to measure morale in the field. *But surely not by a foreign government*, I thought. However, spurning my attempt to change the subject, Colonel Varnwell continued.

"So, Lieutenant Ross, is the U.S. going to be able to win this war, or what?"

"Do you want a political response or a military response?" I asked.

"Military, of course," he replied.

"It is my opinion that it will be very difficult to be successful here," I said.

"Why is that, do you think?" he queried.

"Because, to me, it is crystal clear that because of events I've just mentioned, we, the troops in the field, no longer have what we need most."

"What is that?" he asked quizzically. "Surely you're well supplied?"

"Yes, we are. We're extremely well supplied," I said. "However, what we need that we no longer have is the unanimous support of the American public. Surely, you've seen reports of the various events I've told you about. My God, even Walter Cronkite, probably the most respected news reporter in the U.S., is now expressing his doubts about the worthiness of our presence here and our ability to win this war."

"I know. It must be awfully distressing to you," Varnwell said mournfully.

"It is . . . extremely," came my less than reserved reply. "It's difficult to fight a war on the other side of the globe knowing your country may be tearing itself apart because of the very war in which you are engaged."

Even though the news was censored and we were shielded from some of the worst antiwar reports, enough negative information came through that many of us were beginning to realize our country was involved in a war unlike any other it had fought before.

All of Colonel Varnwell's questions were penetrating, and they gave me pause for thought over the next several days. We had spoken as officers and as professionals, and I had shared my honest, personal feelings about the war with him. While we had also discussed how we had seen war change men, I was reluctant to share my deepest feelings and concerns about—the way I feared the war might have changed me.

It was still very early in the morning when we finally reached camp. I invited Colonel Varnwell to stay for breakfast, but he said he needed to return for meetings that had been scheduled for him in Nha Trang. After arranging a ride back to the city for him, I skipped breakfast myself and sought my bunk and a couple of hours of sleep, which were just about all I had gotten before the sun's late-morning laser-like rays woke me.

"Good morning, Trung Uy," Pop said when I walked out into the team room.

Pop was our Vietnamese cook. He was a small man with large skills when it came to preparing meals for the team. His culinary skills and repertoire had been developed and refined when he learned to cook for the French while they were in Vietnam. Pop was a warm, kind, and soft-spoken man whose cooking skills were only surpassed by his caring manner and the charm of his humble demeanor. Even though he was paid as a civilian employee, Pop had adopted the team and treated all of us as if we were his own sons. In turn, the team had adopted him and cared about him as if he were a close family member.

I was still rubbing my eyes and trying to remember everything I had to do that day.

"You want some breakfast?" Pop asked.

"No, not right now, Pop. I think I'll check on something first. Thanks, though. I'll eat a little later."

"Okay, Trung Uy."

Knowing that one of our other ambushes had contact with an enemy unit the night before, I knew there might be intelligence work that needed to be done early in the day. Certainly, before the sun rose too much higher in the humid air and the day grew really hot. I walked over to the intelligence shack to see if Sergeant Koch and Bau, one of our interpreters, were there yet. When I reached the shack, both were already at work, waiting for me.

"Do we need to go to the river?" I asked.

"Yes, they got three last night. We should go now before the sun is on them too long," Sergeant Koch said.

"Yes, I know. Okay, let's go ahead and go now."

Whenever there was a contact in which VC or NVA soldiers were killed, the common practice was for the camp's Vietnamese units to take the bodies down to the river near Dien Khanh village. There, the bodies would be lined up on the riverbank. Because many of the VC had grown up in local villages, their bodies were left along the river to be claimed by family members. Members of the camp's Vietnamese intelligence network would be positioned at various points along the riverbank in an effort to determine the family names of those claiming bodies. This was done because it seemed reasonable to believe that those families might also be VC sympathizers and supporters. Any bodies that weren't claimed by sundown were buried.

I had been with our Vietnamese intelligence counterparts many times before to search the bodies for maps and any other information that might be of value. Normally, that unpleasant task was theirs, but this morning the job would be mine alone.

Approval had recently been given for a Korean mission into the Dong Bo Mountains. They had three thousand men they could commit to the operation. Colonel Chang was the commander of a brigade-size unit of the Koreans' 9th White Horse Division. With his unit going into the Dong Bo, he asked that A-502 provide him with our most current information on any enemy activity in or near the mountains. Because the ambush the night before involved an enemy unit that had probably come from the mountains, I would personally conduct a search of the enemy bodies.

When we reached the river, the bodies were laid out on display. They had already been lying in the sun for a while, so they were bloated—blown up like huge rubber balloons. The sight, even though I had seen it too many times before, was still a disgusting one. The bodies, riddled with bullet holes, bore testament to the battle that had cost them their lives.

The skull on one of the bodies had been shattered by the impact of the killing bullet. The skin that once covered the skull, including the face, now lay on the ground like a deflated volleyball. The skull of one of the other bodies retained its form but was cracked open like an egg, and the brain was exposed to the morning sun, which was already becoming hot. Swarms of flies were gathering while others already present were crawling in and out of the eyes, nose, ears, and mouth of the three bodies. The sight was extremely repulsive.

I clearly understood the purpose and the intelligence value of placing the bodies by the river. Even though we were at war, it just didn't seem right that a human body, even a foe's, should be exposed to such abuse and disrespect.

As I gazed across the morbid sight, I thought, *Well, I may as well get this over with.*

When I approached the bodies to begin my search, a foul stench was already rising from the corpses. The nauseating odor was gagging—it was the smell of death. Knowing I wouldn't be able to hold my breath for the entire time it would take to complete the search, I took slow shallow breaths through my mouth, hoping to avoid the pungent smell. Unfortunately, that didn't help much. The piquant odor of death was much too strong.

Bending down over one of the bodies, I began to search the dead soldier's pockets for information. The body was so bloated that the worn khaki uniform had been drawn extremely tight around it. Even in death, the body resisted my intrusion. As I was going through the shirt pockets, I noticed a chain hanging around the corpse's neck. Pulling the chain out from under the man's shirt, it slid between my fingers until a medallion popped out and rested in the palm of my hand. It was a gold Saint Christopher's medal—very similar to one my grandmother had given me. Mine was hanging around my neck.

Probably Catholic, I thought.

I placed the medal back inside the soldier's shirt and told a nearby guard who had been posted to keep onlookers away to make sure the medal stayed exactly where it was until the family claimed the body or until it was buried. Continuing my search, I checked the rest of the soldier's pockets but found nothing.

While checking the pockets of the next body, I found the picture of a young woman. *Girlfriend? Wife? Sister?* I wondered. Whoever the young woman was, she didn't know what I knew at that moment. The young man who was carrying her picture wouldn't be coming home. I imagined her grief when she was given the news. *God,* I thought, looking at the faded picture, *this body could easily be mine, and someone could be going through my pockets, finding pictures of my family.* Quickly dumping the thought, I continued to search the soldier's pockets for intelligence information.

In the next pocket, I found a small folded piece of paper. It was a crudely drawn, but clearly detailed, map with Vietnamese writing on it. Potentially valuable, it appeared to be a map that may have guided the three soldiers to the village where they had been killed. The body searches were created to recover exactly this type of intelligence. I put the map in my pocket and would deliver it to the Vietnamese intelligence officers when we returned to camp.

A search of the third body revealed nothing.

With no conception of it at the time, I realized later, when writing about that day, the great irony in what had occurred that morning. These men may have lost a battle, but the army for which they had fought and given their lives would, in the end, be victorious. However, even with that eventual outcome of the war, by finding the map that day, their deaths would result in a similar fate for almost seven hundred more of their comrades.

With my repugnant task complete, I stood and looked at the gathering of onlookers. In the crowd, I noticed an older Vietnamese woman (60s) approaching. She was slender, wearing a traditional peaked straw hat, and was carrying a round basket of fruit and vegetables under her arm.

The woman approached the bodies tentatively—then she shrieked, "Aahhhh!" She dropped her basket and wilted to her knees before one of the bodies, fruit and vegetables fell and rolled among the dead. Now, on her knees, the woman leaned over the body and cried loudly in Vietnamese, "My grandson! What have you done?!"

Obviously, the woman was his grandmother. She straightened up on her knees, back arched, arms outstretched toward the sky, and she screamed mournfully in Vietnamese, "You have become Viet Cong!"

Distraught, the woman fell across the swollen body of her dead grandson. I wanted to comfort the woman but doubted that she would welcome comfort from one of the soldiers responsible for her grandson's death, VC, or not.

Moved by the woman's agony, I did what I could. Turning to Bau, I pointed and said, "Tell that guard no one is to touch this soldier until his family comes for him."

Bau quickly translated to the guard who was standing only a few steps away and the guard immediately nodded acknowledgment.

The grandmother, lifted her face, wet with tears, and looked into my eyes. She nodded what I took as a painful gesture of appreciation, and said what I recognized to be "Thank you" in Vietnamese.

I turned and left, with Sergeant Koch and Bau in trail, to return to Trung Dung. As we walked away, locals hurried to the grandmother's side. I was glad she was being comforted.

During the short ride to camp, I thought about the task I had just completed and realized that as gruesome as the task was, it wasn't affecting me as intensely as it had when I first began the searches. In fact, being a part of such distasteful duty had become all too routine for me. After washing up and changing my clothes, despite what I had just seen and done—I was still able to sit down and eat a hearty breakfast.

As I sat at the table and ate the scrambled eggs Pop had prepared for me, I reconsidered some of Colonel Varnwell's questions regarding the war. While I had answered his questions and expressed opinions honestly, I had failed to mention to him one of my most important concerns: my fear that many of us may have been forever changed by service in Vietnam, and not in a good way. I conjectured–*Are we still who we were before we arrived in Vietnam? When we returned home, will we be the same persons we were before service to our country?*

Without question, we were all being changed in some manner by our experiences. I was saddened to think that I might be so hardened by those experiences that a girlfriend's touch, my mother's voice, or my sister's smile might not mean as much to me as they once had.

When I finally did return to the States, I discovered that my wartime experiences had not affected me as I feared they might. On the contrary, I had a much greater appreciation for life, its beauty, and its gentle accompaniments. My mother's embrace and kiss on the cheek, my sister's tears and welcoming smile when I arrived at the airport in Pensacola, and my father's handshake and spontaneous bear hug when he saw me for the first time, meant more to me than they ever had before—not less.

However, many of those who served in Vietnam weren't as lucky as I was, and they have never been the same. Some of them returned with their lives, but with a large portion of themselves, their essence, left behind in Southeast Asia. One of my teammates, over fifty years later, still takes meds in an effort to live a "near normal" life.

Fighting any war can be a horrific experience. Because of the divisiveness of the Vietnam War, some veterans continue to be saddled with immense guilt and anguish regarding their roles during the war. They have each had to bear the weight and psychological pain of their burden, essentially alone.

Fortunately, I am not one of those veterans, so it is easier for me to make relatively unbiased observations. One such observation is that it was all too easy for some people to blame the soldiers for horrible things that happened as a result of poor decisions made by those at the highest levels of our government. Our troops do not create wars—they fight them.

As true as any statement that can be made about my experiences during the Vietnam War is the fact that virtually every American man or woman that I met was trying to do a good job—patriots who simply wanted to serve his or her country. The Vietnam War is considered by many to be a failure in every way. However, any failure is not the fault of those who were sent to fight it.

It has been said that American forces never lost a major battle in Vietnam. Unfortunately, that isn't true. We experienced many losses that have been well documented. But what is true is that we won a great many more battles than the few that were lost.

Regardless of wins or losses, as time has passed and their numbers thinned, some of the men and women who served with great honor and dedication may still be trying to be who they were before they went to Southeast Asia.

The USO — Doing its Part

The USO routinely arranged for celebrities or shows of a wide variety to visit troops at bases and camps throughout South Vietnam. Some of the celebrities were internationally recognized like Bob Hope, Miss America, and many others. Some of those who visited A-502 weren't famous at all, but their hearts were in the right place and they did their best to entertain us. These events provided service members with the opportunity to be reminded of who they were.

Being Reminded of — Who You Were

Here, South Vietnamese singers offered their version of the "Beach Boys." While they didn't have the sound of brothers Brian, Dennis, and Carl Wilson, their cousin Mike Love, and their friend Al Jardine, when attractive female singers joined them, it didn't seem to make any difference. Their effort and presence were entertaining, if not amusing.

Ngoc and Kim (wearing pearls), were in the front row with two of their sons, Chau and Bau, I was sitting right behind the two boys. So, for a couple of hours, it was like being at a concert with friends. In reality, the war was only a split second and—a BOOM! away.

Hollywood Visiting the War

Actress/comedian Martha "Maggie" Raye with Lieutenant Bill Phalen (L), and Major Ngoc Nguyen (R). Maggie was made an honorary member of SF.

CHAPTER 23

Care, Compassion, and Skill

SEEING THEM IN ACTION would make their families and friends back home feel very proud, I thought, as I watched our medics examine a group of village children.

From time to time, as a part of A-502's MEDCAPS Program (Medical Civic Action Program), our medics would go out to the villages or they would invite the villagers to come to the dispensary at Trung Dung for examinations and treatment.

Jerry Arrants, A-502's senior medic, and his team of medics—Larry Freedman, Chuck McGill, and Juan Sotello—had all gone through an intensive forty-three-week medical training program back in the States. Besides the treatment of battle injuries, animal bites, diseases, and a host of other possible ailments, the training had given them the skills required to perform an array of surgical procedures under field conditions, if necessary.

These men, who wore the green beret and uniform of a military adviser, not only practiced healing skills but they taught them as well. Members of the camp's CIDG units were selected by our medics for medical training based on interest, education, and aptitude. Those selected were trained and they worked in the camp's dispensary, which had been set up and run by our medic team. Because of the unique requirements of soldier, teacher, and healer placed on the A-502 medics, it was not unusual to find them carrying all of the tools of their trades at once, a rifle, a pencil, and a stethoscope.

On this day, Sergeant Freedman and Sergeant McGill were treating the children of Trung Dung's Vietnamese soldiers, camp workers, and some from surrounding villages. Their tone of voice and manner inspired trust and confidence as they tended to their tiny patients. Small children, who frequently arrived hurt and crying, often left with a smile and a good-bye wave for the *bac-si* (doctor) who had taken care of them.

The bedside manner of our medics was only surpassed by their skills and tenacity. On another day that I will never forget, I watched as Freedman and McGill worked under emergency conditions with the focus of skilled surgeons. Pop, our team cook, had been hit by a large military transport truck. He was on his motor scooter riding to Dien Khanh village for supplies when he was struck. The two medics would combine their skills in an effort to save Pop, a man for whom every American in camp had great affection.

It all began when one of our CIDG soldiers zoomed into the camp on his motorcycle and skidded up to the dispensary door. He started yelling in broken English that there had been an accident out on the road. When Freedman ran out in response to the screaming, he was told that a large truck had hit Pop. He yelled for McGill, and the two took off in the ambulance they acquired in some kind of trade with another unit, the details of which were never quite clear—much as Trujillo and Stewart acquired the Beast.

When the two men returned with siren yelping and blue light flashing, I became involved. When I ran over to see what had happened, Freedman yelled, "It's Pop! He's been hit! Help us get him inside!"

With that, he disappeared into the dispensary to prepare a treatment table. By the time I reached the back of the ambulance McGill already had Pop and the stretcher halfway out.

"Grab that end!" he yelled, nodding toward the unattended end of the stretcher.

After carrying Pop into what became an operating room, I watched the two Special Forces medics as they fought desperately, not to take a life—but to save one. Pop's legs had been horribly crushed by the truck and looked like ground hamburger meat. They were recognizable as human appendages only because they were still attached to his torso. Pop had lost a tremendous amount of blood, which was still pouring from his catastrophic injuries. His soft brown Asian skin was now a washed-out, light ashen gray. Despite the feverish efforts of Freedman and McGill, I felt I was watching Pop die.

Working against the monumental odds facing them, Freedman and McGill moved around what was left of Pop's lower extremities, communicating in calm but loud voices as they worked. The two men attached transfusions, tied off profusely bleeding vessels, cut flesh, and sawed bone. The dispensary began to look more like a butcher shop than an operating room as pieces of Pop's legs fell from the table.

Looking at Pop's face, which appeared like that of a corpse, I imagined his skin color returning with his warm familiar smile. I remembered the day he served lunch to a visiting Red Cross girl. Pop had decorated the rim of her plate and beamed as he placed it before her. Imagining the return of his smile would be easier than imagining life in the team house without him.

As word of the accident spread around camp, team members quickly began gathering around the dispensary. After coming in and seeing Pop on the table and how severe his injuries were, Bill Lane, the team's XO, became enraged and angrily declared, "Nothing good ever happens in this f---ing country."

I clearly understood Bill's cynicism. I was becoming cynical myself. If sent, I would have fought in the last battle for Vietnam, but this war seemed far from any resolution. And, I could see what it was doing to our country. I was looking at what it had done to Pop and didn't care to watch it anymore, so I went outside to wait with the rest of the team. Vietnamese medics were now assisting in the effort, and there was nothing I could do anyway.

It seemed like hours, but sometime later Freedman emerged from the dispensary. We all waited for the expected news of Pop's death. Freedman looked weary and was still wiping blood from his hands as he raised his head. "Pop will live," he said. Upon hearing those words, a roar spontaneously arose from the small gathering.

I turned and walked away from the dispensary, deciding my teammate and friend Bill Lane was wrong. Good things did happen in Vietnam, and American medics were responsible for an important share of them. Ultimately, this had been a good day. While seriously injured, Pop had been saved.

There had been the other good days, too, when the medics provided medical treatment for the children and adults in the surrounding villages. Our medics provided important medical treatment and care for local villagers that would have otherwise been unavailable to them. More good days were yet to come days that would truly give meaning to my service in Vietnam.

Pop recovered nicely and was fitted with prosthetic legs. He decided to take a break from work for a while, then he helped cook at a relative's small restaurant in Dien Khanh.

After Pop was gone, I missed getting up in the morning and walking into the team room where I would be greeted by a very cheery, "Oh, good morning, Trung uy!" Pop was a very special man to all of us.

The "Hospital"

When the first twelve men of Detachment A-502 arrived at Trai Trung Dung, the team included a medic. Because he wanted to offer medical treatment to people in nearby villages, the medic asked Thieu ta for space to set up a clinic. When he agreed, the clinic was established. Then, so the facility didn't seem stark and military, banana trees were planted to create a warmer appearance.

As 502 grew and additional medics joined the team, the clinic grew as well. Because the medics were also Special Forces advisers, they came with a unique set of additional skills and a vision for their small clinic. They wanted it to become a hospital. And, what respectable hospital doesn't have an ambulance?

With one of their additional skills being "appropriation" (the ability to acquire things), it wasn't long before they had an ambulance, complete with a flashing blue light and a siren. When I asked how they came by the vehicle, one of the medics simply said, "We made a good trade." I didn't ask more.

Whenever notified of a medical emergency in a village, medics would rip out of camp with blue light flashing and siren screaming. Help was on the way!

These were dedicated men with more than just a bit of panache. When I left A-502, the medics were working on a "trade" for an X-Ray machine. And, why not? After all—they already had a hospital and an ambulance.

The Ambulance

The Medics

These are just two of A-502's extremely skilled and dedicated medics. These are the two who saved Pop's life.

Larry Freedman (above L), who was Jewish, dubbed himself "Super Jew" and he was just that! Larry continued to serve long after Vietnam and he paid the ultimate price in Somalia where he was killed while caring for others.

Above right, Chuck McGill cares for a young girl who has fractured her leg. Notice how carefully and gently Chuck is holding her leg as he examines it.

Our medics were—very special caring men.

CHAPTER 24

Lay of the Land

During my time with A-502, a lesson learned only three days after my arrival at Trung Dung would prove its value many, many times.

The lesson learned on that long-past day began with an intelligence briefing from my S2 sergeant, Paul Koch. As mentioned, it was only my third day at Trung Dung, and we were in the S2 office where he was reviewing maps and pointing out suspected enemy locations.

As Sergeant Koch reviewed the maps, he explained that because of our large TAOR and TAOI (Team Area of Influence), 502's normal staffing had been increased to give it greater capabilities in the achievement of its various missions.

Much of the team's increased staffing in 1968 had occurred because of requests in Major Lee's monthly reports to 5th Group Headquarters. As a result of those repeated requests, my position of S2 (Intelligence) /S3 (Operations) had been created to help meet Lee's needs.

Sergeant Koch was doing his best to break me in quickly and was teaching me some of what he felt were the most important things I needed to know. Within the next few hours, I would learn one of the most important lessons learned at A-502.

Special Forces soldiers, as well as those in every other "Special Operations" unit in the U.S. military, are trained to expect the unexpected and to learn from those experiences when they do occur. This philosophy is not unlike one first taught to me as a youth by the Boy Scouts of America. The simple philosophy, which had been carried into adulthood and amplified by Special Forces training, was embodied in the Scout motto "Be Prepared!"

Shortly, I would be reminded of the value and importance of that motto when a major flap developed over a combat assault mission gone awry and consequently aborted. Despite its failure, the mission gave me a chance to learn a great deal very early in my tour. What I learned would prepare me for the many challenges ahead, particularly during the visit of a group of SF soldiers sent by the 5th Group for an orientation mission.

Sergeant Koch reminded me more of one of my college professors than a Special Forces soldier. But he knew his job well and was extremely dedicated to it. He was still familiarizing me with the maps when Major Lee stuck his head in the door. "Are you coming up to speed, Lieutenant Ross?" he asked.

"Yes, sir, I am."

"Good," he said. "There's an assault mission going out this morning to attack a suspected enemy location. I'm going as the senior US adviser, and it'll be a good mission for you to begin learning our AO. Gather your gear and meet me at the airstrip ASAP. Oh, make sure you bring a map."

"Yes, sir. I'll get my things and be right there."

Lee was waiting for me a few minutes later when I reached the airstrip.

"Let's go," he said as I ran toward the waiting helicopters.

The choppers were ready to go. Their blades were already spinning in anticipation of an immediate liftoff.

"I want you to ride out with us. After we're on the ground, stay overhead until the insertion is complete. Then I want you to be ready to come back with the choppers to pick us up. Is that clear?"

"Yes. sir. Clear."

Lee and I jumped on the lead chopper and were quickly airborne.

"Watch where we're going, Ross," Lee yelled over the roar of the helicopter's engine and churning blades.

"I don't know how long we'll be on the ground, but when we're ready to get out . . . I don't want any screwups. I want to make damn sure one of our team members knows where to find us. And, if we get into trouble, you may need to come in a hurry. I don't want to take a chance of anyone getting lost. That's why I am bringing you as a back-up. No screwups! Are you with me?"

"Yes, sir, understand. I'll find you."

"Good. I don't want you to have to hunt for us, so make damn sure you know exactly where you are when we get out. I'll give you our pickup location from the drop-off point."

"I've gotcha, sir. Don't worry, we'll be there when you need us."

During our flight toward the drop-off point, Major Lee pointed out terrain features that would serve as landmarks on the way back. As he did, I marked my plastic-covered map with a grease pencil. But as the line created by my pencil grew longer and we continued to fly farther out over terrain that was completely unfamiliar to me, I became a little concerned about the responsibility with which I had been charged.

I had been at 502 for only two full days and barely had time to familiarize myself with the area by looking at the maps on the wall in the S2 office. I had only been away from camp during my two trips to Buddha Hill, which was in the opposite direction from where we were now headed.

What if the unit gets into trouble and we do need to get to them quickly? Will I be able to find them as I had told Lee? Surely the pilots will know the way back, but the responsibility has been given to me. That isn't Fort Bragg or Fort Benning down there, I thought to myself.

Then it occurred to me that second-guessing myself had been left on the runway in Nha Trang days earlier. Any doubts about my ability had to be set aside, and dependence on anyone other than myself couldn't be considered. This type of situation was exactly what Special Forces was about and exactly what I had been trained to do. So, in Lee's own words, I would have to "make damn sure" I knew exactly where he and the unit were dropped off.

As the flight continued in a westerly direction, I looked back frequently to remember the route we had taken. Once again, I marked my map as we passed over a distinguishing terrain feature, but then things got strange. We began snaking back and forth over one particular part of the AO. Then, when our pattern of flight became more circular, it appeared to me that something was wrong or someone was lost. I quit tracing our route on my map when lines began to intersect and the ground beneath us became familiar even to me.

When it was obvious that the drop-off point couldn't be located, Major Lee became furious.

"Take us back!" he commanded into the small microphone on the headset that he was using to communicate with the pilot. With that directive, the pilot turned back to the east and we headed toward Trung Dung.

Whoever was guiding the mission was unable to find the drop-off point. At the time, I had no clue who was responsible for the mix-up. However, I later learned that the problem lay with one of the Vietnamese team leaders who was to have guided the unit to the drop-off point. That man was fortunate to be riding in another helicopter. Having worked with Major Lee back at Fort Bragg, I knew he liked a precision operation, and clearly, he considered this one a complete failure.

As noted earlier, my first encounter with then-Captain Lee took place back at Fort Bragg, when he was the Class Leader of one of my Special Forces training classes. Lee was a man of many fine qualities, but he had a reputation for being short on patience and he didn't like excuses. He wouldn't tell you how to do your job, but he expected it done right. If he were displeased by what you had done, he wouldn't hesitate to share his dissatisfaction.

In the present situation, even if you didn't know Lee, you could look at his face and know that he was extremely displeased with the circumstances. There was little doubt that the current circumstances had upset him greatly. Lee had a scowl on his face and sat nearly motionless most of the way back to camp, moving only occasionally to shake his head in disgust. I was sure someone was going to catch the devil for this debacle.

When we stepped out of the helicopter back at camp, Lee looked at me very deliberately and issued a stern warning.

"Ross, don't ever let this happen under your direction or command. Do you understand?"

His message was clear. No misunderstanding was possible.

Later that afternoon, heeding Lee's advice, I asked Sergeant Koch to request a helicopter to take me on observation missions over our AO during the next few days.

"Will do, sir," he said. "This will give you a chance to meet the 281st helicopter guys. They fly most of our support," he said.

"Yes, I know that unit," I told him. "I saw their place the other day when I arrived," remembering their "Intruders" insignia at the Nha Trang Air Base. I also remembered Daily's (the driver) mention of their work with the Delta Project.

Starting that afternoon, I took a map and a ship from the 281st began flying me over every grid square in A-502's area of operation. I spent days flying over Nha Trang City, the Nha Trang Air Base, villages of all sizes, jungle, rice paddies, and flatland, through river valleys as well as around and over mountains.

After spending so much time being flown east, west, north, and south in the Huey helicopter with the call sign "Rat Pack," I started to feel a part of the "Pack" myself. The pilots were extremely patient and perfectly willing to take me anywhere I wanted to go. Because of their total willingness to help, by the end of the third day of flying, I knew every river, hill, and valley in our AO.

Just as I was ready to call it "mission complete" and head back to Trung

Dung, I noticed a small note Sergeant Koch had taped to the back of my map board. His note read "Don't forget Hon Tre Island."

The day before, when the Rat Pack chopper arrived for our second day of observation missions, the crew chief presented me with my very own flight helmet. He said, "It looks like we may be flying together a lot. You'll find this more comfortable and you'll hear better." After they dropped me off back at camp that afternoon, I showed my gift to Sergeant Koch. He said, "Give it to me and I'll have your name painted on it."

I don't know where he took it, but the next morning when I arrived at the office, it was sitting on my desk. In big yellow letters, "TR" was painted on the front and "ROSS" was painted on the back.

So, after finding Sergeant Koch's note, through the mic on my new flight helmet, I asked the pilot to take me to Hon Tre Island.

"Roger, will do," he said, then brought the chopper around and headed east towards Nha Trang. In only minutes we zipped over 5th Group Headquarters on our way out over the South China Sea.

Hon Tre was directly east of Nha Trang and looked as if it were floating in the beautiful crystal-clear blue-green water. When we reached the island, we circled the perimeter slowly. Then we flew smaller circles until we were at the top. Finally, we circled the radio station. The island served as a base for the very important communications center. At the time, I had no idea that I would one day have the opportunity to see it much closer.

After my survey of Hon Tre, the Rat Pack dropped me off at Trung Dung and headed back to their home at the Nha Trang Air Base.

After all the time spent in the air, not to mention my bouts with airsickness, I hoped the effort would one day prove its value. And, it would, time and time again. In the next chapter, you will read about one of those times.

Getting the Lay of the Land

My observation missions with the 281st's Rat Pack took me all over our AO. I photographed key villages that I needed to know and those we suspected of supporting the NVA/VC. I circled the base of the Do Bo Mountains and flew low over river banks looking for trails that might be used by the enemy. I came to know our AO at least as well as I knew my hometown, Pensacola.

This is one of our outposts that overlooked the flats just west of 5th Group.

Bird's Eye View

I circled villages that were near the base of the Dong Bos and searched for trails leading from the mountains into the villages. Those would be places to set up one of our many night ambushes.

Korean "White Horse" Artillery Base

In case we needed to support them, I took several pictures of the Korean base so that I could use them to brief the team. Gilmore also taught me to enlarge photos.

Chapter 25

Flight into Darkness

IT WAS SHORTLY AFTER sunrise. A bright yellow Vietnamese sun had risen from the deep blue depths of the South China Sea and was pouring bright first light over Trung Dung's east wall. The warm morning air was still, and the sound of barking dogs in the surrounding village was perceptible over the background drone of the camp's one-hundred-kilowatt generator. Already up for about an hour, I had been preparing for the arrival of the Combat Orientation class.

All Special Forces personnel assigned to the 5th Group were required to complete the Combat Orientation Course (COC, or "Cock Course") that was conducted by the MACV (Military Assistance Command, Vietnam) Recondo School. The class was an abbreviated version of the Army Ranger Course. The course involved a week of acclimatization and refresher training in land navigation, first aid, communications, directing artillery and airstrikes, patrolling, unit tactics, working with interpreters, and more. Morning runs with heavily loaded packs were part of the physical training.

The second week of training would take the class to Hon Tre Island, just off the coast of Nha Trang. There, they would experience practical exercises in things they had learned the previous week.

The final portion of the course was a three-day combat patrol, which often included a night ambush. Many of these missions were conducted out of Trung Dung by A-502.

This entire block of training is one Bill Phalen, others, and I missed due to our arrival during the TET offensive. We went from stateside duty directly into a combat assignment. And, that was just fine with me. I was ready to put what I had into practice. Oddly enough, I would become responsible for instructing an important portion of the final phase of the COC course.

With my preparation for the COC group's presentation complete, I walked up to the top of the south wall and watched as the sun illuminated the tropical foliage along the far side of the moat. It contained more shades of green than could be mixed on an artist's pallet. The irony of the gentle beauty that filled this war-torn country never ceased to amaze me.

While this day had started quietly enough for me, I sat atop the massive Citadel wall and knew that somewhere else in South Vietnam another young American was very likely fighting for his life. For many, when the sun rose it was not on the soft pastel colors of a tranquil village scene. Rather, it was on a battlefield where the smell of gunpowder and magnesium from burnt illumination flares still lingered, mixed with the growing stench of death—made worse as the rising sun reached and heated the bodies of both friend and foe killed during the night. For those who survived the battles, sunrise often prompted a prayer or simply a hope that they would make it through the new day and following night to the next sunrise.

The Combat Orientation Class would be arriving very soon. My job and the job of the other men at A-502 was to give these men every opportunity not just to make it to the next sunrise, but to make it to the end of their tour—and home. Even though statistics were probably heavily weighted against everyone in this class going home alive or without serious injury, my teammates and I would share every important lesson we had learned, intending to lessen any statistical odds against them.

Unaware of how this day was about to unfold, I relaxed and continued to watch the morning illumination of Dien Khanh village. But, before any hint of the next sunrise, members of the soon-to-arrive COC group would find themselves in a fight for their lives. Ironically, the lesson learned only days after my arrival at Trung Dung would prove its value when a daring helicopter crew launched a midnight flight into the darkness of the Vietnamese sky in an effort to save one of those lives.

With the COC group expected through the gate at any minute, I walked down off the wall and went to gather my presentation notes. As 502's S2/S3, one of my jobs was to plan and coordinate missions for the Recondo School's orientation course. As noted, the course was designed to familiarize incoming Special Forces soldiers with the country before they were assigned to an established unit. Simply put, the class gave them the chance to become acclimated to the Vietnam War before having to face it head-on. Because Tet had interrupted training, my class had begun informally with two nights on Buddha Hill and continued as OJT (on-the-job-training).

After completing the basic course in Nha Trang, the new troops were sent out in trucks from headquarters and would generally spend three days working out of Trung Dung. After an in-camp orientation, the troops were given a combat assignment and mission with a combat patrol, ambush, or combination of both. A South Vietnamese unit and, usually, at least two seasoned A-502 team members would accompany each of the COC units.

While presenting the orientation briefing had become routine for me, the importance of its purpose and message was always critical. The class had been created to give every Special Forces soldier the best chance possible to return home alive. As this class began, it was no different than all the others

I had briefed. However, before ending, it would become unlike any other. What was yet to happen had never occurred before.

"They're here, sir," Sergeant Koch shouted from the quadrangle in the center of the camp. "They just came through the gate."

"On my way," I replied, gathering my presentation material.

The idea of a combat-familiarization period was an excellent one. As I had discovered, Vietnam was very different from training sites back in the States. Besides being a real war zone, the country had its distinct sights, sounds, and smells. The three days that the new men spent at Trung Dung allowed a brief period of adjustment. They were able to work with other men who were already adapted to the Vietnam arena. They were also given the opportunity to experience some of the new and unfamiliar things they had only been told about before they would be thrust into their various demanding Special Forces roles.

Before each of the out-of-camp orientation missions, I would present a briefing. It was usually a standard military operation briefing, along with some dos and don'ts for the new men. Then one of the advisers accompanying the group would provide specific details about the mission. A question-and-answer session normally closed the in-camp portion of the orientation. Of all the groups that passed through Trung Dung during my time there, one group and one individual would imprint themselves in my memory—forever. That group and that individual had just arrived.

As with previous groups, the members of this one milled around outside in the briefing area after arriving. Some of the men were standing and some sitting when I stepped before them to introduce myself. While the program had a formal outline and provided critically important information, my greeting was always warm and informal, as was the briefing. The briefing and information were presented as if I were sharing important information with someone I already knew. This briefing wasn't one where anyone needed to be bored or put to sleep.

If we needed to stop and talk about something during the presentation, we did just that. I had many questions of my own upon arriving in Vietnam, and I wanted every one of these men to leave Trung Dung feeling his questions had been answered. It was important to me to have every chance to make it back home to the southern United States and it was my job to give these men the same opportunity to return to wherever they called home.

As with every other group briefed, I found myself looking at their faces and into their eyes. Often, I wondered what had brought them to Vietnam.

During the briefing, our primary role as Special Forces advisers was always emphasized—we were there to advise. The group was reminded that we were not sent to Vietnam to perform John Wayne or Rambo–type heroics. Despite the courageous nature of Special Forces advisers and even though courageous deeds frequently occurred out of necessity, being heroes wasn't in the job description. We were to provide our military expertise, instruction, and guidance on the use of various types of weapons, combat tactics, equipment, and so on.

Because this group's first mission would be a patrol and night ambush in an area where recent enemy activity had been reported, particular points were stressed. Even though thoroughly taught back at Fort Bragg and refreshed during Recondo School training, one piece of information emphasized was the importance of how a night ambush was initiated.

"I know that all of you know this, but it's important enough to be restated since your patrol today will end with a night ambush. If you are the first to see an enemy unit approaching tonight, pass the word so the ambush can be triggered simultaneously along the line," I instructed. "You should not individually initiate the ambush unless absolutely necessary. Only open fire if you have no choice. If they surprise you and are on top of you . . . of course, take 'em out! Otherwise, hold your fire."

The reason for not being the first to open fire at night becomes obvious with an explanation. When fired, a weapon produces a muzzle flash, a conspicuous and easily seen flash of fire. At night, a muzzle flash is obvious and highly visible, like setting up a target directly in front of your body and indicating your exact location to incoming enemy soldiers.

The point was emphasized for the new men by posing a scenario and question.

"Okay. Let's turn the tables . . . assume you're walking through the dark on a night patrol. You see a muzzle flash and immediately determine that someone is shooting at you. Where would your return fire be directed?"

Several members in the group spontaneously volunteered the obvious and correct response. "At the muzzle flash."

"Of course! And while I know this is basic stuff for you, it's something you need to remember tonight. The enemy will do as you would do and fire at the flash. So, trigger your ambush as a unit with *everyone* placing fire on the target. And remember, when assigned to a new unit, your job will be to survive any initial contact so that you can meet your responsibilities as an adviser—whether that means assisting in the direction of the battle or calling in illumination, artillery, reinforcements, or air support."

At this point in the briefing, heads would always shake up and down in agreement. When heads stopped bobbing, I often became redundant to make certain the point had reached home.

"So, remember, whatever else you do tonight, don't be the first to open fire unless absolutely necessary to protect yourself or your unit. By opening fire with your unit, you give yourself a better chance to go home in twelve months."

Generally, the group grew very quiet after that line and appeared thoughtful.

Typically, at this point, one or both of the accompanying A-502 advisers were introduced to the group. Today, it was Lieutenant Bill Phalen. He was the Dien Khanh team leader, and two members of his Blue Bandit unit were going with the COC group. Bill knew both the area and the type of operation very well, so he presented the field portion of the briefing.

When Bill finished his presentation and after every question had been answered, the time came to prepare for the group's mission. During the preparation and organizing of equipment, I had a chance to visit with several of the men. One officer, a young 1st Lieutenant like me, was also from the South. Dale Reich was warm and very friendly, with bright red hair. When asked where he was from, he said, "Atlanta." As we talked, I learned he had attended the University of the South in Sewanee, Tennessee. After graduating from college and entering the service, he volunteered for Special Forces and, like so many others, duty in Vietnam.

While Reich applied black and green camouflage to his face and hands, we talked about what had brought us to this meeting place and even a little about our families. Dale had a wife whom he spoke about with great warmth and affection. He said she was pregnant with their first child, and he seemed very excited about the prospect of becoming a father.

As we continued to talk, I noticed that he seemed to enjoy camouflaging his face. Earlier, he mentioned playing football in high school and college, so maybe the camouflage rouge reminded him of the smudge of black that many players put under their eyes to reduce glare. One thing was certain, he still had the competitive spirit of a football player waiting to get out onto the field and seemed anxious to get the mission underway.

Just before going to confirm that final ambush locations had been selected and to make sure that the Vietnamese troops were getting ready, I slapped Reich on the back and asked if he remembered everything we had discussed during the briefing.

"You got all this stuff, right?"

"Yeah, yeah," he said with a grin. "I'm ready. How long before we go?"

"About an hour."

"Are you going with us?"

"No. We use a rotation schedule, and tonight isn't my night. Two of Lieutenant Phalen's men are going with you. But who knows? If you guys get into trouble, you may see me."

He laughed as we shook hands. I wished Reich good luck, and we agreed to visit again when he returned from the mission. Neither of us expected it at the time, but our paths would, indeed, cross again later that night.

When the group was ready, everyone went through an equipment check. Then, the two Blue Bandit team members going with the class directed the men onto trucks that would take them to a drop-off point. From there, they would begin their patrol to the ambush site. As the trucks started pulling out, I gave them all the thumbs-up sign as they passed. Many smiled or waved and returned my positive gesture.

Another great group of men, I thought as they disappeared into a huge ball of boiling dust stirred up by the trucks. To the man, they had all been enthusiastic and eager to assume their roles as advisers. Some were even returning for a second tour of duty in Vietnam.

When they reached their ambush location and were in position, their coordinates, along with others out that night, would be plotted on the map in our radio room. We plotted ambush locations on the map so that we knew where everyone was located. If an enemy unit did walk into one of the ambushes and our unit became engaged in a firefight, we could quickly provide support to the unit with illumination, mortars, or artillery. Or, we could send help in the form of reinforcements or air support.

On my way to bed at about 11:00 that night, I checked in the radio room to see what was happening. SPC4 James Miller was on night duty, sitting in his familiar surroundings where he was so capable. He was chewing gum and reading a book when I walked into the small room that was only about five-by-ten feet.

"How's it going, Miller? Any action?"

"No, sir. It's all quiet on the western front. Sergeant Bardsley and Sergeant Key are out on ambush tonight. I heard Sergeant Bardsley on the radio asking somebody where he was, but that's about it. Really, it's a pretty boring night, sir."

"Good. Let's hope it stays that way. I'm really tired. Okay, I'll see ya in the morning."

"Sleep well, sir."

My visit to the radio room hadn't given Miller or me any reason to expect that his boring shift or my sound sleep would shortly be shattered. I left the radio room and headed for my bunk.

After getting into bed, I fell right to sleep. Then, just before one in the morning, with little more than an hour of sleep, Miller exploded into my room.

"Lieutenant Ross! Lieutenant Ross! The new guys are in contact!"

His words meant that their ambush had been successful, and they were in a firefight with an enemy unit.

"Okay, okay! Let's go!"

I jumped out of bed and made my way toward the radio room, still half asleep.

"Any casualties?" I asked.

"I don't know, sir. It just started, but it sounds like a big one. I do know My Loc is firing mortars and illumination for them."

"Good!"

My Loc, one of our remote outposts, was just north of where the unit had set up the ambush.

I grabbed the radio handset and called the unit. It took two or three calls to them before any response was heard, which likely meant that they were in a serious fight and had no time to talk.

"We'll wait for them," I said to Miller. "They'll call when they need us."

Then we just stood helplessly and looked at the X and coordinates written on our wall map that represented the unit's location. I had done that before, the night Bill Phalen was out on ambush.

It seemed like ten minutes, but less than a minute had passed when we received the next transmission from one of our advisers with the unit.

"Bunkhouse, Bunkhouse, this is Blue Bandit, Blue Bandit! Over!"

Heavy gunfire could be heard in the background as the unit's radioman made his urgent call.

"Roger, Blue Bandit. This is Bunkhouse. Go ahead. Over," I immediately answered.

"Bunkhouse, this Blue Bandit! We're in heavy contact! Over!"

"Roger, Roger, Blue Bandit. Understand! Can you give me a SitRep? Over."

A SitRep is a "Situation Report" that would tell us what had happened as well as what was happening now with the unit in contact. Once we had the SitRep, we would know what alternatives existed concerning support.

"Bunkhouse, this Blue Bandit! We've ambushed a major unit! Fire is coming in from everywhere! Over!"

"Roger, Blue Bandit. Are you still at your set-up coordinates? Over."

"Roger, Bunkhouse! We haven't moved! Over!" Each of his communications was urgent, with the sound of gunfire and exploding munitions in the background.

"How far out is the enemy? Over," I asked.

"Damn close! Inside thirty yards!" came the reply.

Later, we would discover that the point element of the enemy unit had been much closer than thirty yards and appeared from nowhere. The larger unit following the point unit was now firing and advancing! Intelligence gathered later would also confirm that our unit faced no ragtag patrol. Two of the enemy KIA (killed in action) were high-ranking officials from a local VC unit. They were dressed in black pajamas and were leading an NVA unit through the area. The NVA unit was suspected to be from a small base several kilometers west of the ambush site, a base that I would later visit.

"Roger, Blue Bandit. Understand. Reinforcements are getting ready and will be on the way shortly. The ROC's artillery battery is being alerted for a possible fire mission. Over." I wanted to reassure the unit that reinforcements were getting ready and to let them know artillery support was available immediately. The Koreans were close, just on the north side of the river, and had once occupied My Loc outpost. They knew it well and could quickly bring their artillery pieces into action.

"Blue Bandit, Bunkhouse. Do you have casualties? Over."

"Bunkhouse, this is Blue Bandit! Standby one!"

"Roger, Blue Bandit. Bunkhouse is standing by. Out."

The first moments in a combat firefight can be hysterically chaotic. It would be difficult enough for the unit in contact to determine what was happening around them if only one military were involved. In this case, there were two, our American COC orientation group and Thieu ta's Vietnamese troops, both firing on the VC/NVA unit they had ambushed.

Both of the units involved in this firefight were communicating information back to their respective radio rooms. We were talking to our Trung Dung advisers with the COC unit while the Vietnamese radio room, only about twenty-five yards away, was communicating with their unit. Information gathered from both radio rooms would be used to coordinate an overall support plan.

While we were on standby waiting for Blue Bandit to respond with information on casualties, we were simultaneously receiving word from our American advisers at My Loc that they and their Vietnamese troops were firing illumination and heavy mortar rounds on enemy positions.

Then came the report from the ambush site. "Bunkhouse, Bunkhouse, this is Blue Bandit, Blue Bandit! Over!" The sound of heavy gunfire and exploding mortar and artillery rounds continued in the background every time Blue Bandit called or answered. It sounded as if they must be in an extremely fierce battle.

"Roger, Blue Bandit. This is Bunkhouse. Go ahead. Over."

"Bunkhouse, it's crazy out here! We know we have men down, but we don't know how many, or their condition! Over!"

"Roger, Blue Bandit. Understand. We've just been told that My Loc is firing mortars. So, you should feel some relief soon. Over."

"Roger, Bunkhouse! I can hear them hitting now! Over!"

"Roger, Blue Bandit. Your reinforcements are rolling out now. Over."

"Roger, Bunkhouse! Understand! Blue Bandit, out!"

From the urgency in our team member's voice and the reverberations of the battle in the background, the COC group members were obviously in a fight for their lives.

With loud sounds in the radio room and the roar of the reinforcement trucks, everyone in the team house was now awake. A few had gathered around the radio room to listen, while others were leaving with the reinforcing units.

After a few minutes, we received a calmer, but still urgent call.

"Bunkhouse, Bunkhouse, this is Blue Bandit, Blue Bandit. Over."

"Roger, Blue Bandit. Go ahead."

"Roger, Bunkhouse. It's settled down a little out here. The Rock Pile [My Loc's call sign] mortars have had some effect, so the incoming is only sporadic now. I've got a casualty report for you. Over."

"Roger, go. Over."

"This is Blue Bandit. We have at least three Vietnamese WIA [wounded in action], and one American KIA. Over."

The radio room fell silent with the news of the KIA. Everyone in and near the radio room was stunned.

My God, I thought, *we've lost an American.*

If true, this would be the first American killed out of Trung Dung since I arrived, and no one in a COC group had ever been killed while at A-502. The thought sickened me. Like others, it was an experience felt in the pit of my stomach. I looked at Miller, who had a grim expression on his face and was shaking his head mournfully. He and everyone else who was gathered around the radio room appeared shocked.

After hesitating for a moment in disbelief, I quickly gathered my thoughts. *Wait a minute,* I thought. I remembered that the medic with the unit was one of the new men. Once again pushing the "press-to-talk" switch on the radio handset, I placed a call to Blue Bandit.

"Blue Bandit, this is Bunkhouse. Over."

"Roger, Bunkhouse. I'm here. Over."

"Blue Bandit, do something for me. Your medic is one of the new guys. Have him go back and check the man reported KIA. Have the medic make sure he's KIA. Over."

"Roger, Bunkhouse. Will do. Out."

I hoped that perhaps in all the chaos of the thunderous gunfire and impacting mortar rounds, a terrible mistake might have been made. Under the circumstances, the new medic could have been wrong unless the wounds were catastrophic. We didn't know who the downed man was and that didn't really matter. But if he was still alive, none of us wanted him out there on the ground with what might be the last of his life dripping into foreign soil.

A few minutes later, we received a reply

"Bunkhouse, this is Blue Bandit. Over."

"Go, Blue Bandit."

"Bunkhouse, the medic says he's gone. Over."

The downed man would have been only the third American lost out of A-502 since the team was formed in 1964. Standing motionless there in the radio room, I thought for a moment about what I had just been told and what my response would be.

Then, speaking in a monotone from an almost statue-like position, I gave a direction to Miller.

"Get the Dustoff frequency on the other radio."

Dustoff was the call sign for the 254th Medical Detachment in Nha Trang. The 254th was our helicopter medical evacuation (Medevac) support unit. Units like the 254th served as air ambulances in Vietnam and the whop, whop, whop sound of their churning blades was welcomed by every injured soldier conscience enough to hear them.

It was generally believed by combat troops that, if you were wounded in action, a Dustoff chopper could have you to a hospital within thirty minutes to an hour. As one of those who walked the jungle floor, that belief gave me great comfort as I did my job.

A Dustoff crew consisted of four people: two pilots, a medic, and a crew chief. Typically, one pilot flew the helicopter while the other served as the aircraft commander. The commander would navigate, monitor radio transmissions, talk to the unit requesting the medevac, and would take over flying if the pilot were injured. The medic was responsible for keeping the helicopter stocked with medical supplies and the crew chief would maintain the helicopter's mechanical condition. The medic and crew chief would load the patients onto the helicopter and the medic would administer any necessary medical treatment on the way to the hospital, often with the help of the crew chief. The Dustoff crews saved countless lives and were universally respected by all of the soldiers in the war, with good cause.

Men of the medevac units in Vietnam often proved to be bold heroes—by any definition. They didn't attack anyone with guns ablaze. Rather, they flew in unarmed helicopters and frequently arrived over a smoking battlefield with bullets ripping through the air in every direction. These incredibly courageous men would swoop in, gather injured or wounded like fearless parents attempting to save a child, then fly them to the nearest hospital.

It wasn't unusual for a medevac chopper to arrive at a hospital riddled with bullet holes or wounded crewmembers. Sadly, it was also not unusual for crewmembers or entire crews to be lost as they risked their lives to save others. These men represented some of the very best our country has to offer.

"Sir, this pickup could be a real bitch. Our unit is still in contact and it will be pitch black out there . . . except for the gunfire."

Miller wasn't easily ruffled and I knew that he was right, but I felt the effort needed to be made.

"Go ahead and get the frequency. Let's talk to them and see what they say. If that guy is still alive out there, he needs to be picked up *now*. He may be dead, but they're going to have to prove it to me."

"Yes, sir."

Miller adjusted the frequency on the radio and began calling.

"Dustoff, Dustoff, this is Bunkhouse, Bunkhouse. Over."

Almost immediately, Miller had a response.

"Roger, Bunkhouse. This is Dustoff. Go ahead."

"Good luck, sir," Miller said as he gave me the handset.

"Roger, Dustoff. This is Bunkhouse Zero Two. We've got at least four men down, and one of them is an American. We need a pick-up ASAP. Over."

"Roger, Zero Two. Understand you need a pickup. Give me your unit's coordinates and status. Over."

I quickly gave him the coordinates and told him that our unit was still in contact with the enemy. "They're still in a firefight," I said. I wasn't going to lie to them, although I was pretty much prepared to do whatever it would take to get them flying.

"Okay, Zero Two. I am alerting a crew right now. You know that this pickup is going to be challenging in the middle of the night with your unit still in a firefight, right?"

"Roger, Dustoff. But one of these guys may be dying . . . he may be dead now."

"Roger. I understand. This will be a very dangerous mission and we just don't want to lose a crew. They are getting ready and firing up their ship right now. They will be prepared to launch in minutes and will need as much information about the pickup location as you can provide. Over."

Clearly, the man on the other end of the radio was doing all he could to help and was obviously as concerned about his men as we were about ours.

"Roger, Dustoff. Thank you. Out."

As I thought about the situation from the Dustoff perspective, it occurred to me, *Now is when Major Lee's advice and the days spent flying back and forth over our AO could be put to good use.*

"Dustoff, Zero Two. Over."

"Roger, go Zero Two. You've got me. Over."

"Dustoff, I know exactly where our unit is engaged. Your chopper will have to fly right over our camp to make the pickup. Your crew could stop and pick me up. Will it help your crew if I go as a guide and show them the way? Over."

After a brief period of silence came the sound of a different voice on the radio and the pounding sound of helicopter blades could be heard in the background.

Later, I would learn that the voice heard next was that of the Dustoff pilot who was to fly the mission, Major Virgil Mielke, the 254th's unit commander. He was already in his helicopter and had been monitoring the exchange of transmissions between his radio room and me while his copilot powered up their ship.

"Zero Two, this is Dustoff. You know the exact location where your men will be for a pickup. Is that affirmative? Over."

"Roger, exactly!" I emphasized.

"Okay, Zero Two, that will definitely help. Get out on your landing pad and turn on the lights. We are lifting off now and coming your way."

"Roger . . . I'm going out the door now. Out."

It was a moonless night and as dark as I have ever seen the night sky. Fortunately, Major Mielke was one of the few Dustoff pilots who had an instrument rating, a primary reason for him taking the mission himself rather than handing it off to one of his pilots.

Just before leaving the radio room, I called Blue Bandit and told them to get their KIA and WIA ready for pickup by Dustoff and made sure they understood the need to be ready to move quickly when we arrived.

As I turned to leave, Bill Lane, the team's executive officer had also been roused by all the commotion, was standing at the door to the radio room.

"I'll handle the radios," he said, "and I'll coordinate the link-up with our reinforcements. Go get our men!"

Because members of his unit were involved in the contact, Bill Phalen was standing at the radio room door fully outfitted. He was about to leave with the last of the reinforcements, said he would run ahead of me to turn on the pad lights while I went for my gear. The helipad was located directly behind his Blue Bandit team house.

When I reached the pad, Bill was standing in the center of the lighted square.

"Who do you think the KIA is?" he asked as I walked onto the pad.

"I don't know. But the odds are it's one of the new guys, and if that's the case, he's been in-country only a little more than a week or so. God, I hope he's hanging on."

We weren't on the pad long before we could hear the distant sound of the inbound helicopter. Then, as the chopper approached over the pad, our lights illuminated its underbelly and nose where white squares with big red crosses were displayed. The red cross insignia indicated to both friendly and enemy units that the unarmed chopper was a medical evacuation aircraft. The whirling machine quickly rested on the pad and, as it did, a jeep skidded up. Two team members jumped out and, over the pounding sound of helicopter blades, one of them yelled, "These are supplies requested by the unit, sir." Then, they hurriedly shoved several boxes onto the chopper.

As the boxes were being loaded, Major Ngoc roared up at the wheel of his jeep. "They tell me you are going after our men," he shouted.

"Yes, I am."

"I just wanted you to know that I am following the reinforcements. Don't get shot down!" he quipped, then roared away.

"I'm going out now, too. Good luck!" Phalen shouted.

"Go! Thanks for the help," I responded, then quickly jumped aboard the chopper.

With the engines still nearly at full power, the chopper quickly rose and we returned to the pitch-black sky from which it had descended.

As we gained altitude over the camp, one of the crewmen handed me a headset. The earphones were barely positioned over my ears when Major Mielke began speaking to me.

"You want us to go west, is that correct?"

I pulled the microphone around in front of my mouth and answered, "Roger. I'm sure we'll see the illumination flares as soon as we gain enough altitude."

Then I quickly added, "Thank you for coming."

"No problem . . . this is what we do," he said. Then he asked, "What kind of terrain are we going to be landing in?"

"It's all lowland rice paddy, but our guys know we're coming and they'll have the injured men on solid ground."

"Good, I don't feel like getting wet."

"That's not a problem. They're in a dry area," I responded.

"Even better," the pilot said calmly.

It was always reassuring to me to hear humor or relaxed calm in the voices of the many helicopter crews with whom I flew, even in some of the worst situations.

This trip would be my first flight in a helicopter at night. The only lights in the chopper were the red ones that illuminated the instrument panel. The reflected red light from the instruments gave an eerie glow to the front portion of the cabin where Major Mielke and his copilot sat.

As quickly as we cleared the trees around Trung Dung, the illumination flares over the contact site could be seen flickering in the distance.

"Our unit is out there under those flares . . . and so are the bad guys," I told the pilot.

"Roger, I see the flares."

After we passed over the populated villages around Trung Dung, I looked out the door toward the ground. Everything looked black, with no lights visible beneath us. With no moon that night, everything was much darker than I had expected. As we cut through the thick, humid, black sky, I strained to see landmarks below. The effort was useless. I couldn't see a thing.

Guided only by the instruments and the distant flares, Major Mielke navigated confidently through what seemed to me to be more like nothingness than sky.

As we neared the contact site, the flares became brighter. We could see occasional tracer rounds streaking randomly across the ground.

Aided by light from the flares, I began to see terrain features.

"Okay," I said to the pilot. "Our unit will be located about a hundred yards out on the southeastern side of the lighted area."

"Roger," Mielke responded.

"Did you get that?" he asked his copilot.

"Roger, the friendlies are about a hundred yards out from the light on the southeast side," the copilot repeated.

At about that point, I contacted the ground unit and told them we were near and needed an LZ (landing zone) marked. The unit acknowledged my request and said they would be ready.

With everything seemingly prepared for Dustoff, Major Mielke began to make his approach for the pickup. The pitch of the engines changed as we started down. It was then that the experience of the pilot and his crew became apparent.

"Keep an eye out for flare chutes" was Major Mielke's first direction to his crew as we neared the ambush site.

The parachute and canister from a burned-out flare could bring the helicopter down as quickly as enemy gunfire if they became caught in the rotor blades.

As if synchronized and practiced, the responses of "Clear right" and "Clear left" came from both the crew chief and medic.

"Damn! I still see muzzle flashes," Mielke said. "You guys keep your eyes open and report. We're gonna drop down and go in as low as we can.

"Zero Two, are there any obstacles we should be looking for?"

"Only the trees between here and the pickup point," I said. "The land is flat except for the paddy dikes. But there's a small hill to the northwest. That's where the illumination and fire support is coming from. If you stay on this line, you'll be fine."

"Roger, understand."

Through the cockpit windows, I could see trees ahead silhouetted by the familiar pinkish-orange glow of the illumination flares. Some of the trees appeared to be higher than we were. But, as we closed on each set of silhouettes, Major Mielke would either fly over them or around them. If the skids got hung up in a treetop, the mission would end—abruptly.

The experience was like flying through an obstacle course. The only sound aboard the chopper as it zigged and zagged toward the hastily prepared LZ was the occasional message of well-being, "Clear right" and "Clear left," from the crew chief and the medic to Major Mielke.

As we neared the pickup point, the crew chief and medic who had been searching the sky for airborne debris turned their attention forward to scan for danger on the ground, which was coming up quickly.

I watched the medic as he scanned the ground for hazards. With flares as a very limited source of light, only parts of his face were visible as he moved his head. Oil forced to the surface of his skin by the heat and humidity of the Southeast Asian night caused the visible parts of his face to shine slightly. Despite the restricted light, I could tell he was young. The apparent lack of fear in his face was surprising. Rather, he seemed as calm as the pilot and appeared composed as he went about the responsibility of protecting his side of our helicopter. He was so focused on what he was doing that I don't think he knew he was being observed.

My own heart pounded in anticipation of what the next few minutes might bring, but as I watched the actions and listened to unexcited exchanges between Mielke and his crew, I felt confident that a better flight team couldn't have been drawn. With absolutely no protection for themselves, these men had dared to take to a very dark sky in an attempt to save others.

I moved to the door and looked toward our proposed landing site, which was now outlined by only four red specs created by filtered flashlights aimed in our direction. The team with the injured men was exactly where they said they would be, but with confirmation necessary, Major Mielke radioed the unit.

"Blue Bandit, this is Dustoff inbound. Over."

"Roger, Dustoff. This is Blue Bandit. Go ahead."

"Roger, this is Dustoff. Describe your LZ. Over."

"Dustoff, we have four reds (red flashlights) pointed right at you. Over."

"Roger. Get ready. We're coming in for your men."

With the extinction of almost all of the flares, everything suddenly became considerably darker again. I had asked our outpost to quit firing illumination to cover our landing. So, besides the stars, the only light in the sky was the occasional flicker of a dying flare.

We had become engulfed in almost total darkness when Mielke cleared the last set of trees and began maneuvering to put the chopper down inside the area outlined by the red flashlights. At that point, the contact had substantially reduced in ferocity, but we were close enough to the ground to hear occasional gunfire and see intermittent tracer rounds and muzzle flashes.

As we dropped toward the ground, I wondered how Mielke could see. I couldn't see anything clearly, and he hadn't turned on any landing lights yet. The ground wasn't far beneath us because the flashlights seemed not much lower than eye level. I braced for the impact that was surely coming. But within the last few feet before touchdown, Mielke turned his lights on for what seemed like only an instant. Then he settled the chopper onto the narrow paddy dike as gently as if it had been high noon.

As soon as the skids touched the ground, the men from our unit immediately rushed to the chopper, pulled off their resupplies, and immediately began loading the wounded. As one man was being lifted onto the chopper, our medic recognized me and shouted to be heard over the roar of the chopper's engine and blades, "This is the KIA, sir."

"Okay, I've got him," I answered, pulling him farther into the chopper.

While the others were getting the rest of the wounded aboard, I knelt beside the man the medic had reported as KIA.

With my red filtered flashlight, I searched for wounds. The circular patch of red light from my flashlight skimmed over his legs, torso, and arms, and onto his face. When the red glow of light illuminated his face, I was stunned by what I saw. It was Dale Reich. His eyes were closed and his face was pale. I immediately reached for his neck to feel for a pulse.

However, upon placing my fingertips on his neck in search of the pulse I hoped could be found, I feared the medic had been correct. His body had an uncommon chill, and despite my hope for any sign of life, no pulse could be felt.

The medic had been watching me check Reich for a pulse. "I'm sorry, sir," he said. "I wish I could have done something for him. I wanted to give you a different report."

"I know you did. It wasn't your fault. I'm sure you did everything you could."

As one of the wounded was lifted onto the chopper, someone yelled, "Watch this one, LT. He's VC!"

The man appeared lifeless and obviously near death, so he didn't appear to be much of a threat, but there was something remarkable in what the men of the American COC group had done. After finding him down in the dry rice paddy bed, they carried the wounded enemy soldier to the chopper and put him on board so that he could receive medical treatment. Many others would simply have left him to die. While I could easily argue both sides of their actions, I know they did the right thing.

"That's everybody!" one of the other team members shouted, letting me know that all of the wounded had been loaded.

I passed the word to Major Mielke.

"That's it. We're clear to go."

"Roger, the power's coming up," he responded.

With the increase in engine power came the familiar "Clear right" and "Clear left" from the crew to let their pilot know that once he had enough power he could lift off.

Mielke lifted off the paddy dike, rose above tree level, rotated the chopper, and headed back in the direction from which we had approached.

With all evidence to the contrary, I clung to the hope that Reich might still be grasping to a thread of life. Pressing the radio switch on my headset, I asked Major Mielke to get us to the hospital as quickly as he could.

"I'm going as fast as and as straight as I can. We're radioing ahead now for an emergency crew to be on the hospital pad when we arrive," he said.

The flight seemed long and slow, but when we arrived at the hospital things happened quickly. Multiple orderlies were waiting with gurneys as we settled in on the helipad at the 8th Army Field Hospital in Nha Trang City.

As the corpsmen rushed to the helicopter doors, I pointed to Reich and yelled, "Take him first."

They carefully lifted Dale onto one of the gurneys and immediately began rushing toward the emergency room doors. I was right behind them. When I looked back, they were lifting the VC soldier onto a gurney, so I yelled, "Watch him . . . that one is VC."

One of the corpsmen yelled, "Okay!" And, they fell in right behind me.

Before we reached them, the emergency entrance doors burst open as we approached with the gurney. An Army nurse had shoved the doors open and the orderlies rushed through. The nurse immediately saw me at the rear of the gurney. As I started through the doors the nurse took me by the arm and gently pulled me aside. Speaking to me in a calm professional voice she said, "Lieutenant . . . please . . . we need information quickly. Can you stay here with me? Our team will take him where he needs to go.

The nurse was a young 1st Lieutenant in the U.S. Army Nurses Corps, small-medium build, delicate features pleasingly attractive, dressed in her olive-drab Army fatigues. She was discernably seasoned and in charge of her arena. And, she was not the least bit intimidated by an armed "Green Beret" in full combat gear.

Responding to the nurse's calm, in-charge manner, I released the gurney and stepped aside. The orderlies and gurney continued through the outer doors, which immediately closed behind them.

As the doors clicked shut, the nurse asked, "Can you quickly brief me on what happened to the Lieutenant while the team begins work on him?"

"Of course, yes . . . his team ambushed a VC unit and during the firefight, he was hit."

Dale Reich was far from home and I wanted to be with him and told the nurse, "I really need to be with him."

The nurse, gentle in her manner, looked into my eyes as she spoke. She seemed to understand the concern I had for a man I felt was a fallen teammate. She gently rested her hand on my arm and she spoke softly and caringly to me and said, "Lieutenant, . . . you've done your part . . . you got him here to us. Now, please . . . let us do our part for him. Our team is already doing and they will continue to do everything possible to save him."

"Yes . . . okay . . . that's fine. I'll wait out here. Just please keep me posted on his condition," I asked.

The young nurse, who was probably my age, quickly reassured me and promised to keep me abreast of Dale's condition saying, "Of course. As soon as I know something, I will come find you."

Then, she quickly disappeared back into the hospital and I walked off into the semidarkness surrounding the hospital.

After what seemed like a very long time, the nurse reappeared. In actuality, it had been only 10 or 15 minutes. I saw her coming out of the emergency room door and walked to meet her.

As soon as I drew close enough to see her face, I knew instantly that she didn't have good news for me. When she was close enough to hear me,

I said, "He didn't make it . . . right?"

When our eyes finally met, we were two young Army officers in a war half a world away from our homes and we were communicating with each other even before she spoke.

"No, I'm very sorry . . . he didn't."

"He was so pale when they lifted him onto the chopper, I knew he'd lost a lot of blood. I just hoped we could get him here in time," I responded.

"Lieutenant . . . you did all you could do and we did all we could do for him. The truth is . . . he was probably already gone when they put him on the chopper with you."

"Yes . . . I suppose I knew that."

Even though Dale and I had spent only brief moments together, I felt a deep loss for a brother in arms. He was the first American casualty that I had experienced and I suspect that the nurse could sense my distress because she tried to comfort me. She offered the simple gesture of her arm over my shoulder—her way of showing compassion for the loss she sensed.

"Lieutenant, would you like to come in and have a cup of coffee with me? You can tell me about your friend?"

"Thank you. That's very thoughtful, but . . . no. The fight that killed the lieutenant may still be going on. I need to get back to my camp. I may have to make this trip again with others before the night is over. Thank you for coming out."

I offered my hand to the nurse and continued, "Thank you for doing what you do."

She gently took my hand and squeezed it as she did. I returned her squeeze with a hurting smile, turned to leave, and walked towards the medevac helicopter. I wanted to thank Major Mielke before they left and before calling my camp for pickup.

As I walked away, I gestured toward the medevac helicopter and said, "I need to go thank those guys before they leave. You stay safe."

"I will . . . you, too," were the nurse's last words.

Mielke had heard what was said and knew the young officer we had transported was dead. He also seemed to sense my distress. As I approached his door window, he was beginning to power up his chopper. He motioned me to get into the chopper and shouted to be heard over the now pounding blades of his Huey, "Get in, Lieutenant. We'll take you back to A-502."

"Do you have time?" I asked.

"Get in . . . the 254th has other ships. We're going to make time."

I boarded the chopper, which was then at full power, and sat in the seat next to the open door. Mielke lifted off and rotated to head west, back towards A-502. And, as we turned, I looked down at the young nurse who was still standing near the hospital emergency arrival door. When she saw me looking at her, she showed me a gentle salute and a hand over her heart— which I returned.

The chopper completed its rotation and we flew off into the darkness.

It was often unspoken moments of tenderness or kindness during difficult times like this one that gave me a deep and very warm appreciation for the doctors, nurses, corpsmen, and medevac crews who supported our combat units in Vietnam. They had to deal with the horrors of war every day. A "Thank you" seemed like so little to offer them for all the things they did.

After we had taken off and were headed back to Trung Dung, I put a headset on and adjusted the microphone. I knew the whole crew could hear me, so I spoke to them collectively.

"I want to thank all of you for what you did tonight. I know this is your job, but I still want to thank you for coming."

"We tried," Mielke said. "We wanted him to make it. We believed you thought there might be a chance. That was one of the reasons we tried as hard as we did."

The rest of the flight back to camp was silent. But, as we flew through the darkness, my thoughts went back to the young nurse at the hospital. She seemed so calm and measured when she delivered the news about Dale Reich's condition. I could only imagine the horrific battle injuries she had seen. I had seen far more than I cared to and wondered why a woman would want to serve during a war and be exposed to such, sometimes catastrophic, sights. It would be many years, but a nurse who served in Vietnam would one day answer my question.

When we reached Trung Dung, I reached up to take my headset off. But just before I did, I squeezed the microphone button one last time.

"I'm really proud to have flown with you guys. Thank you for showing up."

With that, I pulled the headset off, handed it to the crew chief, and jumped down onto the pad. Then, walking to Mielke's window, I shook his hand and thanked him one last time.

"If you need us again," he boomed loud enough to be heard over his engines, "call. You've got our number."

"I will. You guys take care of yourselves."

Then, I backed away from the chopper as it powered up for liftoff. A wave of appreciation was my final offering as the chopper rose above me and back into the inky night sky. It took only a minute for it to disappear in the east, where there was no hint of the morning that would soon be dawning.

A "Thank you" was also all I had given to the very courageous crew of the Dustoff helicopter. It seemed such an insignificant thing to say after they had risked their own lives trying to save another. Somehow, though, I suspected that was probably all they wanted or expected.

My Loc Outpost — Where it Happened

Along the treeline beyond the Vietnamese flag is where Dale Reich and his unit were set up on ambush. The lush exotic look of the area was deceptive. That night, none of the many shades of green could be seen—it was very dark and deadly.

U.S. Army Combat Infantryman's Badge

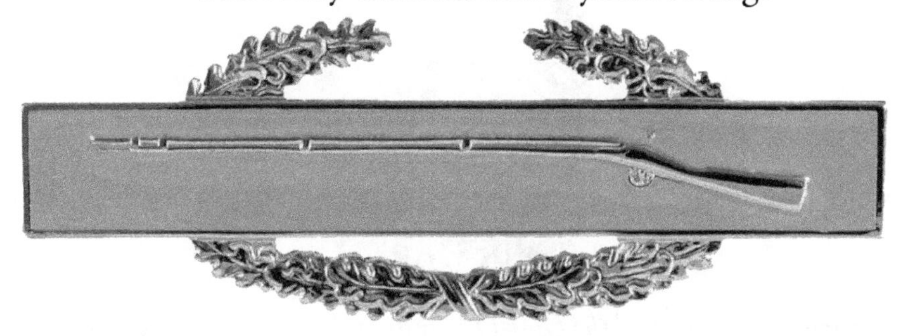

The Combat Infantryman Badge (CIB) is a U.S. Army military award. The badge is awarded to infantrymen and Special Forces soldiers in the rank of colonel and below, who fought in combat while assigned as members of either an Infantry, Ranger, or SF unit, of brigade size or smaller.

Each member of the COC class earned this award the night of their ambush mission. And, most of them had been in Vietnam for fewer than ten days.

It was with great pride that I accepted this award while serving at A-502. The most important aspect of the presentation ceremony was that—I was alive to accept it.

U.S. Army Combat Medic's Badge

The Combat Medical Badge (CMB) is also a U.S. Army military award for Army medics and other members of the Army Medical Department. Individuals who are assigned or attached to a ground combat unit when the unit was engaged in combat are eligible for the CMB. The individual must be performing medical duties while simultaneously being engaged by the enemy.

254th Medevac "Dust Off" Patch

The pilots and crews of all the Dust-Off air ambulance units were amazing men with incredible courage and extreme dedication to those of us who walked the jungle floor. Knowing they were available at a moment's notice made it a bit easier for us to do our job.

More than fifty years after the tragic night we met, I had the good fortune to encounter Major Mielke again. Amazingly, after so many years and although our encounter had been brief, we discovered that we still shared a bond. To remind me of that bond and commemorate our flight together, he gave me a 254th lapel pin crest. I took that opportunity to thank him one more time for his daring—flight into darkness.

CHAPTER 26

They Served with Courage

ON THE WAY BACK from the 8th Field Hospital in Nha Trang to A-502, I wondered how a woman, even though serving as a nurse, could face the bloody and catastrophic wounds of war, often, on a daily basis. It wouldn't be until years later that I would learn the answer to my question. And, I would meet the person who would answer that question in a warm gentile setting, very different from the one in which it was spawned.

After accepting a friend's invitation to be his guest, we drove from Atlanta to the Ritz Carlton at the Lake Oconee Resort to hear a presentation by General (Ret.) Norton "Norty" Schwartz, Chief of Staff of the US Air Force, Washington, D.C. Norty, as he asked to be called, served as Chief of Staff until he retired in 2008. Until that time, he served as the senior Air Force officer responsible for the organization, training, and equipping of approximately 700,000 active-duty, National Guard, Reserve, and civilian forces serving in the United States and overseas.

During the presentation, I was seated with my friend, Dr. Bill Scaljon, at a table of eight. Almost everyone at the table was a veteran and one of my tablemates was a woman, Ginny Dornheggen. Interestingly, Ginny had served as a nurse with the U.S. Army Nurse Corps during the Vietnam War.

We didn't have much time to talk during the event, but after leaving a copy of my book, *Privileges of War*, (the first edition of this book) for everyone at our table, Ginny sent me a thank-you note.

At about the time Ginny's note arrived, I was working with a producer in California who was also a professional screenwriter on a script for a film, tentatively titled *The Rescue*, and based on my book. But, that's another story and the subject for another book.

While working on the screenplay, there was a scene set at the 8th Field Hospital in Nha Trang that involved me and the young nurse you just read about. I wanted the scene to be written authentically and technically correct. But, because I had forgotten her name or never knew it, I couldn't go to the nurse involved. That's when I thought of Ginny.

After finding someone who knew her and how to contact her, I sent Ginny an email, explained my project to her, and asked if she was interested in helping. Graciously, she said she would be happy to help. So, I sent her a copy of the script for the scene as it had been written. After reading the script, Ginny sent a note back to me explaining that a real Army nurse would have handled things described in the scene differently. Pleased that a nurse who had been in Vietnam was willing to help, I said, "Please re-write the script as you would have behaved." And, she did.

The scene as re-written was warm and showed a brief, but a very touching, encounter between two young Americans involved in a war and on the other side of the world from their homes. Ginny had captured the moment perfectly. As I read what she had written, I immediately began to relive that night at the hospital. I hope that scene one day makes its way to the silver screen where it can be shared with others.

When most people envision a war, they imagine soldiers shooting at each other, And, that's pretty much what happens. But, if you are one of the soldiers who has been shot, it's what happens next that is most important. And, unless a fan of "MASH," it's not something most people think about.

In Vietnam, as mentioned earlier, a soldier could expect to be on a medevac helicopter within thirty minutes of the call for pickup. Then, his chances of survival depended on the doctors and nurses at the emergency facility where he was flown.

Wounded soldiers often arrived at field hospitals with their bodies mangled and in conditions near death. The monumental efforts of doctors and nurses often made it possible for many young Americans to return home to their families. But, the stories of healing and survival are not the typical ones you hear about Vietnam.

Determined not to let this edition of my book go to print without a more significant mention of them, I decided to write a chapter about the U.S. Army Nurse Corps and dedicate it, not just to the young nurse I met, but to all of those who treated and cared for the fallen in Vietnam. And, those nurses were both female and male.

As I thought about the chapter and how to write it, I didn't want it to be flat and simply documentary in style. If it were going to interest you, my reader, I believed it needed feeling. Thinking about the night with Major Mielke and my encounter with the young nurse, I remembered my questions of why a woman, or anyone, would become a nurse and then chose to go to Vietnam. It occurred to me that answering those two questions might tell the story I wanted to tell about the Nurse Corps.

While working on the screenplay, Ginny Dornheggen and I had become acquainted, so I once again turned to her for help. I told her what I was doing and asked if she would be willing to answer my two questions. And, again, she agreed to help.

What comes next, is a story that represents and could be about any of those who chose to serve their country and care for its fallen warriors.

In response to my first question, Ginny didn't hesitate with her very assured response, "I always knew I wanted to be a nurse!"

As a young woman, before she was married, she was Ginny Deardorff. Ginny was in the Girl Scouts, was a Candy Striper at her local hospital, and after taking an American Red Cross course, she babysat. She loved the adventures of scouting (camping, backpacking, travel), but most of all, she found satisfaction in volunteering to help others. And, that's probably something you might expect from a future nurse.

Back in the 60s, a three-year nursing school program was an option for year-round learning and that's what she chose. Growing up in Gettysburg, Pennsylvania, Ginny attended the not-too-faraway Harrisburg Hospital School of Nursing. There, she and other students stayed in a dormitory, worked long shifts at the hospital, and took classes between shifts.

Wanting to expand her horizons after graduation, she considered possible options. An upperclassman told her about the Army Nurse Corps. It promised travel, additional education, pay the senior year of nursing, and only required a two-year service commitment.

Intrigued by the opportunity, she said, "I remember going home and telling my parents that I wanted to join the Army Nurse Corps."

She said she was excited and told her parents about all the things ANC could offer her. Then, she said, "I wanted to do something special and meaningful with my life, while learning at the same time. But, most of all, I wanted to serve my country and continue the sense of pride and loyalty I was taught in the Girl Scouts."

Does that sound familiar? So many of us just wanted to serve our country and do something meaningful at the same time.

Ginny told me that, with her parents' blessing, she applied to and was accepted into the Army Student Nurse Program for her senior year. She said, "My Dad was immensely proud as he had served in WWII."

After graduation from the Army Nurse Program, she continued a postgrad course in ICU/CCU (Intensive Care Unit and Cardiac Care Unit). Ginny believed that advanced training would better prepare her for future challenges she might face.

Her first assignment was at Walter Reed Army Hospital in the Recovery Unit. There, she experienced firsthand the horrors of war wounds and learned the meaning of working long—hard hours. She accepted her assignment as preparation for the possibility of becoming a part of the war.

When Ginny was considering Army nursing as a career choice, she said the recruiter told her that there was a 95 percent chance she'd be sent to Vietnam. But she told me, "I didn't really think that would happen."

Well, if I had been around the recruiting office that day, I would have offered the young woman, who I now consider a friend, the following thought—*If I were listening to the radio and heard the weatherman say that there was a 95 percent chance of rain, I would be expecting to get wet!*

After nine months at Walter Reed, it "rained" on Ginny and she received orders directing her to service in South Vietnam. While she wasn't happy about going to a place where she might be killed, she always knew and had accepted that possibility. She understood that she and her skills would be valuable there.

Just like all of those who had gone ahead of her, Ginny experienced an abrupt and dramatic change in her life when she arrived in Vietnam in November 1970. She had just turned twenty-two years old. Arriving as 2st Lieutenant, Ginny Deardorff, she was assigned to the 67th Evacuation Hospital in Qui Nhon, about 235 miles north of Saigon. Because the area was in a designated "Combat Zone," she would no longer be wearing a nicely pressed nurse's uniform. Instead, she was told that jungle fatigues and combat boots would be required dress. After collecting her new uniform, she was assigned to the PAR (Post Anesthesia Room—the same as a Recovery Room in the states) and ICU, two critical care areas where her training and experience would be put to work.

In telling her story, Ginny said, "There was no 'Front Line' in Vietnam, I learned that very quickly! At night, bright-red tracers from M-16s, loud explosions, 'Red Alerts,' and the eerie light of illumination flares, were constant reminders that I was very much a part of the war."

This, or worse, were everyday experiences for those who found themselves serving in "Hot" areas of the country. The world around you could unexpectedly explode at any moment.

On what had been a very quiet evening, I was in the Team House with a few teammates watching "My Fair Lady" on a projector that had been acquired from an "unknown source." And, the film had been dropped into us by one of our Air Force FAC friends. Suddenly, mortar rounds began impacting inside the walls of the fort. Everyone jumped up and reached for weapons that were never far away. Moment to moment, you had to be prepared to defend yourself.

Continuing her story, Ginny said, "As a 'Combat' nurse, my duties, skills, and expectations were to maintain the highest standards of care during any type of situation. Critical thinking skills were of utmost importance. I was trained to visually assess and listen so that I could quickly react to the needs of our soldiers. In Vietnam, there was no computer, iPhone, Wi-Fi, or Google to help with references—you had to use what was in your head."

Ginny explained that our soldiers were the reason she and all the others were there. Their goal was to ensure that every injured soldier received the best of care and respect from every nurse tending to him.

Then, her description of things they did became poignant, "Since a family member couldn't be with them, we would hold the hand of a dying soldier to the last moment of death. We also wrote letters for those who had arms amputated or injury to their eyes. We shared stories, tears, and smiles. Our soldiers were young, strong, and truly terrific to care for. Most of their injuries were life-changing. And, caring for them changed my life."

In the black-as-pitch sky the night Dale Reich was wounded, as our medevac chopper raced him and other wounded toward the 8th Field Hospital, I learned that the definition of "good" and what I considered "evil" could become blurred.

While hovering over Dale, I encouraged the wounded CIDG troops to "Hang on!" Occasionally, checking the VC soldier to keep an eye on him, I could see that his eyes were open and he was watching me. I hated what he and his unit had done to Dale and the Vietnamese soldiers I advised.

At some point, we locked eyes. Looking into his, I could see uncertainty and fear. And, looking into mine, he could very likely see disdain and hate.

As we continued to fly, I again glanced toward the enemy soldier. It was so dark in the chopper that the detail of his uniform wasn't visible. This time, when I looked into his eyes, I could see the pain he was experiencing and began to feel some compassion for him.

Never having been this close to an enemy soldier who might be dying, I became flooded with contradictive emotions. Knowing he was the enemy, I still hated him. But, with his uniform muted by the darkness, I also began to see him as just another human being who was in pain and, maybe, dying. And, my teammates must have felt some compassion for him because, rather than putting another bullet in him, they carried him with our troops to Major Mielke's Dustoff chopper.

Looking ahead, I could see the hospital lights. In just minutes, we would be there and I would learn more about compassion from those in the healing profession.

While our arrival at the hospital has already been described, there is a bit more to tell.

As the wounded were being taken off the chopper, I alerted the medical corpsmen at the chopper doors to the man who was a VC.

On the way to the emergency entrance, I was behind the gurney on which Dale Reich had been placed. The one with the enemy soldier on it wasn't far behind me, so I could easily hear the corpsman at the head of the gurney when he spoke loudly to the soldier, "Stay with me!" he shouted, "We're going to help you!"

I doubted that the soldier understood because he responded in Vietnamese. So, again, the corpsman simply encouraged him in English, "It's okay! We are going to take care of you!"

On the battlefield, we did our best to kill each other. But, there at the hospital, they were going to do their very best to save the life of an enemy soldier, then care for him until he was healed.

After that night, I heard of several more cases where American medical teams, like those at the 8th Field Hospital and the 67th Evac, saved the lives of enemy soldiers along with those of Americans. Preserving life was their job and they did it very well. And, it didn't matter what uniform you were wearing. If you were wounded, you would receive their care—good or evil.

In 1971, Ginny was promoted to 1st Lieutenant. Many things happened as she continued to care for our soldiers and she could easily fill the pages of her own book, but she shared a "most-favorite story" with me.

One day, Miss America, Phyllis George, (and her entourage) visited the 67th Evacuation Hospital. Ginny said she was quite beautiful with perfect makeup, beautiful hair, and she took the time to speak with each soldier in the ICU.

Ginny was caring for a soldier who had both of his arms amputated when Phyllis walked over to speak to him. Ginny helped by holding him up so he could see the American beauty better. Phyllis spoke with him several minutes and Ginny said, "He had the biggest smile!" As she laid him back down in bed, she said, "Wouldn't it be great if all of us nurses could look like that?"

Then the soldier said, "She doesn't hold a candle to how you nurses look and what you mean to us!" Ginny said that she immediately teared up, leaned down, and gave him a kiss on his forehead, and told him she would never forget him. And, as you just read—she hasn't.

Doctors and nurses were typically scheduled to work 12-hour days/6 days a week. When Mass Cals occurred, it was more like 16-18-hour days. "Mass Cals" was an abbreviation for Mass Casualties; when fifty or more wounded patients arrived in a very short time. Ginny said that, during the period the TET Offensive lasted in early 1968 (before she arrived), the 67th Evac sometimes had Mass Cals of more than 150 patients.

Ginny told me that the camaraderie and high degree of professionalism displayed by the nurses and medical personnel she worked with were key to the 67th Evac's esprit de corps. Then, she said, "Joining the Army Nurse Corps was the *best career choice* I ever made. The teamwork and willingness to help each other, no matter how busy, was my most favorite part of military nursing."

Ginny Deardorff Dornheggen was clearly very passionate about both her nursing career and her time in Southeast Asia. She closed her story by saying, "I am a Vietnam Veteran, a souvenir of that War. I have chosen to remember the good things that happened, even though, I do have anxieties remaining. I am proud of the privilege to have served my country with the young men and women I got to know, and they will always be a piece of my heart."

For her effort, Ginny was promoted to 1st Lieutenant in 1971.

Ginny and I were the same age when we served in Vietnam, but we worked on opposite ends of the war. I worked with the tools used to make war, while she worked with the instruments used to heal the results of war. But, when we were both young, we went to Southeast Asia to serve our country.

By answering my two questions, Ginny did indeed help me tell the story I wanted to tell about those who cared for our courageous soldiers like Dale Reich and so many others. Dale didn't survive, but everyone did their very best to save him.

This chapter is dedicated to all of the doctors, nurses, and medical personnel who were on 24-hour standby to treat and care for our country's fallen warriors—they served with courage and dedication.

Dedicated to All of Those Who Cared for Our Troops

1st Lieutenant Ginny Deardorff—U.S. Army Nurses Corps
67th Evacuation Hospital—Republic of South Vietnam, 1971

CHAPTER 27

After Action Report

THE MORNING AFTER THE ambush, when the sun rose and illuminated another day in Vietnam, we held a debriefing for the COC ambush mission. While conditions were exactly as they had been on the previous day, this day didn't seem as clear or as bright. But as the debriefing unfolded, at least a clearer understanding of what happened the night before would emerge.

During a recap of events surrounding the previous night, we learned from one of the men who had been near him that Dale Reich triggered the ambush. Reich and his unit were lying in hidden positions behind a dry paddy dike where they could observe some of the many trails running through the area near our My Loc outpost. These trails were routinely used as infiltration routes for enemy units approaching from the west.

Listening to the account of events, I had to wonder about Dale's reason for being the first to fire, especially since that was one of the things emphasized and discussed thoroughly during the pre-mission briefing. *Surely, he hadn't forgotten,* I thought. Then, I wondered—*Was he so gung-ho on his first combat mission that he was compelled to ignore the cautions about the danger of being the first to fire? Or had he felt that he may have been the only person to see the approaching danger and, unable to pass the word along undetected, acted to protect the men with him?*

As it turned out, and it was no surprise to me when it did, the latter seemed to have been the case. According to one of the other men near Reich, no one saw the enemy until after he opened fire.

"They were just there," the man said. "They came out of the darkness near the edge of the rice paddy and were on top of us before we knew it. If the lieutenant hadn't opened fire, they would probably have walked right into the middle of our unit."

Then he quickly added, with passion in his voice, "He was responsible for saving many of us around him!"

Other Americans confirmed that Reich had obviously seen men in the VC point unit when they emerged from the darkness because he yelled, "VC!" when he opened fire. Because they were wearing black pajamas, often the attire for VC, they were nearly invisible at night. With no time to warn his unit, Dale Reich did what was instinctive for him, he took the lead. He immediately engaged the enemy unit with his M-16 at what was reported to be nearly point-blank range. As a result of his action, Dale instantaneously drew the wrath of the enemy response as he and members of the VC point unit exchanged hellish gunfire.

Having seen his muzzle flash, the VC poured their return fire directly into Reich's position, fatally wounding him. He had taken a stand on the battlefield, just as he must have done many times on the football field as captain of his Grady High School football team. Unfortunately, this one had cost him his life, but his quick action and selfless act gave his COC teammates time to react and the opportunity to survive.

Alerted to the approaching danger by Reich's opening burst of fire, other COC team members and the South Vietnamese joined in the fight, which quickly grew fierce and resulted in a heavy exchange of mixed weapons fire between the opposing units.

The friendly force was composed of four A-502 advisers, twenty to twenty-five COC members, and a similar number of our South Vietnamese soldiers. The combined VC/NVA enemy unit was estimated to be at least the same size.

Considering the rate of fire exchanged between the friendly and enemy unit, it isn't difficult to imagine how loud the initial moments of the encounter must have been. We witnessed some of those moments back at Trung Dung when our radio speakers pounded with the sound of the battle. Despite the ferocity of the fight, the new men of the COC group and their veteran Vietnamese troops held their ground as the battle continued.

Finally, with supporting mortar fire from My Loc, artillery from the ROKs, and Spooky's illumination flares, the unit was able to force the enemy to retreat in disarray. The new men, who became combat veterans that night, had represented themselves well.

When Thieu ta, Bill Phalen, and the reinforcements arrived, the combined unit moved forward and swept the area. While this night would offer the first combat action for most of the Americans, because of the initial advantage given to them by Lieutenant Reich, they would win the battle.

Later in the day, the Vietnamese confirmed what we were told by the Americans who had been near Reich. One of Thieu ta Ngoc's old Vietnamese sergeants told me that he was certain that he and many of his men would have been killed or wounded if the American lieutenant had not opened fire. Because the night was so dark, none of the Vietnamese had detected the VC unit until seeing their muzzle flashes when they returned fire on Reich's position.

His family and those who knew him were very likely not surprised by his selfless action. Despite the briefness of my encounter with Merrill Dale Reich Jr., I will always remember his eagerness to serve and the courage with which he faced it.

After returning to my home in Pensacola when my tour duty ended, my profession would move me and my family around the county. Ultimately, we would settle in Atlanta.

The true irony about moving to Atlanta was that it was Dale Reich's home town. Surprisingly, even though our encounter was very brief and had occurred many years earlier, we would be reunited in a very strange way. As you will read, there is a good reason that I am not likely to forget Dale and what he did that very dark night in Vietnam. And, neither am I likely to forget the courage and bravery of Major Mielke and his evacuation crew who flew the mission, nor the hospital team that tried to save Dale. Their deeds are all indelibly etched in my memory.

The "Ballad of the Green Berets" rings clear and true in many of its lyrics. In Dale Reich's situation—all too true. All of the lyrics really describe Dale, but there two stanzas that I have always found particularly poignant when I think about him. Those lyrics are as follows:

Back at home, a young wife waits,
Her Green Beret has met his fate.
He has died for those oppressed,
Leaving her his last request.

Put silver wings on my son's chest,
Make him one of America's best.
He'll be a man they'll test one day.
Have him win, the Green Beret.

As I have mentioned, Dale had a young wife back at home and she was pregnant with their first child, who would be born a son. But unlike in the ballad, Dale's son would choose a very different path to walk. Rather than choosing "silver wings," he chose a cross and became an Army chaplain. I feel sure that Dale would have approved of his son's choice and been very proud.

Merrill "Dale" Reich, Jr. and His Memorial

This is Dale's graduation picture, taken when he graduated from Sewanee, "The University of the South." The picture was sent to me by a member of the university's staff after I told him about the book and the reason for my effort to locate Dale's family.

Dale's memorial, pictured above, is located in downtown Atlanta. As fate would have it, my career brought me and my family to Atlanta. I have visited Dale's memorial many times and thought about our last day and night together. Before leaving, I placed flags around the granite monument.

Note that the memorial incorrectly shows Dale's rank as captain, while he was actually a first lieutenant. Sadly, he had been in Vietnam barely more than a week.

My search for Dale's family was to let them know about details related to his last mission that would appear when the book was published. I didn't want them surprised by things they might read. During my search for family, I encountered the AVVBA, Atlanta Vietnam Veterans Business Association, the organization responsible for Dale's memorial. A member told me about the memorial they had created for Dale as well as their work on behalf of all veterans. What they have done for veterans and their families is remarkable. I am now a "Life Member" of the organization.

Over the years, I have heard from a number of Dales family members. They were all very proud of his courage and selflessness, as well they should be. No man or woman can give more—Dale's was the ultimate sacrifice.

U.S. Army 8th Field Hospital Patch

8th Army Field Hospital, Nha Trang, South Vietnam

This is where we landed at approximately 3 a.m. on one very dark morning and where I encountered a very caring and dedicated medical team.

CHAPTER 28

Powder-Blue Surprise

WHERE IS IT? The tip of my index finger traced the thin, narrowly divided elevation lines on the map.

Where is it? It has got to be big, and it has got to be right in here somewhere.

Placing another spoonful in my mouth of whatever delicious thing Pop had cooked for lunch, I continued to slide my finger slowly across the map.

The object of my search, while halfheartedly picking at my food, was an enemy base camp that was located somewhere in the now-familiar Dong Bo Mountains. The mountains were located south-southeast of camp and were surrounded by flatlands on the north, west, and south, with the South China Sea on the east. While they stood majestically over the city of Nha Trang, their history was infamous. Several South Vietnamese units searching for the enemy base camp had been run out of the mountains on several occasions with significant casualties. The base camp had a long, mysterious history, and many stories were told about the small but notorious mountain range.

According to one of the stories, the French discovered the heavily fortified position during a patrol into the mountains when they occupied Vietnam. The story also spoke of artillery pieces and large numbers of troops that would emerge from well-camouflaged caves. The position had obviously existed for some time, and 5th Group Headquarters was exerting pressure us to find it and knock it out of action.

Sergeant Koch and I spent days mapping each of the locations where other allied units had made contact with enemy forces. The frequency and location of those enemy encounters in one particular area suggested the Viet Cong stronghold must be somewhere nearby. They obviously were trying to protect something; why not a base camp? The area of greatest activity was along the eastern face of the mountains overlooking the entire city of Nha Trang. It would be an excellent place to construct a base camp from which activity all along the coastline could be observed—a natural. But was it? When sighted and pursued, the VC simply seemed to dissolve into the mountains. They also seemed to be able to vanish with equal ease in widely separated areas, which was an indication that tunnels and hiding places must exist throughout the mountain range.

While continuing to search the map, which was spread across half the table like a Sunday newspaper, people were coming and going for lunch. I could hear others around me talking. Because we were one of the closest A-Teams to 5th Group Headquarters, we often had visitors and provided briefings for high-ranking American and foreign officials and dignitaries. So, visitors in the team house at lunchtime was not unusual.

"We'll seat you here next to Lieutenant Ross," I vaguely heard someone say.

I was so engrossed in my search for the legendary enemy base camp that I didn't look up. Picking up another spoonful of perfectly cooked fried rice and moving it slowly in the general direction of my mouth, I detected a strange smell. I sniffed the rice, but it seemed fine. Putting it in my mouth, I wondered if Pop, who acquired his culinary skills from the French, had discovered some exotic new spice. The rice, with its blend of vegetables and meat, tasted fine—it tasted delicious as usual. But, as I reached for the iced tea pitcher, the aroma persisted.

Can't be, I thought, *but it smells like perfume.*

My tea glass was almost full when I finally noticed the person who had been seated at the table with me. For a moment, I was stunned and couldn't quite believe what I was seeing—I honestly thought I was hallucinating. But, then, the hallucination spoke, "Your tea," my table guest said.

"What?"

"Your tea glass . . . it's full now."

"Oh, geez. I'm sorry," I said, quickly reaching for some napkins.

My glass had been filled and tea overflowed onto the table when I was momentarily distracted by my unexpected table guest, a beautiful young American woman in a powder-blue uniform.

I hadn't seen an American woman in months. So, when this one seemed to appear magically, for a quickened heartbeat or two, my mind simply went blank as I looked at her. She had eyes that sparkled, and her hair shined like satin as it traced the gentle shape of her very pretty face.

Where has she come from, and what is she doing here? I wondered.

Shortly, I regained enough composure to speak coherently. "Hello. Welcome to A-502. Who are you, and where did you come from?" I asked.

"Well, hello, Lieutenant Ross," she said with a chuckling, bright warm smile.

"My name is Molly, and I came from the Red Cross. I wondered if you were going to speak to me."

As with too many of the people I encountered so briefly, she is but a distant memory, but I remember clearly how warmly her presence affected me—as though a little part of home had mysteriously materialized before me.

I had been in Vietnam long enough to miss the sweet fragrance and round eyes of an American woman. Then, suddenly and inexplicably, a captivating example of American womanhood sat easily within arm's reach. In her striped powder-blue uniform, she was an unexpected and very pleasant surprise. It was difficult not to reach out and touch her, just to make sure she was real.

She hadn't been there long when the old, crookedly hung kitchen door creaked open. Pop poked his head out, as he often did to make sure all was well in his tiny dining room.

When he saw we had a visitor, he hurried through the door. He smiled widely at me and wiped his hands on the apron tied snugly around his waist.

"Hello," he said, as he approached the table.

He offered a humble bow to our visitor.

"Can I bring lunch for this lady, Trung Uy?" he asked politely.

Pop's gentle manner and warm Asian features ingratiated him with the many visitors to A-502. As would every other member of the team, I would have adopted him and brought him back to the States if I thought his wife and family would let him go. Pop was more than cared for by our team, he was loved.

I looked to Molly for her response to Pop's invitation and hoped—no, I prayed if you can pray that fast—that it would be yes. She nodded and returned Pop's warm, disarming smile.

"I would love to have lunch. Thank you for asking."

Just the sound of her silky voice made my spine tingle.

Pop disappeared back into the kitchen and quickly returned with a plate of food that he had decorated with lettuce leaves, small vegetable pieces, and a flower. I have no idea where he found the flower, but he proudly placed his creation on the table in front of our guest.

"It looks delicious, and it's beautiful. Thank you very much."

Pop's chest seemed a little more puffed as he once again disappeared into the kitchen.

My heart rate settled back to normal as we ate lunch and continued to become acquainted. We found many things to talk about and laugh about. She bubbled as she spoke and was discernibly very good at what she did. We shared information about our backgrounds, interests, and families. For a while, I could have been back in the States with one of the hometown college girls.

It had become apparent during lunch that there was much more to this woman than met the eye. Not just attractive, she was intelligent and articulate, and beyond her pretty smile and delicate appearance was her unmistakable dedication to a mission.

Dedication to a mission sounds like a quality you expect a soldier to possess, but as I came to know my luncheon guest, and later some of the other Red Cross volunteers who came to visit our camp—I discovered that they were indeed very much like soldiers.

Just as some of the men in military service, the Red Cross volunteers had been recruited out of college to serve their country. A bachelor's degree was required for service in a unique volunteer organization that was referred to only by its initials SRAO, which stood for Supplemental Recreational Activities Overseas, a title created for its members by the Red Cross's Board of Governors.

The unit had been organized for service in World War II. Its mission was to bring comfort and diversion from the monotony and tragedy of that war to the troops who had been sent to fight. The female volunteers shared news from the United States; organized recreational activities and games; and, when possible, served hot coffee and pastries or other refreshments, even in forward or remote combat areas. But, among the most important things they did was to reestablish the humanity and civility of home while providing a patient ear and an understanding heart.

After World War II, SRAO was reorganized for service in Korea, and then again for Vietnam. In all three wars, simply because of their presence in combat zones, it was not unusual for their volunteers to come under enemy fire. As a result, as with soldiers in combat zones, some SRAO members died as a consequence of their decision to serve.

While their service seemed to parallel that of their male military counterparts, at least one important difference existed between the women and the men they hoped to help. Even though they both worked together in a combat zone, the women were unarmed. Rather than weapons, they carried smiles, tenderness, compassion, and tremendous moral support to military servicemen and women in various parts of the world during extremely trying times.

When we finished lunch, Molly and other ladies of the Red Cross spent time visiting with surprised team members who had come to eat. When word spread through the camp of the presence of American women, the small dining area became a bit more crowded than usual.

Later in the afternoon, I invited Molly outside to show her the camp and introduce her to some of the other men. As we walked, I asked a question I hadn't asked during lunch. "What brought you here and why did you come to Vietnam?"

"Oh, I don't know . . . lots of things, I suppose," she said.

She kicked at an old shell casing that was lying on the ground with one of her black leather shoes. It slid and bounced along in front of us.

"Probably some of the same things that brought you and the other men here, I suppose. It became very important to me that I do something to help. I didn't want to simply stay at home and watch it all happen without becoming involved in some way."

The idea that a woman would want to become involved in a war was something I had never given much thought to but found very interesting. It wasn't a chauvinistic matter or a question of courage. My mother was a woman who would have fought physically to protect her family, but I am reasonably certain it was the unconscionable thought of seeing a woman down and seriously injured on a battlefield that had prevented me from considering women involved at all.

After spending time with Molly and others like her, my feelings changed. I discovered that besides courage and skill, they also had a strong devotion to duty and country. You could hear it in their voices or perceive it by just being around them as they did their jobs.

Sometime after meeting Molly, I encountered another "Red Cross Girl," as they were frequently called. Her name was Ann. I posed to her a question similar to the one I asked Molly. "What was your reason for choosing service in Vietnam?"

She didn't hesitate. "A close friend joined the service and went to Vietnam as a medic. He said it was because he wanted to contribute to the war effort. He was in the Special Forces, too."

Her tone was warm and caring as she spoke of him. "He provided primary care and gave inoculations to people who lived in outlying villages. He felt he was doing something very worthwhile," she said, then hesitated for a moment. "When I thought about what he was doing, I wasn't able to think of a reason why a woman couldn't go do something worthwhile as well. So, I started looking for ways to get to Vietnam."

It was easy to hear passion and resolution in Ann's voice as she spoke about her desire to serve. For her, there was no question about whether or not she was going. Her only dilemma was how she would get there.

Passion and resolution seemed to have been a part of every Red Cross volunteer's traits because they had also been evident in Molly during her visit to Trung Dung. Something else was also noticeable about her. She seemed very comfortable and at home as we meandered around the camp, probably because she had done it so many times before. Her interest in anything we had to say seemed genuine. Every time someone showed her or told her something about A-502, even if she had heard it twice before, she acted as though she was hearing it for the first time.

Occasionally, as Molly and I continued our tour of Trung Dung, I would look down at the partially refolded map I had carried with me, then back at her. I wanted to see if she would still be there when I looked up again. And, of course, she was.

It was interesting and fun to watch the reactions of team members when we would stop to visit. The surprise I had experienced when first meeting her was also apparent in the eyes of others who were unaware that Red Cross girls existed. The most common responses after introducing her were, "Where did you find her?" or "How did she get here?" or "Where did you come from?" Each time, she would laugh in response to the question. Then she explained her presence and warmly shared her time.

One thing was sure: When you looked into the faces gathered around her, they looked like children on Christmas morning. They didn't really care where Molly had come from or how she had arrived. They were just glad that she made the trip.

Molly had been brought to the camp with a couple of other girls. Unfortunately, the time came far too quickly when she and the others had to leave. Back at the team house, a small group of appreciative men gathered to say good-bye when the girls got into their jeeps for the return trip to Nha Trang where they were stationed.

Even though their visit had been brief, evidence that it had not been insignificant lingered for some time after they had gone. Off and on during the rest of the day and evening, someone would find a way to work a mention of the girls into a conversation. That went on for days, maybe longer.

Such was my first encounter with the women of the Red Cross and their organization. But after that day, I had several other opportunities to learn the importance of their work.

Occasionally, when in Nha Trang for a briefing or supplies, I tried to find time to stop by the Red Cross facility. Donuts, cookies, punch, and coffee were always available in abundance. There was also an abundant supply of men seeking a few minutes of attention from one of the gals wearing the Red Cross patch on her shoulder.

As warm and understanding as they were, at least one thing would cause some of the girls to raise an eyebrow. Besides being called "Red Cross

Girl," they were often referred to by the affectionate nickname of "Donut Dolly," which to them was not a favored one.

One of the girls, Jean, told me they only served donuts if they were available in a unit's mess hall. She said she didn't care for the name even though she knew a few of the girls thought the nickname was cute. Jean said she didn't care for it because she felt her education and efforts deserved a more responsible nickname and didn't hesitate to vocalize her discontent.

"If they're going to call us anything besides the names we have pinned on our uniforms, I wish they would just stick to 'Red Cross Girl,'" she said.

Despite the too-frequent use of the disfavored nickname or the rare sexist remark made by a serviceman who hadn't thought before making it, the SRAO volunteers went about their jobs with a remarkable attitude and spirit. Most of them were far more than the image suggested by the "Donut Dolly" nickname. Some were quite daring.

In addition to working out of assigned facilities in cities around Vietnam, they would also visit remote camps and firebases that were accessible only by helicopter.

Ann, the woman from whom I learned the most about Red Cross's SRAO volunteers, was one who pushed the limits of where she could go safely. On one particular occasion, her daring and dedication almost cost her life.

Only after being pressed for details, Ann shared her experience. She was on board a C-130 aircraft flying in the II Corps region of Vietnam, the same corps area where A-502 was located. She was headed toward LZ Baldy with a unit of troops. "We had just passed north of An Khe when enemy gunfire began to rip through the thin metal skin of the plane," she said.

In telling her story, something else had obviously captured her attention as much as the continuing bursts of enemy ground fire that ricocheted through the C-130. "Two Second CAV (Cavalry) soldiers, who were also passengers, made their way to where I was sitting," she said.

"They wanted to know if I was okay. We had spoken earlier, so they knew that I had only two weeks left on my tour. Since I was supposed to be going home soon, they told me I was too short to be flying around out there. The concern they showed for my safety was extremely touching. It was my job to make them forget about the war, but there they were, right at my side, trying to make me forget about what was happening."

These amazing young women clearly remembered the difficult and unpleasant times. But, more vividly, they remembered the men, their faces, and how they tried to make the girls themselves comfortable during their visits. During one particular visit, Ann said she and the girls found that the troops had painted the latrine pink and hung curtains in it. "We were quite taken by their gesture and couldn't imagine where they had found pink paint," she said.

While discussing the role of the Red Cross volunteers with Ann, I discovered that she had strong, if mixed, feelings about her service in Vietnam, and still does. As of the First Edition writing (2004), she was still an active member of the American Red Cross. When talking to her about Vietnam and her memories, it became quite apparent how much she cared about her time in Vietnam.

"I remember how young and unworldly some of the soldiers looked. I saw them carrying puppies or holding a child by the hand. You could see the Iowa in their faces. So many were not much more than boys, yet they were doing a man's job."

Because of her position, Ann was not only a veteran of Vietnam but also of many other campaigns against devastating natural disasters. Being experienced in emergencies, she spoke articulately and unemotionally about her Asian experiences until she made one particular comment.

"I just wanted to make it all go away for them, but I couldn't." Her voice cracked almost imperceptibly, but it became noticeably softer. I didn't say anything and just let her talk.

"They had such wonderful senses of humor," she said. "They made us and each other laugh. But sometimes, when they came back from a mission or a patrol, you could see it in their faces. They had been through some terrible experience."

Ann paused, and when she did, I imagined she was seeing those faces once again. Then, she continued, "I couldn't imagine what they must have gone through. Some wanted to talk about it and some didn't. So, we had to be very sensitive and respect their different needs. We would sit quietly and eat cold C-Ration ham and lima beans with them in case they decided, at some point, they wanted to talk. I felt helpless and wanted to make the look on their faces and the pain go away. I wanted to make them smile again. But, I couldn't. I just couldn't."

Ann's sensitivity and understanding are typical of the Red Cross volunteers I met while serving in Vietnam. They were a part of a small, eight-hundred-member female unit, but their contribution was a selfless and very important one.

Other women served in Vietnam and their service was equally important. When you consider the female nurses and administrative specialists, and the long list of other positions filled by women who cared and who served, this small recollection doesn't begin to provide the recognition they deserve.

No story of Vietnam is complete if it does not include the women who served there. Perhaps without knowing words he had written, military men who met the Red Cross volunteers in Vietnam understood something that Charles Dickens wrote long ago about women, "Nature often enshrines gallant and noble hearts in weak bosoms; oftenest, God bless her, in woman's breast."

For me, the women of the Red Cross, the Donut Dollies, will always hold a very special place in my heart and they will always be remembered as the—powder-blue surprise.

Red Cross Patch

Red Cross records reflect that more than 1100 hundred women volunteered to serve during the Vietnam War. Over 600 of those volunteers were sent to Vietnam where they served in the SRAO program and wore this patch.

Sadly, the true role of women involved in the Vietnam War has not been fully recognized by the American public. Few Americans are aware that female members of SRAO died while wearing this patch in South Vietnam. There were three and I am proud to recognize them here. Those women were—Hanna E. Crews (died 10/2/69), Virginia E. Kirsch (died 8/16/70), and Lucinda J. Richter (died 2/9/71).

Another SRAO volunteer who had worn the patch, Sharon Wesley, stayed in Vietnam after her Red Cross tour ended to work with a civilian agency. Sharon was killed on April 4, 1975, while participating in "Operation Babylift," a humanitarian effort to airlift orphans out of the country before the fall of Saigon that same year.

For me, the encounter with the women who wore the powder blue uniform was memorable. They brought caring civility and a reminder of home to the otherwise harsh days of the war. I will never forget the smiles, the laughter, and the caring that, for a few special moments—reminded me of home.

CHAPTER 29

Unexpected Gentleness

THE SWIRLING CLOUD OF stifling dust chased us across the old wooden planked bridge until it met a warm breeze that blew down through the wide riverbed. The breeze wafted above the river's surface, and glistening ripples traced its path toward the South China Sea. Bridge planks vibrated rhythmically as our jeep rolled over them, and the breeze offered a momentary respite from the dust it chased into the trees at the river's edge.

The warm westerly breeze felt good for the short time it lasted. It disappeared when we bounced back down onto the road on the far side of the bridge where we reentered the tree line. With the breeze gone, the dust resumed its pursuit as the tread on the tires spun and regained their grip on the hard, sun-dried dirt road.

I rotated my map when we turned and began driving west along the road on the north side of the river. We followed the road for a few kilometers until we found the location on the map outlined with a circle from my grease pencil.

"There it is," I said, pointing to our destination. "Pull in over there."

After getting out of the jeep, we moved slowly. They hadn't seen us yet and I didn't want them to be frightened when they eventually noticed our presence. Some were sitting and some were standing, while others ran here and there. It had been some time since any of us had seen a sight like this, so, for a while, we just stood and watched.

Then, watching as one group tried to form into a line, I locked eyes with her and knew we had been seen. With her big almond eyes, she looked almost like Bambi and every bit as delicate.

This moment can't pass without a picture of her, I thought.

Raising my camera slowly, so as not to scare her, I found her in the viewfinder and focused.

She's very pretty, I thought as the shutter snapped and I muttered, "I got her."

"Which one?" one of the other men asked.

"The little girl over there next to the one in the sunbonnet. The one looking this way."

With our presence at the small Vietnamese elementary school detected, we walked farther up into the schoolyard. Still moving slowly so none of the children would be frightened, we smiled as we made our way to the chairs that had been prepared for our visit.

The school was in the Korean AO. As a part of their community action program, they had arranged to conduct a karate demonstration for the school children. One of the Korean officers who visited our camp occasionally, one with whom I had just finished exchanging intelligence information, asked if any of the Americans would enjoy seeing their demonstration. We had a training mission going out that afternoon, but since all the preparations had already been made, I accepted his invitation and took a couple of other team members with me.

Because of the close scrutiny we got from the children, we understood we were possibly the first Americans some of them had ever seen. Our round eyes likely seemed very strange and foreign to them. Even though we smiled and tried to greet them warmly in their own language, just as children anywhere, they were reluctant to return our greetings with any enthusiasm.

We took our seats for the demonstration and the children sat on the ground around us. We were all entertained as the Koreans broke boards and concrete blocks with their hands, elbows, feet, and heads. The children seemed particularly amazed at the feats of the Korean karate masters and applauded enthusiastically when the demonstration ended.

As we rose from our chairs, one of the teachers who spoke fluent English walked over to me and asked, "Would you care to see our school?"

Despite our tight schedule, I told the very polite young teacher that we would be honored to visit her school.

"Oh, wonderful," she said. "Please come this way. I would like for you to see some of the things our children have done."

When we reached the small one-story building, the young female teacher showed us through some of the classrooms. She took great pride in the students' work, which was displayed on the walls of her classroom. As I studied the papers around the room, it came to mind that it could have been a classroom at almost any school in America. There were numbers on some papers and letters on others that formed the basis of their language, all meticulously written by her student's small hands. There were also brightly colored pictures that depicted life in and around their small village community. Drawings of rice paddies weren't likely to appear in an American child's picture, but the clouds, trees, grass, and sun all looked the same.

When our brief tour finished, we thanked the proud young teacher for showing us the school and started back across the schoolyard. We smiled and waved friendly good-byes as we walked. This time, unlike when we arrived, our smiles and waves were returned. Those few returned tiny smiles brought an unexpected gentleness to the morning and provided a pleasant start to the day as we headed back to camp to meet our own students who would soon be arriving.

The Innocent—Caught in a War

Korean Karate Demonstration

Chapter 30

Mystery Meat and Scorpions

AFTER THE KARATE DEMONSTRATION and visit to the Vietnamese school, we arrived back at Trung Dung just as the trucks from Nha Trang were arriving with students from another Combat Orientation Course group. After we parked the jeep, I went to the assembly area to greet everyone and outline the long-range patrol we would be conducting. After the usual pre-mission operations briefing, we began final preparations and equipment checks. This time, I would serve as the group's senior American adviser.

When everyone was ready, we climbed onto the trucks and headed to our drop-off point. The group was not unlike the one that Dale Reich was with when he came to Trung Dung. Hopefully, our mission wouldn't experience a tragedy similar to the one that had taken his life.

Unfortunately, because tragedy lives on the battlefield, we would find ourselves attempting to dodge death in an ironic twist of war. This infrequent occurrence would demonstrate that tragedy is not alone on the field of battle. Shrouded and waiting to claim an opportunity, tragedy can be challenged by the courage of those who would face it.

No time was wasted when we reached our drop-off point just west of My Loc outpost. We dismounted and immediately headed farther west.

With approximately one platoon of thirty-five Americans and an equal number of CIDG soldiers at five-meter intervals, our patrol was nearly a quarter-mile in length and wound along through the lowland terrain like a long, slow-moving train. We were going in search of an NVA unit reported to be in the area. Only on the trail a short while, we passed a small herd of red deer grazing in an open field. They grazed on the new growth of plants in an area that had been burned during a fire created by exploding artillery shells. Our point unit guided us through a maze of craters opened by shells that had impacted and started the blaze.

We walked for some time, threading our way west over and around small hills, along the dikes of overgrown rice paddies, and through the abandoned villages of those who once tended the paddies. As we passed a natural or man-made feature that would serve as a landmark, it was noted on my map and became an indicator of the path back to camp.

Toward the end of the day, as shadows grew long and night began to fall, we stopped and made camp. Security was set out in a 360-degree circle around our position. Shifts were established with American and Vietnamese soldiers sharing security responsibilities. My position was established near the center of the circle to make it easy for me to reach any point on the circumference of our perimeter with equal speed if trouble developed. I then called Trung Dung and gave them our location coordinates.

When we stopped, my feet were hot and sweating. After stringing my hammock between two trees, I sat down in it and unlaced my boots. Normally, I would not have walked around without my boots, but, because the ground was dry and fairly clear of debris, I took them off and set them under the hammock. Since it was dinnertime and lunch had somehow been overlooked, I pulled my pack over and took out one of the freeze-dried meals. It was rice and shrimp, which was one of my favorites. And, as any good jungle chef might, I carried an array of seasonings to improve the taste.

After boiling water in my canteen cup over a small can of Sterno, I dumped the rice and dry shrimp in and waited for everything to puff up. Everyone had their own way of improving military cuisine to make their meals more appealing. Mine was to season it with red pepper and soy sauce. Many of the Vietnamese and some of the Americans carried small cans of sardines, which they would eat with their rice. The smelly little fish weren't my cuisine favorites though.

While my dinner was absorbing water, I walked over to a small tree and cut my utensils, a pair of matched chopsticks. Previously, I had seen many of the Vietnamese cut theirs from a small, thin tree branch and had started doing the same thing, just as a rapport builder. When I first started trying to use chopsticks, it took a few awkward attempts to develop the art, particularly with rice. My unskilled attempts to feed myself amused the Vietnamese, who seemed to take pride in demonstrating the proper use of their ethnic tableware. Eventually, eating with chopsticks became as easy as eating with a fork or a spoon. A knife wasn't needed because meat and fish were already cut into bite-size pieces.

After learning to use chopsticks, the only challenge involved in eating food that had been prepared by one of the camp's Vietnamese cooks was to determine exactly what type of meat the small bite-size pieces were. Fish was never difficult to identify because it had a distinctively fishy aroma. Chicken and pork were other easy ones, chicken usually tasted like chicken, and pork usually cooked to a white color. The difficulty came in separating the red meats: beef from venison, monkey, or dog.

I am thoroughly convinced that, at one of the camp's Saturday get-togethers, the Vietnamese fed me my own dog.

If it had been a particularly hard week, the Vietnamese CIDG soldiers would be rewarded by Thieu ta with an afternoon party-type affair to which the American advisers were always invited. Along with a special meal the parties often included local entertainment. This entertainment usually took the form of twanging strings from various musical instruments and an array of Vietnamese solo or group vocalists with varying degrees of talent.

A day or two before one of the Saturday parties, a small dog I had adopted—disappeared. The small mixed breed and I became fast friends after he wandered into the camp early one morning. He looked hungry, so I found some leftover scraps to feed him. He ate until he looked as though he might pop. I named him Frank after a crazy but lovable uncle who had seen me off at the Seattle/Tacoma airport when I left for Vietnam. Every night after our first meeting, Frank would sleep outside the door at the end of the team house where my room was located, and every morning he would bounce around and bark when he saw me look through the bamboo blinds to check on him. Frank, nothing more than a scruffy little mutt, was good company and a very pleasant reminder of our family's dog, Bingo, back home.

Because he would occasionally wander off, I didn't think too much about it when Frank wasn't outside my window one morning. But when he wasn't back by dark, that was unusual. He had never been gone overnight before. When he still wasn't back the next night, I assumed he had found his way back to wherever he had come from. I imagined him back home with his Vietnamese family in one of the nearby villages. The next day at the camp party, though, another more disturbing possibility crept to mind.

As we ate and listened to the high-pitched strings and voices of the village band, one of the CIDG soldiers asked an intriguing question, "Trung Uy . . . what are you eating?"

Looking down at the things on my plate, there were vegetables and what appeared to be beef in some thick, gooey steamed rice.

"I don't know. What am I eating?" I asked, knowing that I probably shouldn't have asked the question.

"What is the meat?" the questioner persisted. It didn't require a high IQ to assume the meat wasn't going to be what it appeared to be, given that the question had been posed.

"Beef? Cow? I don't know. What is it?" I responded apathetically.

When my guess was met with laughter, little doubt remained that, whatever it was, it wasn't beef. But since the meat was sweet and tender, exactly what it was didn't make much difference. I assumed it was probably monkey, which made it a little less appetizing. But, since it tasted good, I continued to eat.

Snake eating had been demonstrated during a Special Forces survival exercise and I had tasted it, so I was certain this wasn't snake. While my curiosity was growing about the identity of our entree, I wasn't about to let the Vietnamese see even the smallest sign of distress on my face.

When the question, "Trung Uy, what is the meat?" came again, I was sure it must be something strange like goat, horse, or cat. Turning to one of the Vietnamese sergeants, I asked, "Okay, Trung Si, what is it?"

He laughed a little and said, "Don't worry, Trung Uy, it is only deer meat." Then, speaking in Vietnamese to those sitting around me, he gave what sounded like a stern admonishment. The question didn't come up again until after the meal was finished.

The party was over and I was on my way back to the team house when a couple of CIDG soldiers who appeared to have had one too many beers approached me. They were giggling when one asked, "Trung Uy, did you enjoy the food?"

"Yeah, it was number one." In Vietnam, everything was either "number one," which was the best. Or, it was "number ten," the worst. As was pretty much the case, there was little in-between.

"You like it . . . yeah?" They were still giggling between themselves, just like two little girls.

"Sure, it was numba one." The word "number" often deteriorated and became "numba."

Persisting, the other one asked, "What was the meat?"

"I don't know. Trung Si said it was deer. Was the meat deer?"

"No, it wasn't deer meat." They had fallen to the ground and were, literally, rolling with laughter. They couldn't wait to tell me the identity of the mystery meat. "Oh, Trung Uy . . . it was dog!"

While I would like to think that he lived a full life with a village family, to this day, I'm reasonably sure it was Frank because—he never came back.

When my canteen cup became filled with puffed rice and rehydrated shrimp, it was time for the red pepper and soy sauce. After a long walk and no lunch, the concoction actually tasted very good, and because we had set up camp in an abandoned orchard, the meal was complemented by an unexpected treat of fresh fruit for dessert.

Taking advantage of our presence in the overgrown orchard, I walked over and pulled something that resembled an orange from one of the trees. However, once peeled, it tasted more like a grapefruit. Whatever its botanical identity, it was sweet and it was fresh. I considered myself fortunate. Small things like a piece of fresh fruit was a treat to soldiers in the field.

As I dropped the last piece of fruit peel, something tickled my leg just below my knee. Thinking it was nothing more than my fatigues against my skin, I brushed at my pant leg. When the tickle persisted, I stood up. When I did, whatever was on my leg—moved. At first, I thought it was probably a piece of weed that I had picked up while walking around without my boots, but then it started to crawl farther up my leg.

That's no weed, I thought.

Easing myself back down onto my hammock slowly, I kept my leg straight so whatever was making its way up my leg wouldn't be disturbed. Then, just as it reached a place on my leg where the fabric rolled, I made a quick jabbing grab at it and squeezed very tight. Liquid from the crawler oozed onto my leg. Quickly, I jumped up and shook it out of my pants.

One of the old Vietnamese sergeants, who was sitting on a stump not far away, saw my dance and started to laugh until he saw what fell out of my pant leg. It was a large, dark-brown scorpion. As soon as he saw it hit the ground, his mood changed and he became serious immediately. He ran toward me and was speaking frantically in Vietnamese to the interpreter.

"No, no . . . it's okay. I'm okay." I tried to tell him that I hadn't been stung, but he continued to speak rapidly in Vietnamese to my interpreter, kept pointing at my leg, and very quickly pulled out a very large knife.

"Trung Uy, he wants to know where this bug has bitten you."

Of course, he meant stung, but it had done neither.

"No, Light. Tell him I'm fine. It didn't sting me. I'm okay."

Light translated quickly and the old sergeant looked at me and asked, "Sure, Trung Uy?"

"Sure, Trung Si," I responded.

Satisfied I hadn't been stung by the scorpion, the old sergeant put his knife away, turned and walked over to where it had fallen out of my pants and crushed it under his boot and said, "Numba ten, Trung Uy . . . numba ten!" Obviously, his way of telling me it was very bad.

Having grown up in Florida, scorpions were not unknown to me, but I'd never seen any as big as this one. It was almost four inches long, not counting the tail that curved up over its body.

After shaking my pants out thoroughly, I did the same with my boots and put them back on. While lacing them up, I thought *At least it wasn't a two-step or three-step snake.* Those were extremely poisonous vipers and they struck quickly. Their name was well earned. If you were struck by one of them, depending on which one it was, you could expect to take two steps or three steps, collapse and die shortly thereafter. Never again did my boots come off my feet while in the field.

Aside from the human enemy; tigers, snakes, scorpions, and mystery foods were just a few of the many other absurdities and threats soldiers had to contend with in Vietnam—there were many other dangers.

254th DustOff in Action

The pilots and crews of the helicopters with the callsign "DustOff" were some of the most courageous men I met in Vietnam. Their choppers were unarmed, yet they would fly anywhere, anytime, and under virtually any conditions. This chopper is about to pick up a man who had a heart attack while on patrol.

CHAPTER 31

Friendly Fire

AFTER MY ENCOUNTER WITH the scorpion, the rest of the night was long but uneventful.

Periodically during the night, I would walk the perimeter, then nap briefly with Ahat watching over me. Then, I would walk it again to make sure perimeter guards were awake. There was never much sleep for me while in the field, so I was always glad when morning finally dawned.

The sun's first light filtered through the trees and spread golden beams across our campsite. Examining them from my hammock, each beam appeared as though it were made of hundreds of soft golden threads. Despite its venomous inhabitants and the war within it, the jungle often looked beautiful to me. Within hours though, the morning's ethereal beginning would be forgotten when we were forced to deal with an unexpected attack that ripped into the natural beauty of the jungle that surrounded us.

Reaching up and unhooking my radio handset from the hammock rope where it hung, I checked in with the radio room at Trung Dung to let them know we would soon be moving again. Within thirty minutes of my check-in, we were packed up and continuing west. We were headed in the general direction of the Cambodian border, which was far beyond our position.

We forded small creeks and streams and walked—and walked some more. In all that distance, we found no sign of recent enemy activity, other than occasional holes filled with sharpened bamboo sticks. The sticks, however, were not innocuous. The VC had contaminated them with either animal or human waste. We were just about to stop for lunch when one of the American members of the training class ran up behind me.

"Lieutenant Ross, hold up, hold up." He was nearly out of breath from having run up the column to find me.

"What's the problem?" I asked.

"I think one of the men is having a heart attack," he said.

"What? Where is he?"

Pointing back down the trail, he said, "Back that way about a hundred meters or so."

"Okay, let's go check him out."

I asked my Vietnamese counterpart to call the point unit and have them stop while I checked on our man.

When we reached him, he was sitting under a tree. He was an older man, a sergeant on his second tour in Vietnam. His breathing was labored, his face was pale and he was complaining of chest pains. Whatever his problem, it seemed obvious he couldn't continue with the patrol. Juan Sotello, one of A-502's team medics, was with us. After confirming that the man's condition could be grave, we requested a Dustoff medical evacuation chopper from the 254th.

We were lucky in that a clearing not far away was large enough for the chopper to make a safe landing. I quickly reorganized our patrol to provide security around the clearing.

While we were moving the downed man to the opening, he apologized for being sick and said he thought he could continue after a short rest. Sotello assured him that there was no reason to apologize and told him he needed to go back to be examined.

While we were waiting for the medevac chopper to arrive, and since we were stopped anyway, members of the patrol were told to have lunch.

It took the 254th Dustoff chopper about twenty-five minutes to reach us. When it appeared over the trees, the pilot was directed to the secured LZ. In a matter of only minutes, he was in and out. As the chopper turned east with the ailing soldier, we packed up and once again headed west.

Our primary objective was an area of trails the Vietnamese suspected were being used by enemy units moving up and down the country. The mission was planned after Air Force FAC, Colonel Baer, reported seeing activity on the trails and he believed they may have established a camp.

We had been walking for at least two hours over, around, and across an unending assortment of hills, gullies, streams, and finally into denser jungle. We were a long way out, farther than any of our units had ever been on foot. The farther away from Trung Dung we got, the closer I watched the jungle.

Are the NVA out here today? If they are here, I hope we see them before they see us? I thought. I always positioned myself near the front of our unit, right behind my point team or squad.

While walking on a long patrol you had to constantly watch the jungle. It could explode in your face at any moment. Despite that and other dangers I've described, your mind could wander. Hundreds of thoughts could flood your mind while you walked or were posted out in the middle of nowhere on an ambush. On patrol, you didn't talk while you walked, chopped, crawled, climbed, or sloshed your way along in search of the often-elusive enemy.

On ambush, you had to be still and very quiet, sometimes for many hours, as you simply waited for the enemy to walk into your position. Often, you not only had to be prepared to fight a yet unseen foe but also fight the urge to sleep. While these weary blocks of time could become painfully boring, it was absolutely necessary to stay alert because your life depended upon it. If you didn't see the enemy before he saw you, odds were better than good that you would not survive the encounter.

It was late afternoon and our patrol continued to follow the long course marked on my map. We were a long day-and-a-half walk from camp when the quiet of our stealthful movement was broken by the rhythmic drumming of a helicopter somewhere in the distance behind us. Occasionally, a burst of machine-gun fire could be heard.

Probably from the chopper, I thought. *But what are they shooting at?* I wondered. *Maybe they've spotted an enemy unit.*

As the sound of the chopper moved still closer and the gunfire continued, I could see some of the men in front of me looking back over their shoulders. I didn't blame them. The chopper was beginning to sound very close, and the gunfire still burped intermittently. I turned around to take a look myself. The chopper wasn't visible through the thick double canopy growth of jungle, but it certainly seemed to be coming our way.

Motioning to Ahat, who was walking behind me, I moved my rifle to my left hand and took the radio handset from him.

Even though we had walked beyond the western border of our official AO, I first tried reaching the helicopter on A-502's frequency. My thought was that if the pilot had flown through our AO, or simply because he was near it, he would be monitoring our radio frequency and would recognize my call sign.

"This is Bunkhouse Zero Two to the unidentified helicopter in Bunkhouse's western AO. Over."

I waited for an answer, but nothing. No response.

Once again, "This is Bunkhouse Zero Two to the chopper firing in Bunkhouse's western AO. Over."

Still, there was no response.

Because it seemed to be firing in different places, I was uncertain about the chopper's target. It didn't seem likely that it was shooting at a hard target on the ground, because nothing in the jungle could move as fast as he was flying. The only thing that made sense was that the chopper's gunners were firing randomly in an attempt to draw fire. That was sometimes a tactic to locate VC camps or hiding places. If return fire were received, an airstrike would be called in to destroy the source of the ground fire. But, if that were the case and they were going to attempt such a mission so near our AO, we should have been notified.

Then, as with many things in war, what should have been was no longer of consequence. Machine-gun fire rained into the trees above us.

"Take cover! Take cover!" came the urgent yells in both English and Vietnamese up and down the patrol line. With the call being repeated in two languages by dozens of voices, everyone scrambled to get behind a tree opposite the incoming gunfire. Pieces of leaves and branches that had been shredded by the incoming fire fell all around us like green snow.

Maybe it's one of the 281st's choppers, I thought.

Reaching for the frequency knobs on the radio hanging across Ahat's back, I changed the frequency from ours to the 281st's.

"This is Bunkhouse Zero Two to any chopper in Bunkhouse's western AO. Over." But, again, the radio remained silent. Then, much stronger and more aggravated, "This is Bunkhouse Zero Two to any chopper who can hear this transmission! Over!"

The chopper sounded like an American Huey. But, in case it was one of the older Vietnamese choppers, I yelled up the line for my Vietnamese counterpart to try to reach them on his radio.

The Vietnamese sergeant tried several times to reach anyone in the air or on the ground, but with no luck. We were so far out in the middle of no-man's-land that his signal wasn't even reaching the Vietnamese radio room at Trung Dung.

Seeking help from anyone, I tried to reach our radio room, hoping they might know something about the chopper and have him called off. But again, there was no answer. I was only receiving a fuzzy unintelligible response from someone in the radio room trying to respond to my call.

For a few minutes, the gunfire stopped as the chopper moved off ahead of us, but then a change in its engine pitch could be heard.

"It's coming back!" someone said.

What a terrible mistake, if they've seen us and think we're VC or NVA, I thought.

Once more, the chopper opened fire and was coming back in our direction. The sound of its blades pounded against the jungle canopy, causing vibrations that could be felt as well as heard. The sensation was like being on the inside of a huge drum. The chopper flew over us on a course almost exactly parallel to ours. I could hear cursing as hot lead and pieces of shredded tree leaves once again snowed down on us.

"Idiots!" someone exclaimed. "They're going to kill one of us!"

"What now, LT?" one of the COC class members asked.

As the patrol's senior American adviser, the responsibility to do something was indeed mine. But what was there to do? The only obvious thing was to keep everyone down or behind trees. I could have thrown a smoke grenade, which would have given the pilot a visual clue to our presence. However, because of our location, that would not have necessarily established us as Americans in his mind. There was one thing it would have done for sure. It would have alerted the NVA/VC to our presence and exact location, which was the last thing I wanted to do.

When the sound of the chopper started to fade, I felt reasonably certain that, at least, we hadn't been spotted or they would have pressed their attack.

It seemed the potentially deadly encounter with the unknown chopper had ended, but that wasn't the case at all. Just as the sound of the chopper seemed that it would slip back into the inaudible distance, a subtle change in the pitch of its engines could again be heard. Then, they began to get louder. It was coming back!

Looking around, I noticed a tiny clearing not too far away. I patted Ahat on the shoulder and motioned for him to take the radio off his back and give it to me. Then, after dropping my backpack, I donned the radio. Motioning for Ahat to stay put—I headed for the clearing.

Damn! This is crazy! I thought. But something *had* to be done, and it was my responsibility to do that "something."

Moving quickly, I ran through the undergrowth with vines and branches slapping me in the face nearly every step of the way. My thought was that the damp thick jungle canopy could be interfering with our radio signals. Reaching the clearing might make it possible to establish radio contact.

If the chopper couldn't be reached by radio, throwing smoke and trying to establish visual contact would be the only other option, short of trying to shoot it down. Obviously, we weren't going to do that, even though the idea had been suggested.

Upon bursting into the open, I ran toward the center of the clearing and tried, as before, to make contact with the chopper by radio.

"This is Bunkhouse Zero Two, Bunkhouse Zero Two to an unidentified chopper! Over!"

Even though my call was repeated several times, there was still no answer.

Again, occasional bursts of gunfire burped from the rapidly approaching helicopter. Quickly, I changed frequencies on the radio and tried one last time for a radio response. Not a thing, there was no response.

Reaching for one of the smoke canisters on my equipment harness, I glanced back toward the area where the patrol was located.

One of the Americans from the patrol was coming out of the jungle and he appeared to be in a hurry. *What is he doing?* I wondered.

Even though I couldn't tell who he was yet, he was distinguishable as an American simply because his size was much larger than that of the average Vietnamese. As he came closer, he became easily recognizable. It was the young medic from the orientation class who had been a few men behind me in the patrol column.

Whatever he wanted, the urgency of his message was evident on his face as he neared me, but just as he opened his mouth and before he could communicate anything, the chopper passed just to our north. It couldn't be seen, even from the clearing. But it was very low, close, and loud as a seemingly indiscriminate spray of machine-gun rounds once again ripped into the trees around us.

Suddenly, I was hit and knocked completely off of my feet and to the ground. No, a bullet hadn't struck me. The medic who was afraid I might be hit by the incoming gunfire had tackled me!

As we rolled along the ground, I asked, "What are you doing out here?"

"I came for you, sir," he said.

"Why? Has someone been hit?"

"No, but we're afraid you'll get hit out here. You need to come back into the tree line."

Rolling over onto my stomach and propping myself up on my elbows, I said, "Listen. They've stopped shooting."

Jumping to my feet quickly, I got a momentary glimpse of the American chopper as it crossed and disappeared over the far end of the clearing. I pulled the pin on the red smoke canister and prepared to throw it.

The sound of an occasional angry curse could be heard from the jungle where the patrol had taken cover not from enemy fire, but from—friendly fire. While it would kill you just as quickly as enemy fire, the disquieting term "friendly fire" was applied to bullets or ordnance that emanated from American or allied sources.

"Come on, sir, throw it from the trees. You've got to get out of this clearing," the medic urged.

Just as I prepared to heave the small olive-green canister that would pop and belch a huge cloud of bright red smoke into the sky above us, something happened.

"Listen to that," I said. "They've moved away."

The chopper sounded as though it was now several kilometers beyond our strung-out patrol, and it was no longer firing.

"You know, I don't think they've actually seen us. They aren't attacking or they'd be all over us," I said.

We were intentionally in an area where recent enemy activity had been reported through both Vietnamese and U.S. intelligence channels. So, our frustrating situation was possibly due simply to poor communication.

While it seemed unlikely, one of the other headquarters in Nha Trang could have requested the chopper's mission, whatever that might have been. Or, it could simply be passing through on its way to someplace else and decided to take some unauthorized target practice. Whatever the reason for its presence, unless the chopper pressed an attack that indicated we might have been mistaken for an enemy unit, the smoke grenade should remain unused. If the enemy did see it, besides pinpointing our location, it might cause them to flee or, worse, prepare an ambush for us.

When the chopper's engines strained in another turn that seemed to be bringing it back yet again, why and how it got there wasn't going to be as important as what I was about to witness. What would become remarkable were the continuing actions of the young medic over the next few minutes.

When we realized the chopper was coming back, the medic began to move as he spoke, "Sir, please . . . it's coming back. Let's get the hell back into the jungle."

The fact that he moved to position himself between the approaching chopper and me wasn't immediately apparent.

"Come on, sir. That chopper could cut us down out here."

As the sound of the choppers' beating blades grew louder above and behind him and its pass became almost parallel, his movement seemed more purposeful.

The chopper's gunners weren't firing as it passed, so I didn't throw the smoke canister. But, as it passed, the young medic moved around me in such a manner that I noticed he was keeping himself between me and the chopper. If we had received fire, the medic would have been hit before and, probably, instead of me.

When I realized that he was making himself a human shield, I asked, "What are you doing?"

"I don't want you to get hit. You know the safest and best way back," he said. "If something happened to you, where would that leave us?"

I almost laughed but didn't, knowing the young medic hadn't been in Vietnam for much more than a week. It was easy to see that he was truly concerned. While admirable, his concern and daring deeds were for naught. He had apparently forgotten that another A-502 adviser was with our patrol unit. Even without American advisers, the Vietnamese would have easily led the unit back to camp since they were acting as our guides. Additionally, as well trained as they were, any member of the orientation unit, including the medic, could have found his way back to camp with little difficulty. However, I'm sure that after being in-country for such a short time, it wasn't something any of them really wanted to have to do.

Despite his needless concern, the medic's action and initiative on behalf of his unit spoke loudly and impressively about his character.

The chopper's next heard, but unseen, west-to-east pass was a little farther north than it had been the last time. Also, its less frequent fire was no longer impacting near us.

"I'm sure they don't know we're down here," I said, "and I'm fairly sure they must be running low on ammunition. Okay, I'm with you. Let's get back to the trees and see what he does next."

When we rejoined the patrol in the jungle, one of the other lieutenants from the training class asked, "What do you think? Are they shooting at us?"

"No, I don't think so. And, as much as they've been firing, they're probably running low on ammo."

"Good!" he said. "I'm getting a little tired of this."

"Yeah, I know. Me too."

Finally, though, the concern of being discovered waned when the sound of the chopper dissolved into the distance, towards Cam Ranh Bay.

As everyone stood up and we began reorganizing the patrol, I asked the medic once more why he had come into the clearing. He explained by saying, "When I heard the chopper coming back, I was concerned about you getting hit and how we would get back."

"And, what about you?" I asked. "What if you'd been hit?"

"I don't know . . . I didn't really think about that."

The medic's thinking might seem a bit muddled, but his reasons for acting were crystal clear to him. And, to me, they were remarkably selfless. I ran into the clearing because I had to, not because I wanted to. It was my job; responsibility for the safety of the patrol was mine alone. The medic ran into the clearing because he wanted to, not just for himself, but for all of us—his team. His genuine care and concern for others are very likely among the many things that prompted him to become a medic.

Countless stories exist about men and women like the medic, individuals whose thoughts and purpose were crystal clear in their own minds when they disregarded personal safety to act on behalf of another. In this account, the medic survived his actions—not everyone did.

Dale Reich, a previous COC group member, and others like him can't be asked the question, "Why did you do what you did?" The reason they can't be asked the question is because they didn't survive the situation in which they had willingly placed themselves at risk. It is likely, however, that their thinking and purpose for what they had done were also clear. It is just as likely that they would have responded as the medic had: "I didn't think about what might happen to me."

Certainly, countless other stories of war, far more sensational or stirring than this one, took place under decidedly more intense situations. However, if someone had been killed in the rain of seemingly less lethal, but equally deadly "friendly fire", I might be telling a more upsetting story. My reason for sharing this particular occurrence is very simple. It is to convey the frequency with which Americans serving in Vietnam, often very young ones, displayed qualities of courage and selflessness. Sometimes the results of their actions were tragic, while other times they were glorious. Today was simply a very good day—one we had all lived through.

This was simply another example of the selflessness I encountered regularly as we all did our jobs and tried to survive our experiences.

Exhilarating Highs — Gut-Wrenching Lows

This picture was taken the morning after I fired artillery in support of my friend Bill Phalen when he and his unit ambushed a much larger enemy patrol. Fortunately, my friend survived, but many of the enemies were killed when the ambush was triggered and, some, presumably during the following artillery fire.

When the reinforcing unit took over, they collected all of the enemy bodies. Thieu ta asked me to fly with him to the ambush site to determine if the unit was VC or NVA and search for intelligence information. Only half of the picture is shown simply because the bottom half is far too graphic. The incident is mentioned to demonstrate that any day could be a blend of both highs and lows.

CHAPTER 32

Building Bridges

ONE WOULD THINK THAT being shot at by the enemy and sometimes your own friendly forces would be reason enough to lie low or hide when things were slow or when you had free time. Remarkably, that's not the way it was at A-502.

When they weren't on other missions, our medics were out in one of the local villages treating anyone who needed medical attention. The rest of us worked on many projects around the camp that would improve our conditions. From building a runway to a two-story motor pool. We were busy beavers.

One day, when several of our NCOs were taking a concrete mortar position apart, they were using a jackhammer they had "borrowed" from another unit. It was a hot day and the work was tiring. So, even though an officer, I stripped down to a pair of cut-off shorts I had made out of a pair of old tiger fatigues, and my jungle boots and took my turn at the jackhammer.

In the villages surrounding Trung Dung, the team developed a reputation for being builders as well as "men who fight by day and night" (words from the "Ballad of the Green Berets"). As a result of what the villagers believed about our many skills, an elder from a nearby village came to visit Major Lee one day. He explained that his village was situated along a large stream and an important bridge crossing the stream had been washed out during a recent storm. He asked Lee if the team could help the villagers repair the bridge.

Well, that was right down Will Lee's alley, he was a former Civil Engineer and loved working aspects of his previous civilian occupation into his military career. So, he told the elder he would go back to the village with him and see what needed to be done.

The men of A-502 never shied away from accepting a challenge and Lee had no thought of dodging this one. After surveying the condition of the old bridge, he told the village elder that the men of A-502 would not help them repair the bridge. Rather, they would help them build a brand-new bridge. And, that's exactly what we did.

Lee designed the new bridge and helped procure the needed pilings and other lumber. Thieu ta even got involved in the collection of supplies for the bridge and offered his troops as workers. Then, when we weren't fighting the war, we began building a bridge.

One of the most amusing days I spent in Vietnam occurred at the site of the new bridge. I had gone over to check on progress and see if there was anything I could do to help. As soon as I stopped my jeep and turned off the engine, I immediately heard the sound of group laughter. I couldn't imagine what could be causing such a reaction. But, after watching the construction process for a few minutes, I began to laugh along with everyone else.

Lee had developed, and the villagers had constructed, a piledriving system. Once a piling was positioned, a tripod was set up over the piling. Then, the villagers would haul a larger concrete pile driver to the top of the tripod by pulling a long rope attached to a huge pully. And, it took fifteen to twenty of the small Vietnamese villagers to work the rope. Once the piledriver was at the top of the tripod, the signal was given and the villagers would release the rope. The pile driver would fall, hit the piling, and drive it farther into the stream bottom. Watching the process was a lot like watching the pyramids being constructed.

The laughter I had heard came not long after the rope was released. When the concrete pile driver hit the piling, it would then fall into the stream and create a huge splash that sent gushing water everywhere. Every time, one or more of the workers would get wet. Well, this was hysterically amusing to the villagers and they would all burst out laughing. Proof that laughter is contagious, all of the Americans and every onlooker, including me, would also burst out laughing. It couldn't be helped!

Days spent helping build the bridge were happy ones and a great diversion from the rigors of the war for team members.

When the bridge was finished, it was attractive and five times stronger than the one it had replaced. The villagers were so appreciative of what the team had done for them that they hosted a huge dinner party at the site of the bridge. Their dinner was seated and every table was filled with a wide variety of delicious Vietnamese food. Pictures of the dinner appear at the end of the chapter.

When the party was over, the team left the bridge with a sense of accomplishment and pride in what they had done for the village.

In addition to being trained to use virtually every killing weapon on the field of battle from knife to nuclear, the men of A-502 also had an extensive array of other personal skills to offer those in need. And, those Special Forces soldiers who serve today bring similar sets of skills to their service. Surely, "These were men, America's best" (more words from the ballad) and they still are.

You can see both the bridge and the "Bridge Party" on the next few pages. Great fun was had by all as people from different sides of the world celebrated the completion of a project that was important to both.

The Bridge

The Party

As soon as we arrived, tables were immediately filled with a bounty of food.

The Party Continues

Chairs were then placed at all of the tables, and we were invited to choose a seat. The District Chief (military) and Village Chief (civilian) offered a brief ceremony of thanks for what the team had done, then we had a wonderful meal.

Bridging Cultures

In many cases, tablemates didn't speak the same language, but that didn't seem to matter. Smiles and warmly spoken words, even though not understood, were more than enough to bridge the gap in language. Do you eat rice left-handed or right?

CHAPTER 33

Take Them Alive

MANY AILMENTS THAT VIETNAMESE villagers suffered were a result of poor diets and lack of medical care. Because rice was their basic or, often their only, food, they also lacked many of the vitamins and nutrients contained in fish, meats, and vegetables required for a healthful diet.

When the villagers did come by fresh meat, regardless of what kind it was, nothing was wasted. The Vietnamese villagers' lesson of "don't waste anything" had been taught to me one night in a small village a few weeks earlier.

In November 1968, "Vietnamization," the act of turning military responsibilities for the war over to the South Vietnamese, had just begun.

Vietnamization was a Nixon strategy with the goal of reducing American involvement in the Vietnam War. The president believed his Vietnamization strategy would prepare the South Vietnamese to take more responsibility for their own defense against the North Vietnamese as we prepared to withdraw.

If successful, the Vietnamization strategy would allow the United States to withdraw from the Vietnam War with dignity and honor. Unfortunately, the strategy failed miserably.

The president's Vietnamization program affected A-502 in a significant way. Once the program began, 502 didn't receive an equal count of men to replace those who were leaving the team. As a result, other team advisers and I were often in the field alone with the Vietnamese soldiers. On ambush, the only Americans available to me—were on the other end of my radio. As a result, I relied on everything I had learned since entering the Army and depended totally on myself for survival.

The number of advisers at 502 was being reduced, and schedules often allowed for only one American adviser to go out on a night ambush with each of our Vietnamese units. Such was the case for me when my next ambush rotation came up. I was scheduled to serve as the only U.S. adviser to one of my favorite old Trung Sis (sergeants). Being the lone American with the unit didn't bother me at all. By this time, I had been in-country for many months and felt comfortable with the assignment. Besides, I knew that if anything happened, there would be plenty of support on the other end of my radio.

It was between dusk and full dark as we walked across rice paddy dikes toward our ambush site. The night air was still hot and laden with humidity. My skin was moist with beads of perspiration as I slapped at mosquitoes buzzing around my face and neck. Flickering candlelight could be seen in the small village ahead, the village where Trung Si lived and where we would be setting up our ambush for the night. Our men would be set out along the south side parallel to an approach used by looters believed to be VC or NVA from the Dong Bo Mountains.

When we reached the village, the old Vietnamese sergeant told me our position would be in the center of the ambush, which wasn't far from his house. He then told me that he had asked his wife to prepare a special meal for us, knowing I would be with him that night. As usual, before a night ambush, I had already eaten at camp. But, because it would have been impolite and a dishonor to the Trung Si not to accept the extremely rare invitation to a Vietnamese soldier's home, I would eat again.

After establishing the ambush and reporting our exact location to 502, we went to Trung Si's home for dinner. His wife greeted me warmly at the door to their tiny dwelling and gestured for me to enter. The table, like the rest of the house, was lit only by candlelight. There was no electricity. The small dining table was set with a humble flower centerpiece, painted rice bowls, oriental soup spoons, and chopsticks.

When Trung Si's wife served dinner, it consisted of a heaping bowl of rice, chicken soup, and warm Ba Mui Ba (Vietnamese beer) for Trung Si and me. Sipping a spoonful of hot broth, it didn't taste or smell quite like anything Mom used to make. Even so, I complimented Trung Si's wife on her wonderful soup. Even though she spoke no English, she smiled broadly and thanked me in Vietnamese. Then, spooning deeper into my bowl, I felt a large piece of chicken and began lifting it to the surface of the soup. As it emerged, I discovered that special surprises had been placed in my bowl. Pausing to let my spoon rest on the edge of the bowl, I reached for my beer glass and pondered what to do with the surprises.

After taking a drink of my beer, I looked back down at the chicken head lying in my soup spoon. Its glazed blue eye seemed to stare straight up at me. The head didn't look appetizing, nor did the chicken foot that was hooked to the spoon by its claw. My method of dealing with the situation was to simply let both slide off my spoon and back to the bottom of my bowl. Not wanting to hurt the feelings of Trung Si's wife and knowing I was probably the only American ever invited to his home, I hoped to leave a good impression of my visit. So, eventually, I ate everything—except the foot and the head. Later, Trung Si told me those pieces had been used to give more flavor to the soup. One thing was certain, none of that chicken had been wasted. Every piece of it had been used, from head to toe.

Continuing to watch our medics treat the village children, I noticed something interesting. The medics themselves appeared to be gaining something from the healing process in which they were involved, a great sense of satisfaction. How do I know? The look on their faces just after putting a treated child back in its mother's arms showed everything.

The medics were a special blend of sensitivity and courage. Sergeant Freedman, for example, besides being a skilled medic, was also a seasoned military adviser. I learned that my first night at A-502 when we were on Buddha Hill together. When he wasn't conducting one of his many monthly MEDCAP visits, he served as a primary adviser to Vietnamese Combat Reconnaissance Platoon 558 and saw action with that and other units on several night ambushes and patrols. He was a man the Vietnamese liked, trusted, and respected. Freedman, Sergeant Arrants, and his entire team of medics were a unique breed of men.

My observation of the MEDCAPS program at work was interrupted by one of our radiomen.

"Lieutenant Ross, Walt Three Zero is on the horn for you."

"Okay. Tell him I'm on the way."

When I arrived at the radio room and called Walt Three Zero, he seemed fairly excited. "Zero Two, I've got two VC suspects in the open. Can you get out here?"

"Where are you?"

When he gave me coordinates for his location, I realized it was going to take a chopper to get to the area he was circling. Because of the demand for them, it could be difficult to obtain a chopper unless it had been previously scheduled. However, the 281st AHC always seemed to come through for us. They had a chopper available and dispatched it immediately.

The men of the 281st, whose company designation was "Intruders" and whose motto was "Hell from Above," were divided into three platoons. "Rat Pack" and "Bandits" were lift platoons, which means they were used primarily to deliver troops to a battlefield. "Wolf Pack" was a gunship platoon, which means they were primarily used to cover the lift platoons during troop insertions and extractions. They were also called upon to provide cover and/or support for ground units. They were like having a big brother, and I was always more comfortable when the Wolf Pack was nearby.

The pilots and crews of these UH-1 helicopters sat exposed to any and every danger on the battlefield as they entered and exited. The pilot and copilot sat in a cockpit surrounded by little more than Plexiglas, clearly visible to any enemy gunner who might be on or near their LZ. While they had small armored shields on both sides and under their seats, it was always my opinion that they provided little more than psychological protection. On the lift platoon choppers, the two crew members, who served as crew chief and door gunner, sat on each side of the helicopter manning .60-caliber machine guns, fully exposed with no protection beyond the flak vests they wore.

The pilots and crew of these extremely vulnerable aircraft were supremely courageous men who never failed to respond to A-502's calls for support or help. Their bold and frequent intrusions into dangerous situations confirmed the appropriateness of their "Intruders" designation. But their response to our most recent call for assistance would demonstrate that they weren't just bold, they were skilled, intelligent, and compassionate.

With the 281st inbound, I sent a message to Thieu ta asking that he have four members of his Vietnamese Special Forces Eagle Team, his quick response unit, meet me at the chopper pad. Our A-502 radio operator called Walt Three Zero and advised him that we would be airborne shortly.

It only took our ride about ten minutes to reach us and about the same to reach the place where Colonel Baer was circling in his 01 "Bird Dog" aircraft.

On the way out, I told the pilot we needed to capture the VC alive, if possible. It had been a while since we had received any fresh intelligence information, and this offered us a great opportunity to learn what was going on in Charlie's (slang for the enemy) head out west.

"Just show us where they are," the pilot said.

"They ought to be somewhere under that 01," I told him, then checked in with Colonel Baer.

"Walt Three Zero, this is Bunkhouse Zero Two. We're coming in on you from the east. Can you see us? Over."

"Roger, I've got you."

"Do you still have your targets?" I asked.

"Roger, I just chased them into that abandoned village directly beneath me. They ran into one of those houses down there."

"Okay," said the chopper pilot. "Let's go find 'em."

Then, he swooped down toward the village like an eagle after a fish near the surface of the water. My insides felt as though they had stayed somewhere a few hundred feet above us as we continued our steep dive toward the village.

"Let me know when you see our targets," the pilot told his crew as he finally leveled off and swooped low over the village.

After making about three passes over the village at around fifty feet, one of the door gunners spotted the two men.

"I've got 'em at five o'clock running between two small houses," he said.

The gunner had barely gotten "five o'clock" out of his mouth before the pilot pushed the chopper up around to the right and back down. It felt as though we had gone from one direction to the exact opposite instantaneously, and I wasn't sure exactly where my insides were that time. We all just hung on as the pilot maneuvered to locate and lock in on our prey.

We were still coming out of our U-turn when the copilot said, "Yeah, I've got 'em. They just ran behind that house with the blown-out roof."

"Be alert," the pilot said to his door gunners. "We're going to rock around behind that house."

That's exactly what we did. The nose of the chopper continued to point directly at the house as its tail started to swing around. In just a few seconds we were looking at the backside of the house and the two VC suspects. When they turned to run, we could see they were in civilian clothes, but it was similar to clothing we had seen on VC before. Because they were turning, our view was obscured. We couldn't tell what kind of weapons the men were carrying.

Obviously, they were trying to elude us and bolted for the corner of the house. Darting around the corner and along the side of the dwelling, they crossed an open area and ran toward yet another vacant house. But this time they were in full view as they made their crossing. The door gunner swung his M-60 machine gun around and had the two in the center of his sites the entire way. I watched the face of the young door gunner, whose focus on the men was intense. He had a tight grip on his M-60 and he was clearly ready to fire. I wanted the men alive and was concerned he might open up on them. One or two bursts from his weapon and the chase would have been over. The two men weren't very fast on their feet and would have been very easy targets if the gunner had intended to kill. Despite the intensity of the situation, the gunner never opened fire and simply kept his weapon trained on the two men as they ran into a house.

"Were those carbines they were carrying?" the pilot asked.

"Yeah, I think so," the copilot responded. "We could have nailed them," he added.

The pilot circled the house to make sure his quarry hadn't run out the back door. When he saw there was no back door, he said, "We've got 'em." Then, he moved back around to the front side of the house and hovered in a position that, once again, gave the left door gunner an ideal firing position. Immediately, three Eagle Team members moved with their M-16s to the chopper door to provide backup for the door gunner.

The pilot was hovering little more than twenty-five feet off the ground, dust was blowing everywhere. The door gunner had his M-60 machine gun trained on the front of the house to cover the door and two open windows.

In our low hovering position, our chopper was an easy target for the two men inside the house if they chose to duel. We waited to see either the men or their weapons. Then, finally, we saw their faces looking up at us.

When I waved and yelled for them to come out, they backed out of sight. When they appeared at one of the windows again, I waved and yelled once more for them to come out. But, as they had done before, they simply backed out of sight. That went on one or two more times. Then, the pilot very calmly said, "I'll run 'em out for you."

The pilot's next action was unorthodox and, frankly, amusing to me. He moved the chopper directly over the house and set it down on the roof. Then, he bounced on it a couple of times. When he roosted on the roof the next time, it started to collapse under the weight of the chopper, and the two men burst out of the house, unarmed with their hands in the air. The pilot then quickly moved off the house and set the chopper down in front of it.

As soon as the chopper's skids hit the ground, three members of the Eagle Team and I jumped out to retrieve the two men. Without a gunship for covering protection, we didn't hang around. As quickly as everyone was back on board, the pilot lifted off with the quarry bagged and uninjured.

The two men that the pilot and his crew had skillfully captured could have been killed by either door gunner or crew chief, who also manned an M-60, on multiple occasions. But, given the challenging mission of capturing the two alive, that's exactly what they had done.

Even Colonel Baer who had stayed close at hand and seen the capture called with compliments for the chopper's pilot and crew.

"Zero Two, Walt Three Zero. Over."

"Roger, go ahead Walt Three Zero."

"Tell your pilot that was some mighty fancy flying. I especially enjoyed the rooftop landing. Ask him if he learned that at flight school. Over."

The pilot, who was monitoring the frequency, grinned as he listened to Baer's remarks and replied, "No, that one came out of my hat."

"Walt Three Zero, this is Zero Two. Seems that one wasn't in the book."

After thanking Colonel Baer for his tip on the two VC suspects, who were now prisoners, our communications were ended. But, with shared feelings of satisfaction, the Air Force 0-1 Bird Dog and Army UH-1 Huey flew together back toward Trung Dung.

It had been another good day that started with healing and ended with mercy—an unusual and welcomed event in Vietnam.

UH-1 Huey, AKA — "The House Bouncer"

The is a 281st helicopter on A-502's runway and it is exactly like the one used to capture the two Viet Cong soldiers. The pilot of the helicopter that flew the capture mission positioned the chopper over the house with those two skids on the bottom perpendicular to the roofline. The roof was covered with clay tiles, so there was the ominous sound of "crunching" as the pilot settled in on the roof. Unfortunately, I didn't get the name of the daring pilot or any of the crew members, so I can't recognize any of them by name—I wish I could.

Vietnamese Jump Wings

Vietnamese Special Forces troops were also required to be parachute qualified. A-502's American advisors helped the VNSF train Thieu ta's LLDB soldiers in parachute operations. As part of the training, we jumped out of the old Sikorsky H-34 helicopters too, and earned the wings as well. Thieu ta presented mine.

Earning My Wings — Again

This was my perspective the day I jumped out of another perfectly functioning aircraft and earned my Vietnamese Jump Wings. That is the Song Cai River below. We landed in a large sandy area just south of the river, which is directly under the helicopter from this line of view.

While I never landed in the river, after returning to Pensacola, I did end up in the Gulf of Mexico one evening when parachuting into a beach party.

CHAPTER 34

Death Lives in the Mountains

THE DONG BO MOUNTAINS stood tall and imposing against the magnificent star-studded southern sky, which was the only suitable backdrop for their enormous mass. Behind them, the night changed from deep purple in the east to a glowing bright blue along the horizon in the west. The air lacked its usual humidity and was occasionally stirred by a gentle breeze from the distant South China Sea. It was the type of setting and evening meant to be shared by candlelight with someone special.

Unfortunately, while candlelight flickered nearby, anyone special to most of those Americans in Vietnam was more than ten thousand miles away. And, as beautiful and soft as the huge Dong Bo Mountains appeared from a distance, I knew how treacherous and deadly they had been to assaulting units in the past. Tomorrow, A-502 and its key CIDG companies would face the danger confronted by those who had gone before us.

My role as one of a handful of American advisers for the Dong Bo operation would take me deep into the heart of the mountains that I had found so picturesque since my first day in Nha Trang. But, for the first time since arriving in-country, there were unusual feelings of apprehension about the coming mission. Every trip into the field could be dangerous, but this one felt different in some way. This was the first mission that I felt it could be one from which I might not return.

My feelings of foreboding were uncomfortable and a little more than distracting, but not altogether unexpected. During the past several months we had gathered considerable intelligence about the vast mountain complex. Sergeant Koch had collected information from the camp's Vietnamese intelligence section and every other source in the Nha Trang intelligence network. Our operation would be mounted under less-than-favorable conditions, so we needed to know as much as possible about our objective.

For some time, we had been trying to pinpoint the location of the NVA base camp that we knew existed somewhere on the eastern-facing slopes of the Dong Bo Mountains. Finally, we had a break. One of our night ambushes had captured a prisoner who came from the mountain camp. During their interrogation of the man, the Vietnamese intelligence section "convinced" the prisoner to serve as a guide and lead us back to his base.

This opportunity was extremely meaningful, if true. My concern was that our NVA guide might also be planning to lead us into a trap. After all, the mountains had belonged to the VC and NVA for years. It was difficult to believe that the captured soldier would lead us to the base camp, knowing his fellow soldiers would probably kill him if he survived any ensuing battle.

Much of the information provided by the prisoner matched what we had already accumulated. His report of the NVA strength in the mountains was about six to seven hundred men, approximately what we had estimated. Fortifications and supplies were also reported very much as we expected them to be. Other than sharing the general location of the base camp, which he told the Vietnamese he couldn't find on a map, the prisoner hadn't told us anything we didn't already know. So, his only value was his ability to lead us to the base camp.

The fact that the enemy base was well manned and supplied had been demonstrated previously when they ran other allied units out of the mountains after inflicting significant casualties on them. We clearly understood the very dangerous challenge we were facing.

A month earlier, when the current assault into the Dong Bo was being considered by Corp Command in Nha Trang, I had been asked to present a briefing on what we knew about the mountain complex. My presentation was given at First Field Force Headquarters to Lieutenant General William Peers and some of his staff officers.

After describing in detail, the suspected location of the base camp, its fortifications, estimated troop strength, supplies, and other details, the briefing concluded with an outline of the South Vietnamese plan of attack. A-502 would be supplying the military advisers for the operation, which included me.

The plan, which was not ours, seemed very weak to those of us who would serve as advisers. The plan involved the use of most of Trung Dung's resources, three light Vietnamese CIDG companies, and some support platoons. In all, fewer than five hundred men would be used to attack what was believed to be a superior enemy force that was well entrenched in a location they had held and successfully defended for many years. This option seemed almost foolhardy when considering the results of similar missions.

There was, however, an alternate plan to attack the mountain complex, one that was tactically sounder. I asked General Peers if he cared to hear it.

"Absolutely, Lieutenant," he said. "I want to hear everything you can tell me about that hell hole and how we can get rid of it."

With approval to proceed, I wasted no time outlining a second option.

The Koreans, our allies on the north side of the Song Cai River, knew of the legendary enemy stronghold and they yearned for a major involvement. From our perspective, the most important part of their desire for a fight was their ability to commit almost three thousand men to such a mission. These would be exceptionally well trained and highly motivated soldiers. We had no such resources.

General Peers immediately recognized the tactical advantage of the Korean option, but he pointed out that the Dong Bo Mountain complex was located in the Vietnamese AO.

"I'm with you, Lieutenant," the general said. "But the authority to give the mission to the Koreans rests with the Vietnamese High Command."

The decision, tactically, should have been such a simple one to make but, politically, it seemed far more difficult.

For the South Vietnamese High Command, it may have been a matter of saving face. Whatever the issues, after taking several days to consider all the information and options, the final orders came down. CIDG companies 557, 558, and 559 and other Vietnamese support units from Trung Dung along with their U.S. advisers from A-502, would seek, then attempt to destroy the enemy stronghold in the Dong Bo Mountains.

Aside from the war itself, this was the first time I could remember being personally affected by a political issue. The decision to send our units into the mountains had clearly been a political one, not a tactical one, and I was astonished by its absurdity. Word made its way to me from First Field Force that, because the Dong Bo were in the Vietnamese AO, they felt that they would appear weak in the eyes of allies if they didn't make at least one more attempt to find and destroy the enemy base themselves.

With the Vietnamese units at Trung Dung going into the mountains, the American advisers from A-502 were committed to accompanying them. The Americans would do what they had been ordered to do and exactly what they had been trained to do—provide the best support possible.

Because of my work on the operation plan and knowledge of the Dong Bo history, my presence on the mission was a given. So, looking out across the darkening mountains, I anticipated the next day with some trepidation. Strange, but I had never given much, if any, thought to my mortality before any previous mission.

Perhaps it is because of an innate will to survive, but military personnel often feel that if someone is going to die in battle, it will be someone else. I suppose that's the only way you can do the job. There wouldn't be many people in line at the recruiting station if dying were a sure thing. Whatever the cause of the phenomenon, I no longer felt exempt from serious harm, particularly because, with the NVA prisoner as a guide, an encounter with a major enemy force seemed inevitable. And, my friend, Bill Phalen, had very nearly been killed on a mission in the Dong Bo Mountain complex.

Watching as the mountains lost definition and became a silhouette against the starry Vietnamese sky, I organized my thoughts. And, as those fell into place, I began to feel a sense of inner peace.

In anticipation of the coming operation, there had been both military planning and personal preparation. Earlier in the day, while in Nha Trang to coordinate artillery support, I visited the Catholic chaplain who heard my confession. As I turned to leave the chaplain's office, he offered his own mission support. "Lieutenant, I'm going to say a special prayer for you and your unit's safe return."

Everyone in Vietnam dealt with their fears and concerns in various ways. For me, it was a brief visit to a priest dressed in a military uniform who simply listened as I cleansed my soul. Almost smiling when his promise of a "special prayer" was recalled, I realized, standing there alone in the dark, that my concerns about being killed had nearly vanished. While I still recognized the possibility intellectually, I was emotionally prepared for *whatever* was to come. *If the worst happens*, I thought, *at least I am prepared to meet my maker.*

By the time the sun edged above the eastern horizon and illuminated our destination, we were already at our airstrip waiting for pickup. A short while later, we were being airlifted to a location about three-quarters of the way up one of the western slopes of the Dong Bo. Our search-and-destroy mission was officially underway.

Since the NVA prisoner was captured after we were given the mission orders, there had been a good deal of discussion about how we would proceed. We weren't sure what information disloyal Vietnamese in our own unit might have leaked. So, we had decided to enter the mountains from above by helicopter high on the west side of the mountain complex at the last minute. Our original plan had us entering from the low ground on the east side. That was where all the other previously defeated units had entered. If we had anything in our favor, hopefully, it would be some degree of surprise.

Clouds hung close to the mountain's summit as the old Vietnamese H-34 choppers began the many ferry trips required to transport all of us to the drop-off point. In case the NVA had lookouts on the mountains, which were generally southeast of our camp, we took off and headed directly west before circling around behind the suspected enemy location.

While it took a few hours to insert everyone on the mountainside, the process went very smoothly. As soon as each chopper landed, its offloading unit organized and immediately started moving farther up the mountain.

At this point, I have included a couple of pictures so that you will have an idea of the dramatic terrain we were entering and would be walking through as we searched for the enemy base camp.

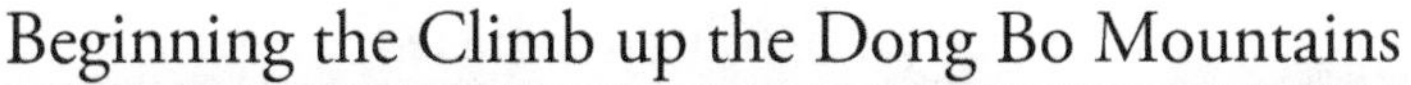

Beginning the Climb up the Dong Bo Mountains

Shortly after being inserted by the Vietnamese helicopters, we began our claim and, almost immediately, encountered this stand of elephant grass. We made our own trail, but often crossed those created by the VC/NVA. We were already on enemy ground. "Light," my Vietnamese interpreter in the last in line.

When on any mission, especially those in the dangerous mountain complex, it was important to be alert because the enemy could be close—very close!

In Search of an Enemy Base Camp

Dense Jungle—Dong Bo Mountains

An enemy base of more than 700 men was hidden in these mountains and an enemy soldier could easily be hiding within feet of you—and never be seen.

Again, Light is right in front of me and the troops ahead of him quickly disappeared into the very dense jungle. In some places, the jungle was so thick that I couldn't see Light even though he was only a few meters ahead of me.

Thieu ta Ngoc was in charge as the Dong Bo mission commander. The senior American adviser was Major Richard Dubovick, who would soon replace Major Lee as A-502's commander. Having completed his tour of duty, Lee was scheduled to return to the States in only days.

Major Dubovick was an even-tempered man who was less intense than Lee but seemed equally experienced and militarily skilled. Because this mission was his first out of 502, my role was to provide him with whatever information he required. Along with Major Dubovick and me, two Americans would advise each of the three CIDG companies.

We had been walking for about an hour and were on a very steep incline when I began to feel winded. The Vietnamese didn't seem to be affected by the climb at all, but the farther up we went, the worse I felt.

How are they doing it? I asked myself.

After watching the two or three Vietnamese in front of me for a while, I noticed that for every one step I was taking, they were taking two or three. I changed my stride to a much shorter one. In only minutes, my respiration became less labored and more normal as we continued up toward the clouds.

As we neared the summit of the mountain on which we had landed, we actually walked into the clouds. It was like walking into a dense fog. The air was cooler and thick with humidity. Trees dripped with condensation—so much so that, at one point, it felt like rain as we were pelted by water droplets falling from the jungle canopy.

We followed our point unit quietly through the cloud layer and around the summit to a point on the southeast side of the mountain. We stopped there for a late lunch of cold C rations. While I sat on a rock and picked at the contents of one of the tins, the aroma of cinnamon became very distinct.

"Do you smell cinnamon?" I asked Light, who was serving as interpreter.

"Yes," he said. "It comes from the trees." He stood up and cut a small piece of bark from a nearby tree. Handing it to me he said, "Smell it, Trung Uy. It smells very good."

I suppose it was cinnamon, it smelled like cinnamon. Whatever it was, its aroma mixed with the fine mist of the low hanging clouds to give the air a pleasing scent. The surprise of any pleasant sensation was always welcomed in Vietnam. In reality, the country was beautiful, and pleasant experiences were more frequent than I expected.

After a brief lunch, we moved behind the point unit down the mountain through jungle growth so thick that at times you couldn't see either the man in front of you or the one behind you. We were all hot and wringing wet with sweat when we finally broke into a clearing. Our NVA guide then led us onto a trail that ran along a narrow ridge toward another portion of the mountain.

Walking on trails in enemy territory was one of my least favorite things to do, even when it was quicker or there was no other option. The possibility of ambush always existed when walking on trails, simply because one of the easiest places to set up an ambush is along an existing trail. In this case, though, traveling on the trail was a must situation if we were going to reach the suspected base camp location quickly enough to take advantage of our element of surprise. We hoped to find the hidden camp and attack not later than the afternoon of the second day.

As we moved along the trail, everyone watched the jungle as it thinned on both sides of us. With the jungle opening, the pace quickened. No one wanted to get caught in an open killing zone. Ahead, on a short, straight part of the trail, I could see a dip and an open clearing in the growth. As each Vietnamese soldier reached the dip and the clearing, he bolted and ran across it to the far side. There was no sound of gunfire, but I wondered if a sniper was shooting at them.

When it was my turn to cross the small open area, there was still no explanation for why everyone had run across it so quickly. One of the men about two people ahead of me shrieked something in Vietnamese to the man behind him, but I couldn't understand what he said. Then, he bolted.

They must know something I don't, I thought as I began my sprint. There was still no apparent reason for our hurry other than to simply cross the clearing quickly. I couldn't understand why the soldier had cried out since we were trying to move as silently as possible. Then, about halfway across the opening, I discovered the reason for the hurry.

WHACK! I was suddenly hit in the neck. The pain was excruciating, but I kept running and was glad that I could.

At least I'm not dead, I thought. Quickly, I reached for my neck to locate the wound and assess the seriousness of my injury. Since I felt an intense stinging sensation, I expected to see my hand covered with blood when it reached my line of sight. But when I looked at it, there was nothing—not a speck of blood on it. I couldn't understand what had happened.

After running back into the jungle on the far side of the clearing, the pain was still extremely intense. Again, my hand searched for a wound and source of the crippling pain, but nothing. No apparent injury.

Ahat, who was running behind me, had seen me grab my neck and knew I had been hit by something. When he came up beside me, I pointed to my neck. He pulled my collar down and looked for the wound.

"No wound, Trung Uy," he said. Then he started making a buzzing sound.

I called Light back and asked him to check my neck and told him to ask Ahat what he was trying to tell me.

"Feel your neck now, Trung Uy," Light said.

Touching my neck for a second time, it was beginning to swell.

"You were stung by a hornet," he said.

As a young boy playing in the woods around my home, I had been stung many times by both bees and wasps, but I had never experienced that kind of pain before. Even though the pain was intense, there was something for which to be thankful—I hadn't been shot.

A military combat column doesn't stop for a hornet sting, no matter how badly it hurts. So, we continued moving along the ridgeline. It was almost dark anyway and nearly time to stop for the night.

When we finally stopped for the evening, each of the CIDG companies consolidated their positions and set up security. Thieu ta, Major Dubovick, and I picked a cave-like opening under a rocky overhang to spend the night. As we ate our evening meal, Dubovick asked, "How's your neck?"

"It doesn't hurt anymore. It's just numb feeling."

"Good, that has to be better."

"Yes, sir. It is . . . much better. I don't think I've ever felt a searing pain that intense before."

Then, pointing toward a small group set up not far away from the opening to our cave, the major said, "We have to make damn sure we keep an eye on that joker. He'd like to do more than sting us. He'll crawl in here tonight and crack our skulls with a rock if he has the chance."

He was talking about the NVA prisoner who the Vietnamese had tied to a tree. Ironically, it wasn't the enemy soldier that was going to injure the major that night. The rock that would take him out of action would be launched by another.

Thieu ta was talking to one of his lieutenants after we had all finished eating. Major Dubovick and I were both propped against the rocks to relax. It had been a long hike up the mountain to where we now rested. Eyeing our surroundings, the major noticed a small rock wedged between a couple of larger ones in the overhang above his feet. He pointed toward the smallest one in the center with the toe of his boot.

"I wonder if that rock's the keystone," he said, kicking at it. It didn't budge. Then, he kicked it again. To our surprise, mostly his, the rocks suddenly broke loose and fell. One of the larger ones landed on his ankle. He grimaced, and I could tell he was hurt. Immediately, I lifted the rocks off his legs.

Slowly and gingerly, the major unlaced his boot and pulled it off. Again, he grimaced as the boot slipped free of his foot. The boot had kept his foot from being cut, but it was swelling quickly and already showing signs of being badly bruised.

"Do you want me to get one of the medics?" I asked.

"No, it hurts, but I think I'm fine." The pain showed in the expression on his face as he rubbed the ankle, which was swelling even more.

"Are you sure you don't want me to get one of the medics up here to look at that? It really doesn't look very good."

"No, no. I can move it. I don't think anything is broken." Then, demonstrating his ability to move the blackening appendage, he wiggled it around a little. "I think it'll be fine by morning. Being able to stay off of it tonight will help."

Neither of us slept much that night, the major because of his ankle and me to check our perimeter, make sure the NVA prisoner was still securely tied, and discuss strategy with Thieu ta.

Nightfall in the jungle isn't just dark; it's very dark. Sometimes you could barely see your hand in front of your face. So, even though the prisoner was guarded, I never felt comfortable having him only feet away from us. Many times, when I looked over at him, even though his form was barely discernible, I could see his eyes were wide open and moving around. Even when he appeared to be sleeping, I was sure he was just waiting for his guard to fall asleep. Because of our location and our mission, not many of the troops slept well that night. Everyone knew we were on dangerously unfriendly ground.

The next morning, light filtered through the jungle canopy to once again bring color and form to our campsite. The overnight rest did little to heal the major's injured foot. He couldn't do much more than stand or hobble. When Thieu Ta Ngoc and I tried to convince him to let us medevac him out, he wouldn't hear of it.

"No," he said. "I'm staying till we find the base camp."

Since he wasn't going to leave, after a meeting with company commanders to review our attack plans, our force began moving again. Dubovick limped along with it.

Based on information provided by the prisoner, we expected our recon patrols to find the enemy base camp by mid-morning. When there was still no sign of it by noon, we began to believe we were being led on a wild goose chase.

By mid-afternoon, we still hadn't found anything of substance. A couple of our recon units had made contact with small enemy patrols and exchanged gunfire, but that was it. When we stopped for a break, it was easy to see that the Vietnamese had finally had enough of the rugged mountain terrain. Some of the officers felt certain the prisoner was intentionally misdirecting us and had no intention of taking us anywhere near his base camp. They questioned him and even threatened him with his life. He cried, apologized, and begged to live, claiming he had never come to the camp this way and was lost. None of us believed him, and some of the Vietnamese wanted to kill him. Thieu Ta Ngoc intervened and didn't let that happen. He told his men that we would simply continue our search, and the prisoner would be handed over to the District Chief for punishment when we returned to Trung Dung.

Since our recon units had encountered and fired on the enemy patrols earlier, every VC and NVA soldier in the mountain complex would soon know we were there. Our element of surprise had been lost, and we had become vulnerable to attack ourselves.

Because our units might have to divide and move quickly, Thieu Ta Ngoc and I tried once more to convince the major to let us have him medevacked off the mountain. His ankle had become extremely discolored and so swollen that he could hardly walk. This time he agreed. He recognized that his condition was getting worse and that his presence could impede or endanger our unit if things suddenly got crazy.

We moved the major to a large boulder that hung out over the mountain. From the overhang, we had a commanding view of the Nha Trang Valley below. The boulder would serve as our LZ for the Dustoff helicopter.

The 254th Medevac chopper took only about twenty minutes to reach us from the time our medic requested the pickup. Shortly after the call, we could see the helicopter clearly when it rounded the base of the mountains and started up to our location. We communicated frequently as the chopper made its way to the outcropping where the major was waiting.

Whenever warned of possible danger, the pilot displayed calm, confident professionalism and simply replied, "Roger. Understand."

When he arrived and set up for his approach, we advised him one last time to use caution since we were uncertain about enemy presence. The pilot's only response this time was, "Roger. Get your man ready. We're coming in."

The speed and efficiency with which the 254th Medevac pilot and his crew functioned were smooth and practiced. The chopper swept in boldly and began to settle in on the outcropping. Because the rocks weren't level, the pilot rested only one skid and stayed at a hover. We loaded the major onboard quickly and in only seconds he was on his way. He wished us well and showed us a thumbs-up as the chopper lifted off and began to rotate. Once clear of the rocks, the pilot dropped its nose and dove down between the mountain ridges toward the valley floor. Even though a great churning machine, it flew down between the ridges with the smoothness and authority of a soaring bird of prey.

While this one hadn't been a life-saving mission, there were countless others during the Vietnam War that were. As with Major Mielke and his crew, who had attempted to save the life of Lieutenant Dale Reich near My Loc a few months earlier, it took incredible courage and devotion to fly those low-flying air ambulances. Unarmed, they were easy targets for enemy gunners. Even though on mercy missions and clearly marked with large red crosses, many were blasted from the air. When that happened, another pilot and crew would confidently take their place.

With the major safely onboard the chopper and on his way back to the field hospital in Nha Trang, the role of Thieu Ta Ngoc's Senior adviser fell to me. By that time, we had developed a close bond and I knew him very well. I always enjoyed our time together, especially on a mission. The role of Senior adviser to Thieu Ta had typically belonged to A-502's camp commander. But, as the medevac chopper disappeared around the base of the mountain, Thieu Ta said, "I am glad you are with me in this place, Trung uy."

When I asked how he wanted to proceed, Thieu Ta said he wanted to search for the base camp a while longer before requesting a planned resupply mission. Even though many of the men were already out of drinking water, he felt we needed to attempt to find the enemy base camp and attack before dark, which was only a few hours away.

"The VC and NVA know we are here now, Trung Uy," he said. "We must find them because, after dark, they will have a great advantage over us. These mountains are their home."

In agreement with his assessment of our situation, I shook my head and said, "Let's go find them."

We spent what remained of the afternoon crawling over rocks, following trails, and chopping our way through the jungle in search of the enemy hideaway without luck. As evening approached, I suggested to Thieu Ta that he call for the resupply. Almost everyone was out of water, and it would soon be dark.

Thieu ta agreed to the resupply and we sent a receiving unit to secure another large outcropping of rocks that projected out over a valley between two ridges.

Just before dark, lumbering H-34 helicopters began to appear in the air above the rocks, but their resupply mission soon turned into something more closely resembling a bombing mission.

Either because of updrafts from the valley beneath the rocks, lack of flying skill, fear of hitting the trees near the rocks, or a combination of all those factors, the chopper pilots couldn't get in close enough to deliver their loads. Time after time, each chopper tried to maneuver near enough to set down or hover so that water containers and boxes of food could either be handed to or tossed to the waiting troops. Frustratingly, none of them could make it. So, as a result, the chopper crewmen would simply try to drop the containers of water to the men on the ground. Unfortunately, when the troops attempted to catch the heavy containers being dropped from eight to ten feet above them, they would pass through their arms and burst at their feet. There was water everywhere, but it quickly seeped into the dry hot rocks.

As the long day began fading to darkness, the Vietnamese crewmen became less cautious and simply shoved things out of the chopper door. Cases of sardines and rice fell into the jungle around us and the ones that hit the rocks burst like bombs. When the resupply mission was over, cans of smashed sardines and broken bags of rice covered the rocks. As far as the much-needed water was concerned, we had only salvaged from the broken containers little more than a quarter cup for every man.

Thieu Ta was very angry about the results of the botched resupply attempt and called Trung Dung. He commanded an aid to arrange for another mission the next morning and threatened disciplinary action if it failed. That night was a long, dry, and hungry one. It also became restless and a little crazy when an unexpected intruder attempted to kill a perimeter guard. We were expecting the NVA or VC—but not this attacker.

At around two or three in the morning, the radio handset hooked to my hammock buzzed as I tried to briefly nap. Occasionally, radio checks from Trung Dung's night ambushes caused it to crackle when the frequency was used. When the noise from the radio aroused my attention, I checked to make sure the NVA prisoner was still secured. I had just put my head back down when the still of the night was broken by the drumming of running footsteps and a frantic Vietnamese voice. In the dark, I didn't know if it was one of our troops or an incoming NVA assault.

As the person ran in closer, he began to scream. His screams roused all of the Vietnamese around me, and many of them thought we were being attacked. They started yelling to alert everyone else. I still didn't have a clue about what was happening but grabbed the M-16 lying across my hammock and rolled out onto the ground. Just as I hit the ground, the runner hit my hammock and fell right beside me. I grabbed him and Ahat jumped on him as he still chattered away.

"What is he saying, Light?" I yelled.

"He is one of our men, Trung Uy. He says a tiger tried to eat him."

"What?"

There was a frantic exchange of words between Light and the soldier, then a clearer explanation.

As it turned out, the man was one of our perimeter guards. He hadn't noticed the tiger stalking him—he may have fallen asleep. Whatever happened, a tiger had walked to within just a few feet of him before he saw it coming out of the darkness. When he finally did see it, he panicked, believing it was going to jump on him and kill him.

Things calmed down after the word of what had actually happened was circulated, but that took a while. I don't remember sleeping another wink that night. Occasionally, though, my eyelids closed just long enough to moisten my hot, dry eyes.

The next morning, when it appeared there was enough light to fly, Thieu Ta Ngoc summoned the second resupply. Unfortunately, because of an overcast sky that produced slightly higher winds than the day before, things didn't go much better than they had the previous evening. Water containers dropped from Vietnamese choppers that were once again hovering too high, burst when they hit the ground.

As a crewman shoved one of the last water containers out of the chopper door, a thirsty and frustrated Vietnamese soldier raised his carbine as if to fire at the chopper, only to have it slapped down by one of his sergeants.

With a water resupply apparently impossible, we salvaged what we could of the food that was still scattered on the ground from the evening before and moved out. Hoping to find water in a mountain spring along our way, we headed for another location that intelligence had once targeted as a likely spot for the NVA base camp. In reality, the entrance or entire base camp could have changed or been moved many times over the past many years of its existence. And, the NVA were exceptionally skilled at camouflage.

Again, we spent the day walking and climbing up and down in the Dong Bo Mountains. We had nothing to show for our efforts, other than isolated contacts with very small enemy units, which had probably been dispatched simply to report on our movements and current location. I felt that we were probably being stalked by the NVA as our perimeter security guard had been stalked the night before by the tiger.

By the end of the day, we hadn't located either the enemy base camp or water. We were at the end of our third day in the mountains and were all very surprised that we had not encountered or been attacked by larger mountain-based enemy elements. It seemed the NVA might intentionally be avoiding contact with us. But we couldn't understand why that would be the case since we were on ground they knew extremely well. Previously, they had been very aggressive in their defense of the mountains.

That night, Thieu Ta, clearly frustrated, decided that we had no other good locations to search. We agreed that we had been through every area that we and Vietnamese intelligence suspected as likely locations for the elusive NVA stronghold. Thieu ta said we could spend weeks in the mountains following trails and never find the base if they didn't want it found. Then, he added, "These mountains probably have as many tunnels as an anthill!"

Many of our Vietnamese were fatigued and some had become dehydrated and sick without water, so we obviously were not the fighting unit we needed to be. Thieu Ta decided we would try to make it out of the mountains before the next evening. Because our present location wouldn't permit a resupply, I suggested that we pick a slightly flatter place farther down the mountain. The next morning, to ensure the success of our water resupply, I suggested to Thieu ta that it be brought by U.S. choppers. When he quickly agreed, I called Trung Dung and asked them to make arrangements with the 281st.

While the night was uneventful, it was every bit as sleepless as the two previous nights had been. Just before sunrise the next morning, I thought I detected the aroma of coffee in the air.

Where did they get the water for coffee? I wondered. *Maybe someone found water,* I hoped. But I couldn't imagine why anyone would be cooking anything. That was insane! I was sure that the VC and NVA not only knew we were in the mountains but knew our exact location!

As I got out of my hammock, I noticed the coffee had a peculiar smell about it. Light was trying to open one of the smashed sardine tins he had put in his pack when I walked over to where he was sitting.

"Is that coffee I smell?"

"Yes, Trung Uy." Pointing to a small group of soldiers around a can of Sterno. Then, he added, "Some of those soldiers are making it."

"Where did they find the water?" I asked.

Making a grimace and shaking his head, he said, "They make it with pee-pee Trung uy."

"What?"

"Yes, I watched them do it," he said.

It was disgusting. They had made coffee out of urine. Yes, we had been out of water for a day and a half and my lips were dry and cracked, but I wasn't that thirsty. Nor was Thieu Ta, who ran up and kicked the Sterno can. He yelled at the men who had been responsible for permitting the smell of coffee to drift over the mountainside, then turned to me and said, "We must move out of this area quickly."

A short while later, after hurriedly deciding on our path out of the mountains, our column began to move. We had only been in motion for minutes when one of the Vietnamese medics ran up to Thieu Ta to say that two of the men who had been drinking coffee were very sick. Thieu Ta showed little sympathy and told the medic to tell the men that if they didn't keep up, they would be left behind. Then, barely fifteen minutes later, the medic returned to say that three other men were sick. They had become ill after sucking on plants in a failed attempt to get moisture from them. Thieu Ta sent the same message to those men, and we continued moving toward a resupply site.

It took about two hours to reach the place we had chosen for our resupply effort. While it was still jungle and wasn't level, it was reasonably flat. We would clear it with explosives, those we carried with us to blast the NVA from their base camp. They would now be used to create an LZ in the middle of the jungle. While some of the Vietnamese soldiers chopped small trees, others placed the explosives near the base of larger ones.

I had taken the radio and climbed up on a large boulder near the edge of what would become our LZ to check in with 502. They were coordinating our resupply, and we needed to make sure they were ready. With their confirmation that everything was set, I clipped the radio handset on my web harness and turned to check on progress with the demolitions. Before I completed my turn, an immediate and very abrupt change in my surroundings took place. I was little more than halfway into my turn when the world around me, quite literally—exploded! Boom! Boom!

Several of the soldiers placing the explosive charges had walked past me while I was sitting on the boulder. So, it was difficult to believe that no one realized that I was there. Maybe they thought I had moved or had been given the warning, I have no idea. But they set off the explosive charges attached to the trees—all at once. Chunks of trees, bark, branches, leaves, dirt, and small rocks filled the air. I crumpled and rolled off the large boulder down between two smaller ones, where I waited for the debris to quit falling.

Pulverized pieces of trees and earth fell for several seconds. A large severed branch slammed down within inches of my head and because of its weight was driven far into the ground. Finally, when it sounded as if everything had quit falling, I crawled out from under the trees and branches that had fallen over me. The boulders had kept me from being injured, but I was covered with small pieces of splintered wood and dirt, and my ears were ringing from the explosions.

After shaking my shirt out and letting my head clear, I examined the opening that had been created in the jungle. With all the stumps and fallen tree trunks, it was impossible to accurately pace the diameter of our new LZ. It looked a little tight but appeared large enough for the choppers that would bring our water. We were all ready for a drink, so I made the call and got our resupply started.

Once again, as so many times in the past, it was the 281st AHC that would be responding to our call for support. When the choppers began to arrive over our hole in the jungle, the first pilot on-site expressed some concern that the opening might be a little too tight. Normally, the touchdown area would be cleared to a diameter large enough to ensure several meters of clearance for the chopper blades. And, under best conditions, stumps and remaining pieces of trees should be short enough not to interfere with the landing skids. In this case, the opening appeared very tight and large trees had simply fallen like pick-up sticks, lying in every direction.

With the first chopper now hovering above the opening, it was obvious the fit would indeed be tight. We estimated that, at best, there would be only about a two-to-three-meter clearance from the tip of the chopper blades to the edge of the jungle.

The pilot asked, "What are the chances of making that hole a little larger?"

"I think we've used all our explosives to clear what you're looking at, but let me check," I said.

Thieu ta quickly confirmed that all our explosives had been used to make the LZ its present size. If we had to cut more trees it could take the rest of the day to clear some of the large ones that still surrounded the LZ.

"I'm afraid we've done the best that we can, but if you think it's too small, don't risk it," I told the pilot.

"It looks very close," he said. "Let's check your measurements. We'll try to get you guys a drink of water."

Evidently, the team member at 502 who had arranged our resupply had also shared the urgency of our situation.

The hovering chopper began descending through what now seemed to be a very, very small opening. As it dropped beneath treetop level, its rotor blades clipped leaves and pieces of small branches as it settled down through the cylindrical hole we had created in the jungle. Standing beneath the helicopter was much like being under a huge fan creating hurricane-force winds. My hair and clothing were being violently whipped in the turbulence. Looking up at the slowly descending chopper, I could see the copilot's and crew member's heads moving quickly back and forth as they passed information to the pilot regarding their position inside the opening. Dust and dirt created a sandblaster effect on those of us around the chopper as it neared the ground. Huge trees littered the base of the LZ, but the pilot brought his chopper to rest across two of the fallen tree trunks that were lying parallel to each other. Once his chopper was stable, he motioned through the window that it was safe to retrieve the water cans.

As quickly as we could, we off-loaded the heavy but welcomed containers of water. As soon as all the cans were off, several sick and injured men were on-loaded to be ferried out. Then, directly in front of the chopper, from just inside the tree line, I mouthed a "Thank you" to the pilot and copilot. Both shook their heads, and the copilot offered a familiar thumbs-up as they powered up.

Once again, we were buffeted by churning winds as the chopper ascended back into the sky. Then, one by one, the other 281st helicopters came down inside the small opening to drop off water. As each chopper descended toward the rubble at the base of the LZ, it was like sticking an eggbeater down inside an opening that was barely large enough to accommodate its spinning beaters. After each one touched down, sometimes maintaining a precarious balance across the trunks of the fallen trees, we unloaded the water as quickly and carefully as possible. Despite our dire need for the resupply, I was relieved when the last chopper cleared the top of the trees safely on its way out.

While we were distributing the much-needed water, it occurred to me that any one of the helicopters could have beaten its occupants to death if unbalanced by a branch falling through the rotor blades. The feat that each pilot and crew dared and successfully completed was fraught with countless dangers. I was amazed that they had actually attempted a landing when it would have been so easy and understandable for any one of them to say, "The opening is too small. We can't make it in safely."

Fortunately for us and many, many others in Vietnam, helicopter pilots and crews had earned their "God's Own Lunatics" tag by doing more than they had to do and by going where they didn't have to go.

As if another example were necessary, another chopper pilot I know was on a routine mission when he overheard a call for a medevac from one of our Special Forces LRP (long-range patrol) units. When he heard that no medevac choppers were available, he responded to the call and immediately diverted to the emergency. Even though he didn't have a medic on board, he knew the wounded men would have a better chance with him than if they had to lie on the ground and wait for a medevac that might be hours away from arriving.

The situation he encountered was very similar to ours. The unit had to create a landing zone in the jungle. After arriving and settling into the opening, the men were loaded onto his chopper. In attempting to clear the trees, he realized he had too much weight and couldn't rise above them. The obvious answer was to leave someone behind. But, for this pilot, that wasn't even a remote consideration. After trying once again to clear the trees, he was only able to get within just feet of making it out. Dropping back into the jungle, he landed momentarily as he studied trees around the LZ.

"Don't be scared by what I'm about to do," he told his copilot. "I've done it before."

Powering up once again, he rose up through the opening. Then, as if using a lawn tool, he began trimming the tops out of the trees with the chopper's blades. When the opening seemed right, he settled back to the ground. Then, with his engine straining at full power, he ascended one more time and carefully guided his chopper through the stubble of the remaining treetops. Finally—they were clear!

This man did what he knew how to do and what he felt he needed to do, not for himself, but for the benefit of others. He could have easily landed and said, "Some of you have to get off. I can't get all of us out." But that isn't what this pilot chose to do. He didn't take the easy way out; neither did the pilots and crews who brought us water and rescued our sick and injured men there on the mountain. The most important observation I can make about these men is that they were Americans—simply being American.

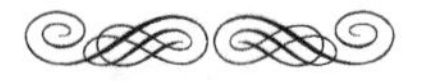

With bellies and canteens once again filled, we worked our way down the rugged northeast side of the mountains. Because of the weak condition of many of the Vietnamese soldiers, our movement out of the mountains was far slower than it had been when we entered. It was nearly dusk by the time we reached the river where boats were waiting to pick us up.

As we skimmed along the river's quiet, mirror-smooth surface, I looked at the reflection of the soldiers in the boat around me. Noticing my own, it appeared slightly weary and a bit dirty. Then, as my gaze moved to the reflection of the mountains and onto the mountains themselves, it occurred to me that I had returned from the Dong Bo tired and dirty—but alive. *Surely, the chaplain's prayer must have been a good one*, I thought, remembering the 5th Group chaplain's promise to say a special prayer for me and our unit's safe return.

Interesting, but that was the first time since stepping foot on the mountain complex that I was reminded of my initial concern about surviving the mission. However, within days, it would be strangely surprising to discover just how close I had come to being killed in the Dong Bo. Then, in little more than a month, everyone in the Nha Trang area would be reminded of just how deadly the mountains really were.

The reminder would occur when the Vietnamese High Command finally agreed to the joint allied operation I had outlined for General Peers. Using fresh intelligence, the operation would once more attempt to locate and attack the Dong Bo base camp of the infamous North Vietnamese Army Regiment 18B. The operation would involve Vietnamese, American, and Korean units. The Vietnamese would provide a point unit to locate the base camp. Americans would provide advisory and air support with the Koreans White Horse Division providing the main attack element of approximately three thousand men.

The point unit would consist of Vietnamese troops from Trung Dung accompanied by members of A-502's Blue Bandit advisory team. My friend, Lieutenant Bill Phalen, would serve as the unit's senior American adviser.

Bill's point unit would be much smaller than ours had been so that it could move more swiftly and with a bit more stealth.

Acting on our newly acquired information, Bill and his point unit entered the mountain complex and quickly located an entrance to the huge base camp, but with disastrous results. The team sustained heavy casualties.

Even though he believed he and his unit were being sent on a suicide mission, Bill did what every other professional soldier in Vietnam did. He took his orders and carried out his mission.

It was common knowledge among Nha Trang military units that any foray into the Dong Bo Mountains was potentially dangerous and could cost one's life. While our unit had been extremely lucky, Bill's wasn't nearly as fortunate. Upon locating the base camp, a firefight erupted and lasted for torturous hours. During the battle, Bill was blown several meters down the side of the mountain by an exploding grenade. While stunned and wounded, he survived the blast that could have easily killed him. However, six of his Vietnamese soldiers were killed, and another seventeen were seriously wounded.

Having successfully located the enemy base camp, Bill and his CIDG Company 555 disengaged, carrying their dead and wounded with them down to the base of the mountains. There, they encountered troops from the Korean 100th White Horse Division who were waiting and more than ready to attack.

In preparation for the Korean attack, Air Force C-130 aircraft bombed the mountain complex where Phalen's unit discovered the well-camouflaged enemy base camp. After the bombing, the Koreans quickly moved into position and surrounded the portion of the mountain where Bill's unit had located the base camp. In a heavily supported massive assault, they cleared it from bottom to top and, quite literally—took no prisoners.

Intelligence gathered during the Korean operation revealed that the enemy base camp was far more than myth or legend. It was very real. Information supplied by the Koreans confirmed that the mountain complex had been occupied by the North Vietnamese Army's 18B Regiment. The regiment comprised the 7th, 8th, and 9th Battalions, the Dien Khanh NVA District Force, and one sapper (demolition) company. The regiment even had a finance unit and a makeshift hospital in the multi-cave headquarters that Thieu ta believed were there. Captured documents also indicated that, while assigned to the mountain unit, the 7th Battalion was actually in Cambodia on R&R (rest & recuperation) when the Koreans attacked.

Whatever the actual disposition of enemy units in the Dong Bo Mountains at the time of the attack, the 18B Regiment was functionally destroyed. While the Koreans suffered casualties of their own, they reported more than seven hundred NVA and VC killed, with none being reported as wounded—or taken prisoner.

The Korean mission, first suggested by A-502, was extremely successful. Besides destroying the enemy headquarters, it revealed the true size and makeup of the force that had been entrenched in the mountain stronghold since the days of the Viet Minh. It also explained why the Dong Bo Mountains had been such a dangerous place to go.

Just as in any other war, American soldiers in Vietnam went where they were ordered to go, regardless of any danger they might face, just as Bill Phalen and his unit had done. Then, there were others, such as the pilots and crew members who brought us water and carried out our injured, who rather than acting simply on orders seemed to rely on some higher and deeper calling to complete their mission.

The Intruders

Vietnamese H-34 Helicopter

These were the big lumbering choppers that carried us high on the side of the Dong Bo Mountains. They are also the ones from which I parachuted.

They Often Went Where They Shouldn't

This is a 281st re-supply of our Dong Bo outpost sometime after our mission, but it looks very similar to our water re-supply. The key difference is that our opening was totally surrounded by trees as thick as those opposite this helicopter.

The View from High in the Dong Bo Mountains

This is a view of the Nha Trang Valley and I took the picture from the rock outcropping in the Dong Bo Mountains where we were waiting to medevac Major Dubovick to the 8th Army Field Hospital.

The Mountains Where Death Lived

As a part of the Korean assault of the Dong Bo Mountains, C-130 aircraft flew low over the mountains and crew members shoved bombs off the tailgate that hit and exploded into huge orange fireballs—the beginning of the end.

Chapter 35

Life Spared

WHILE MANY YEARS HAVE come and gone since American soldiers served in Vietnam, nearly everyone who was there can cite one or more occurrences that remain vivid in memory. The following is an account of such an event that causes me to simply shake my head when reminded of the episode.

One morning not long after we returned from our patrol through the Dong Bo Mountains, I was on my way over to visit Thieu Ta regarding an upcoming briefing we were scheduled to present to a group of visiting officials. About halfway up the steps to Thieu Ta's, I heard a commotion coming from near the Vietnamese radio room. Backing down the steps, I walked around the corner to see what was happening. Everything had grown quiet as I approached the doorway, but that changed shortly after I entered the room.

The Vietnamese were interrogating another VC suspect they had captured near the base of the Dong Bo the night before. They had begun to threaten him with the possibility of a death sentence if found guilty of supporting the NVA, which is what caused all the commotion. The Vietnamese were yelling at the suspect and he was screaming, claiming that he had only helped the NVA by carrying food and supplies to drop-off points in the mountains but had never fought for them.

After being in the room long enough for him to get a good look at me, the VC suspect pointed at me and began chattering frantically in Vietnamese. He was almost yelling again. I couldn't understand what he was saying but knew I was somehow involved in whatever it was. There was considerable back-and-forth conversation between the suspect and interrogator before the following story was related to me.

This man, along with two or three of his comrades and one or two armed NVA guides, were on a routine delivery trip into the Dong Bo at the same time we were there. While carrying supplies up the mountain, they detected our point unit. Fearing discovery themselves, the men quickly hid in the rocks and thick jungle growth. As we passed by, one of the NVA soldiers noticed me in the slow-moving column. Recognizing me as an American, he leveled his AK-47 rifle on me and was preparing to open fire. Killing an American, any American, would have brought him special recognition at the base camp. In many cases, a financial reward would also accompany that recognition.

The suspect being interrogated quickly pointed out that he had saved my life by keeping the soldier from pulling the trigger. However, then as now, he was likely trying to save his own life as well. The interrogator said that the suspect claimed he argued with the soldier and told him that if he fired, they would probably all be killed. So, it was simply the fear of being killed by return fire from the men around me that kept the NVA soldier from killing me.

After hearing the tale repeated by the interrogator, I was a little skeptical. I'm reasonably sure it showed in my expression, but the old Vietnamese sergeant who was conducting the questioning seemed convinced the man's story had merit. He had been on the mountain mission with us and expressed his belief in what the prisoner had just said.

"No, I think he is true, Trung Uy. He says to me the day and the place.

The day is true, and I think also is true the place." While the interrogator's English wasn't clear, the implication of what he had conveyed was perfectly clear.

In the still of the darkened interrogation room, which had fallen quiet, I considered the old sergeant's assertion. *If the story is true*, I thought, *I wonder how much closer you can come to the event that actually claims your life.* Then I pondered the enigma of who lives and who dies in war, who comes home and who doesn't, and why.

During the Vietnam War, more than fifty-eight thousand Americans would meet a fate I had escaped. Each of those names appears on the Vietnam Veteran's Memorial Wall in Washington, D.C.

Only days earlier, I had been amazed when two of our team members had survived a blazing close-quarter firefight. That incident began when Colonel Baer, Walt Three Zero, was flying an observation mission in support of one of our Vietnamese CIDG units. Sergeant Richard Bardsley and Sergeant John Key were the American advisers to the unit. They were returning from a three-day patrol and were coming down mountain foothills into a flat area divided by a raised railroad berm. Colonel Baer, in his O-1 Bird-dog aircraft, was almost directly overhead when he radioed Sergeant Bardsley with a question.

"Blue Bandit Three Five, this is Walt Three Zero. Over."

"Roger, Walt Three Zero, this is Bandit Three-Five. Go ahead."

"Roger, Three-Five. Have you got troops on both sides of the railroad tracks? Over."

"Walt, Bandit Three-Five. No, there shouldn't be anyone on the other side, but I'll check it out. Over."

With that, Sergeants Bardsley and Key headed for the railroad tracks. As the two started up their side of the berm, the men Baer had seen were coming up the other side. When Bardsley and Key reached the top of the berm, they were suddenly face-to-face with members of an NVA enemy unit. A fierce firefight immediately ensued at near-point-blank range. Each unit fired at the other, and both followed up by throwing grenades. During the exchange of munitions, the Americans either dove for cover or were knocked to the ground by one of the exploding grenades.

When the dust cloud created by the grenades had settled and calm was restored, the two Americans and their Montagnard radioman were the only ones standing. A heavy rapid-fire machine gun was lying on the ground next to one of the dead NVA soldiers. It had a bullet hole, put there by Sergeant Bardsley, directly through the center of its housing. The weapon was taken as a trophy from the battle and placed in our team house where it also served as a constant reminder of our tenuous situation as soldiers. It wasn't always the Americans who were left standing.

While he survived what amounted to nothing short of a Western-style shootout, Sergeant Bardsley didn't escape the encounter uninjured. During the firefight, his Montagnard radioman had taken cover next to him near the top of the railroad berm. In an attempt to return fire quickly, the radioman simply stuck his M2 carbine up over his head and started pulling the trigger, firing as fast as he could. Unfortunately, while pointed in the right direction, the muzzle of his carbine was only two or three inches from the steel railroad track. So, every time he fired, his rounds hit the track and splintered into multiple pieces, which then ricocheted all around him and the two Americans. Sergeant Bardsley had to have several pieces of that ricocheting shrapnel removed from his back and shoulder. He was extremely fortunate that he hadn't been hit in the head or hit by a larger piece of the exploding projectiles, for how paradoxical if he were killed by one of his own men.

Certainly, this would have been an unfortunate, but not uncommon folly of war—further complicating my consideration of the enigma of who lives, who dies, and why.

Once, I was reminded of my experience in the Dong Bo Mountains and, in particular, the subsequent incident in the interrogation room. I imagined myself in the NVA soldier's gunsight and felt his finger as he applied pressure to the trigger. For whatever reason, my life was spared that day, and I am very grateful that it was. That incident and the many others that I had survived gave me tremendous respect and appreciation for life—all life.

Special Forces Shoulder Patch

This is the patch that was stitched onto the shoulder of my uniform when I first arrived at Fort Bragg—it would be worn until my service and experiences with Special Forces were complete.

The gold and teal Special Forces patch is worn by members of Special Forces units around the world. The arrowhead shape represents the craft and stealth of the Indians, America's first warriors. An upturned dagger represents the unconventional warfare missions of Special Forces. Three lightning bolts represent blinding speed and strength, and the three methods of infiltration – land, sea, and air. The gold represents constancy and inspiration, and the background of teal blue represents the Special Forces' encompassing of all types of assignments, land, sea, or air—anytime, anywhere.

It must be confessed that knowing this patch was on my shoulder and that much was expected of me—helped me rise to face many difficult challenges.

The Assault of Hon Tre Island

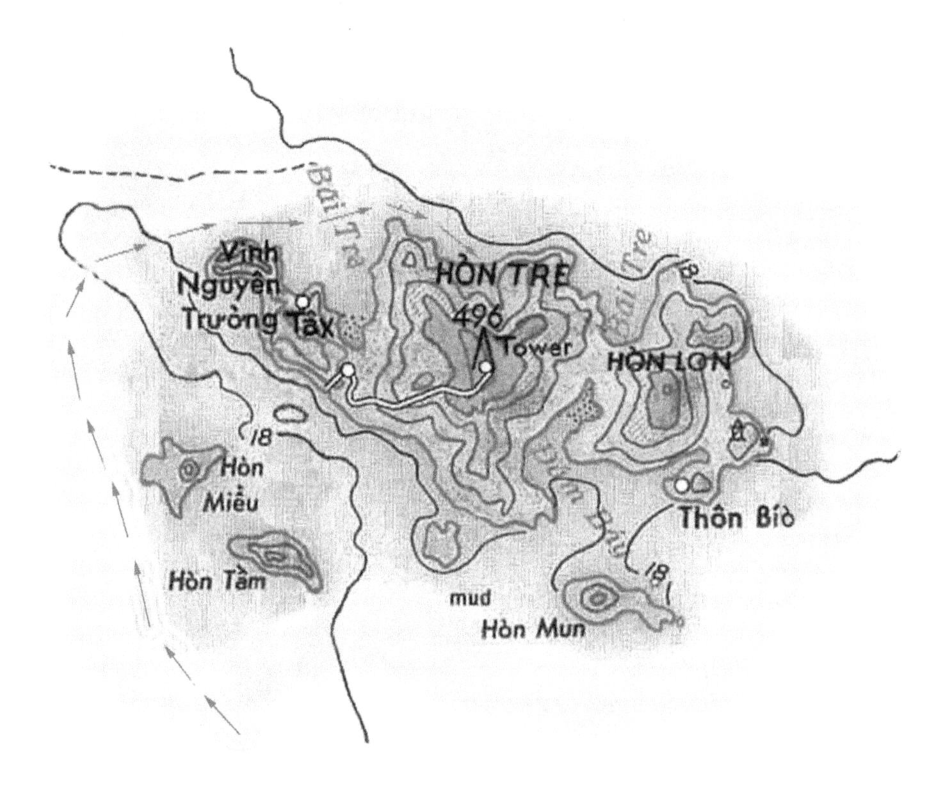

In the next chapter, you will read about an unusual operation A-502 was given after an enemy patrol was sighted on Hon Tre Island. Special Forces don't usually train to make an amphibious assault. Those missions typically fall to our very capable brothers in the Marine Corps.

However, in the Special Forces spirit of "Anytime—Anywhere," 502 quickly accepted the unique mission challenge. The map above is provided so that you can see the route our rapid response team took to the island.

CHAPTER 36

Still Alive

EARLY ONE EVENING, DURING the days when my tour of duty was drawing to a close, I took a cold bottle of Coke and walked to the west wall of the fort. At the top, I created a chair of sandbags and sat, just wanting to watch the sunset alone. If I were back in Pensacola and watching the sunset, you could bet a great deal of money and win—that I wouldn't be alone.

Slowly, as I watched, the sun tucked itself into the distant mountains of Southeast Asia. The bluish-purple mountains stood in silhouette against the fading yellow-orange glow of the setting sun, everything was deceptively peaceful. Even though I had been there for many months and witnessed the often-tragic results of its existence, it was sometimes still difficult to believe that a war could exist in such a setting. But it did and I knew it.

Considering my time with A-502, it had been both demanding and challenging, but I wouldn't have asked to be any other place. My job was certainly never dull and it had introduced me to some amazing people.

In my role as 502's S2 and S3, I worked with nearly every branch of Uncle Sam's military, including the, sometimes overlooked, Coast Guard. And, as I discovered on another of many memorable days, they were as courageous as any unit I worked with.

In the middle of the night, just a couple of weeks earlier, one of the technicians working at the radar station on Hon Tre Island reported seeing an enemy patrol of 9-10 men.

During the Vietnam War, Hon Tre was the site of an important radio tower and radar installation. The importance of the radar facility made it vulnerable to probes or attacks by enemy units attempting to destroy or damage the station.

A-502's responsibilities did not end at the sea. For that reason, whenever the island was threatened, it was the team's responsibility to respond. So, on the night the probe was detected, an emergency message was immediately sent to 5th Group Headquarters. In turn, they quickly requested a rapid response team from A-502.

Knowing Hon Tre Island, having flown over it a couple of times during my many observation missions, I decided to serve as the responding unit's senior American adviser. And that was where I encountered the U.S. Coast Guard, they would provide cover for our response.

Before dawn, a CIDG platoon, with me and another American as advisers, loaded onto an amphibious assault craft in Nha Trang and headed east for Hon Tre. In case the enemy patrol could see us, I suggested that we head north, circle around the island, and land on the eastern shore. My Vietnamese counterpart agreed, so that's what we were going to do. The Coast Guard would first provide escort, then cover when we landed.

Upon approach to Hon Tre, the Coast Guard and our landing craft took the path followed by routine patrol boats. However, on the east side of the island, both craft abruptly turned directly toward the beach. At the last minute, the Coast Guard pulled out of the way when the water shallowed, and we continued ahead. Then, the ramp was dropped when we were in about two and a half or three feet of water. Since they hadn't done this before, the Vietnamese troops hesitated. I believe they thought we were going all the way to the beach, so I yelled, "Go!" They immediately jumped into the water and headed for the beach and I was in the water with them.

As our assault team waded through the crystal-clear water that surrounded Hon Tre, I held my M-16 over my head and closely scanned the hills and cliffs that were the island. I looked for movement and hoped I wouldn't see the bright orange flash of enemy weapons. We were sitting ducks and very easy targets for any enemy gunners on the higher ground. Hopefully, our diversionary landing had provided us with some measure of surprise.

With our team in the water, the landing craft had pulled away and the Coast Guard boat was covering us. If the enemy had seen us and decided to take potshots at us, they would have quickly been engaged by Coast Guard gunners. Knowing that gave me some comfort but, still—I couldn't believe we were doing what we were doing. I was used to being in the jungle, not wading ashore. But I was also used to being prepared for—anything.

That day gave me a greater respect for our country's Marine Corps troops who had, throughout military history, routinely, and on countless occasions, exposed themselves as we were that morning.

When I glanced back at the Coast Guard boat, I was surprised to see it so close. Having grown up in Florida and knowing something about boats and the depth of the water required to keep them afloat, I was surprised they hadn't already run aground. And they were close enough to shore that they could have easily received enemy fire. In water shallow enough that the boat propellers were churning up big clouds of sand, they were a much bigger and better target. As I turned back toward the beach, it was my opinion that they were offering themselves as a target to protect us.

Once on shore, we climbed the hills of Hon Tre and began our search. We crisscrossed the island looking for the enemy patrol, but an all-day search failed to locate the enemy unit. I believe that when the unit was first sighted, it was on its way off the island and not onto it. It seemed clear to me that they were gone long before we arrived because the Coast Guard had ringed the island and we had searched every square meter of it.

While we hadn't encountered the enemy patrol, the operation demonstrated A-502's ability to immediately mount an operation in response to even the most unusual situations. And, as was often the case, it was supported by an array of American resources. This time it was the U.S. Coast Guard, who had selflessly exposed themselves to danger and hovered over us when we were wading ashore and extremely vulnerable.

The Coast Guard, the Air Force, the men of the 281st, the artillerymen, Colonel Baer, Major Mielke, doctors and nurses, the female reporters, the Donut Dollies of the Red Cross, and my teammates—just a few of the many people I encountered while serving my country. A complete list of the noteworthy units and individuals with whom I worked and served during my time in Vietnam would require pages. And, even then, I would surely overlook one or more of those who had inspired me to write this book. The list would certainly begin with the three young Marines I had watched on television nearly three years earlier. It was watching their courage under fire that had compelled me to serve. I'm not sure where the list would have ended, maybe with my friend Ngoc.

The sunset had been replaced in the western sky by graduated colors of dark blues and purples that were beginning to twinkle with the first light of evening stars. My Coke bottle was empty and I was getting hungry, so I left my sandbag chair and started for the team house. After dinner, I would go say goodbye to Thieu ta.

As I walked to the team-house and prepared to leave Vietnam and return home, it occurred to me that the very best thing about my time there must surely be the fact that—I was still alive.

CHAPTER 37

Saying Goodbye

ABOUT TO LEAVE VIETNAM, I wanted to say goodbye to Thieu ta. By that time, we had become very close, almost like brothers. While I would still see him and there would be an "official" goodbye, I wanted this one to be personal. So, after dinner, I walked over to his quarters and found him where I often had, in a bench chair on a small patio just outside his quarters with a beer in his hand.

Thieu ta saw me coming, "Chau, Trung uy."

Even though close, I always greeted him respectfully, "Chau, Thieu. How are you this evening?"

"I am very good now. Come up and have a beer with me."

Over the next hour or so, Ngoc and I sat and shared a couple more beers while talking and, occasionally, laughing about some of the many experiences we had shared. Then, at some point, he asked me what I was going to do when I got home. I told him that I was already enrolled for my next semester in college and planned on finishing a degree in Finance while joining my Dad in the family jewelry business. When I told him that working in the jewelry business beat being shot at, he laughed one of his Ngoc belly laughs—I was going to miss him.

We talked some more, then Ngoc became quiet for a while as if contemplative, so I didn't interrupt the silence. Then, he turned and looked me directly in the eyes as if he were about to say something important. When he spoke next, he did something he had never done in all the time that I had known him. He used my first name. "Tom, he said, "I want to thank you for coming to my country and helping me fight this war." Then, he extended his hand.

I was touched and very much appreciated Ngoc's gesture, but no thanks were necessary. Responding to his remark as we shook hands, "You're welcome Thieu ta. I am very, very glad I came. As you know, I will go home with the belief that I accomplished something meaningful while I was here. And you made that possible, so thank *you* for both your confidence and your support."

TO YOU, MY READER—some explanation may be necessary at this point. If you remember that, more than once, I mentioned my hope of doing "something meaningful" while in Vietnam, then, after reading the paragraph above, you may be asking yourself if you missed something. *When did the something meaningful happen and what was it?* would be perfectly logical thoughts.

Well, here's an explanation. As mentioned in the "Introduction" to this book, after finishing the manuscript for the second edition, the word count and page count were so high that a very experienced publisher told me that what I had written was two books, not one. He suggested the single book be divided into two separate publications. You have nearly finished the first of those two books, *Along the Way*.

As mentioned in the Introduction, the second book is titled *Rescue in the Valley of the Tigers,* and it was originally PART II of the first edition. The new book describes in greater detail when the *something good* happened and what it was. The story of the *Rescue in the Valley of the Tigers* made national news, was reported on the first page of at least one major newspaper, and was reported on the CBS Evening News with Walter Cronkite. If you would like to see that report as a preview of the book that follows this one, you can go to YouTube and type *Rescue in the Valley of the Tigers*. There will be more than one video you can watch.

To finish this book, my purpose for writing the first edition was to shed light on the selfless deeds and courage I witnessed while serving as a military adviser in Vietnam. At the same time, by telling my stories, I intended to encourage others to tell theirs. The same purpose and intention have continued with this edition. If you are one with a story of service to our country, I encourage you to tell it.

When I got up to leave Thieu ta after our thank yous and goodbyes, I reached in my pocket and pulled out a folded piece of paper. It contained my parent's home address and phone number. I handed it to Ngoc and said, "If you ever get to the States, my parents will know how to reach me. I hope you will call me."

We shook hands and as we did, I said, "We had a lot of close calls Thieu ta, but we survived."

Ngoc smiled big, then as he was fond of reminding me, just as he had the first day we met, he waved his finger and said, "Day not over yet, Trung uy."

My reasons for going to Vietnam were uncomplicated. I went of my own volition, perhaps because of the way I was raised. It was something I felt compelled to do for myself and my country. However, as you have read, there were many who inspired and supported me—along the way.

Thieu ta Ngoc's Quarters

Ngoc and I spent innumerable hours together on that small bench in the upper left of the picture discussing missions, military strategy, our families, and the things of life. It was during those times—that we became friends.

Epilogue

MY TOUR OF DUTY COMPLETE, I and my duffle bag were once again on the asphalt runway at the Nha Trang Air Base. This time, I was waiting for the helicopter shuttle that would ferry me back to Cam Ranh Bay, where I would board my flight home to the United States. Since sitting in that very spot nearly a year earlier, much had happened. My time in Vietnam had been a unique life experience and I was going to leave with many things to ponder and for which to be thankful. Most importantly, I had survived the experience.

Just as I noticed the incoming helicopter, an Air Force airman walked out to the edge of the runway where I was sitting and pointed toward the inbound chopper.

"Lieutenant, that's your shuttle on approach. Have a good trip home."

"Great. Thank you."

A collective cheer arose as the wheels of the big transport jet lifted off the runway in Cam Ranh Bay. Everyone on board seemed very happy, some euphoric, to be headed back to the United States. As we turned east out over the South China Sea, I looked back to watch the Vietnam coastline drift into the distance. A year in the place that I first imagined to be a tropical paradise left me filled with many impressions, both good and bad. Turning to look ahead along the way home, I began to think about my arrival back in Pensacola. My homecoming would be quiet—very different from the one my family had planned for me.

Near the end of my time overseas, my mother often wrote about the plans that she and my Dad were making for my homecoming. They had arranged for a band from Rosie O'Grady's, one of the local nightspots, to welcome me at the airport. I, however, didn't want a band or any other fanfare at my homecoming. There was now too much controversy over our country's involvement in Vietnam. And, I didn't need or want a parade. I had volunteered to go where I went and do what I did. All I wanted or needed was to see the faces of my family and have a quiet trip home from the airport. For those reasons, I hadn't told my parents when I would be returning, so they had no way of knowing that I was already—on my way.

After a very long flight back to the West Coast of the United States, another long coast-to-coast flight loomed ahead of me. After a plane change in St. Louis, we finally turned south. It was late afternoon when we landed in Birmingham, Alabama. We were scheduled to be on the ground just long enough to drop off and pick up passengers. So, anyone who was continuing to Pensacola and beyond was asked to stay on board. When we took off again, the flight to Pensacola would take only about 30 minutes.

Knowing my mother would barely have time to get to the airport in Pensacola before I did, let alone organize a reception, I thought my family should probably know that I was near. Going to the front of the plane, I introduced myself to a flight attendant and told her that I needed off for just a few minutes to call home and I explained why. Before she could respond, a voice from the cockpit said, "Go ahead, Lieutenant, we'll wait for you. Just make it as quick as you can." One of the pilots had seen me board the plane and heard me speaking to the flight attendant.

When my mother answered the phone at home, I asked, "Do you have a place for a tired soldier to lie down?"

Taken by surprise, her voice began to quiver, "Oh, my God. Is that you, Tom? You sound so close. Where are you?"

"Birmingham," I said.

"Oh, thank God," she sighed. "But we wanted to do something special for you." Then, she started to cry.

"Mom, I have to go. The plane is ready to leave. I'll be home in about forty-five minutes to an hour. Will you call Dad and let him know I'm coming home?"

"Yes. Are you all in one piece?" she asked with a mother's concerned voice.

"Yes, I'm fine. Mom, I have to go now. I love you."

"I love you, too. I'm so glad to get you back from that terrible place."

About forty-five minutes later, the propeller-driven Eastern Airlines Silver Falcon circled in over Pensacola Bay and touched down on the airport runway. As we taxied to the terminal, I could see my mother and sister, Polly, at the gate. I had barely cleared the bottom of the steps before being rushed and smothered in their embraces—I was home!

After collecting my bags, we went to see my father at work. He was in the back of our family business and had his back to me when I walked through the front door. When he heard the door, he turned, and in an instant, his face lit up. He beamed with a huge smile and quickly surrounded me with a bearhug.

Such was my homecoming—the only one I needed or wanted.

During the first few days after my return to the United States, I was surprised by the degree of anger being expressed over the Vietnam War. The true nature of the descent hadn't been this clear to me before I came home. I read the paper every day and watched the evening news every night. The news broadcasts were often painful to watch. There seemed to be protests everywhere, sometimes with rioting and fighting in the streets. For me, the occurrences were truly very sad.

As I watched and listened to various reports on the Vietnam protests, I found the abuse leveled at military personnel difficult to believe. When I heard some of the terrible monikers shouted at Vietnam soldiers and veterans, my heart sank and my stomach turned. I now understood why my mother was so relieved to have me home.

Nearly every time after reading, watching, or listening to news reports, I found myself dealing with feelings and emotions that were sometimes contradictory. Even though having served in the military, I began to understand the civilian anger and frustration with the government's conduct of the war. The more I read and the more time passed, the more I felt that the American men and women serving in Vietnam weren't going to be allowed to win the war.

On the day the South Vietnam government collapsed and Saigon finally fell in 1975, I watched all of the television coverage. By that time, all I could do was shake my head. *This can't happen again,* I thought. To me, it was clear that those in government responsible for directing the war had made very serious mistakes. It was and is my belief that we should never become involved in war if not prepared to see the battle to a victorious conclusion.

Whenever I think of those who didn't make it home from the war lost in Vietnam, I feel sincere regret for the loss of so many lives. I also regret the life-altering physical injuries and mental scars brought home by many of those who survived the Vietnam experience.

It was not only those who served who were affected by what occurred in Southeast Asia. When the Vietnam War ended, it was obvious to me, as to most Americans, that we as a country and a people had suffered very deep wounds. And, healing those wounds would take a very long time. But I would like to believe that along with our wounds there also came learning. And, there were certainly lessons to learn. For me, the single most important one was that those who commit our military to combat should do so with far greater prudence and a commitment to winning.

Because I don't want their loss or injuries to seem meaningless, I have convinced myself that those who didn't make it home, or those who were seriously wounded, didn't give their lives or suffer their wounds in vain. I feel certain that what happened in Vietnam has given and will continue to give our leaders a good reason to think more carefully before committing other brave men and women to war.

While Vietnam remains a controversial topic and our involvement there may have been ill-conceived, there is no doubt in my mind about my reasons for serving our country. I am still at peace and perfectly comfortable that my decision to serve was the correct one for me. And, if I had it all to do over— I would do it again.

The stories shared here about time spent in Vietnam are not as remarkable as some of those yet to be told. There are thousands of accounts that, if told, would demonstrate the way young men and women served and represented their country under difficult circumstances. This book is offered as encouragement to others to tell their stories of dedication and patriotism before they are gone. By so doing, our country and the families of those who served in Vietnam will know that the great majority did so with honor while attempting to deliver the gift of freedom.

The chance to meet and serve with American men and women, such as those I have described—was a very special privilege.

The American and South Vietnamese Flags

These are the two flags under which I and other Americans served our tours of duty.

AUTHOR'S FINAL NOTES

When I went to say goodbye to him before returning home, Ngoc offered his hand and gripped mine firmly, but warmly. Then, looking intently into my eyes—he thanked me for serving in his country.

Ngoc Nguyen, "Thieu ta," was the first and only person to thank me for my service for many years. Later, it became custom for Vietnam veterans to thank each other for their service and offer a "Welcome home!" Eventually, thoughtful and appreciative American civilians also took up the practice. Since I had volunteered for service in Southeast Asia, I never really expected or required thanks from anyone. Nonetheless, I must quickly add that each of the many, many times I have been thanked for my service or welcomed home, I felt warm appreciation and a sense of pride.

Still, when I think of all the many very kind gestures of thanks offered to me, Ngoc's is the one that stands above the rest and is the most important. For me—his was enough. My presence had meant something to someone.

Sadly, my friend Ngoc died on February 5, 2011, in Houston, Texas. Ironically, the man who fought so fiercely for the freedom of South Vietnam was born in Son Tay, a very well-known suburb of—Hanoi, North Vietnam.

I miss my friend Ngoc and will never forget him.

Tom — “Trung uy”

Adviser

Author

THEN

NOW

Ngoc — “Thieu ta”

Commander

Lifetime Friend

More than fifty years have passed since my friend Ngoc and I were last together on his small porch at Trai Trung Dung, but I am still very thankful for the time we shared. Ngoc made it possible for me to leave Vietnam feeling that I had accomplished—something good. Years later, I could return the favor.

Lifetime Friends — Ngoc and Kim Nguyen

Ngoc, Kim, and I shared many lunches and dinners during my time at Trung Dung. Here, I had been out on ambush the night before and arrived at lunch after it started. When he saw me coming, Ngoc called to me, "Trung uy, come and please here . . . I saved you a place next to Kim." That was a seat of honor.

The Final Farewell

One of Ngoc's last pictures was in uniform with the flag behind him of the country he had fought to free, a country he still remembered and loved very much. And, that doesn't surprise me—I am proud to have written about him.

With Honors

When he died in 2011, Ngoc was buried with the full Vietnamese honors, which he had earned and to which was entitled. I still miss my friend like a brother.

About the Author

Thomas A. (Tom) Ross was raised in Pensacola, Florida where he lived and attended college until he enlisted in the U.S. Army. Tom's commitment to both community and country was apparent at a young age when he earned the rank of Eagle Scout in the Boy Scouts of America.

In early 1966, Tom enlisted in the U.S. Army and was commissioned a 2nd Lieutenant after attending Infantry OCS. He immediately applied to and was accepted for training with the Army's Special Forces, the unit also known as the "Green Berets." After completing an intense course of unconventional warfare training, he was assigned as the Intelligence Officer of Company B, 3rd Special Forces, stationed at Fort Bragg, North Carolina.

After a year of focused training, Tom was assigned as the Intelligence and Operations Officer of Detachment A-502, 5th Special Forces in Vietnam.

During his time as a military adviser, he was privileged to witness many courageous and selfless deeds performed by both American men and women.

After returning home in late 1968, Tom joined his family's custom-design jewelry firm. Then, after serving as the company's General Manager for several years, he sought the challenge of a larger arena with family blessings.

As his career evolved, Tom was recruited to and served as an executive with two internationally recognized jewelry companies. At one of these companies, he hosted a "Breakfast at Tiffany's" with Audrey Hepburn as the honored guest. Tom sipped tea and enjoyed warm pastries with Ms. Hepburn, a very different environment than the jungles of Southeast Asia.

Committed to the Atlanta community, Tom was recognized for his community service when he was presented the "Georgia Outstanding Citizen" award by the Georgia Secretary of State and, later, the "Florence McDonald People of Vision" award for his dedication to the community.

In support of those who have served and are serving our country today, Tom has become a "Life" member of several veterans or military support organizations.

In 1999, Tom and his wife, Amy, reestablish their family's jewelry firm, The Ross Jewelry Company, in the Buckhead area of Atlanta. Today, they live in Peachtree Corners, a suburb of Atlanta, Georgia.

Peachtree Corners, Georgia . . . My Hometown

Veterans Monument

I am very proud to live in the community that created this beautiful monument to honor all veterans of every service branch for their service to our country, its citizens, and to the preservation of freedom throughout the world . . . past, present, and future.

As long as there are wars, there will be courageous American men and women who will step forward to protect and defend us and our country.

The Men of Special Forces Detachment A-502

MEMBERS ARE LISTED BY THE YEAR THEY JOINED THE TEAM

1964
Day, Kenneth J.
Chastain, Joyce F.
Combs, Harold J.
Fields, Arthur
Foxworth, Louis G.
Grabey, Stanley G.
Hobby, Oscar L.
Johnston, James M.
Miner, Louis F.
Spradlin, Earnest J.
Wilson, Carl L.
Wilson, Gerry W.

1965
Batteford, Frank P. Jr.
Berg, Charles L.
Chestnut, John
Cincotti, Joseph G.
Foshee, Edgar E. Jr.
Grady, Clyde E. Jr.
Hughes, James E.
Mallare, Gerald E.
McClellan, Henry
Moore, George R.
Peters, Larry J.
Rice, Homer L.
Schreiber, Robert D.
Smeltzer, William L.
Switney, Robert
Sweeney, Robert T.
Vasquez, Jose E.
Watson, Roger

1966
Chaplin, Robert W Sr.
Charest, Robert A.
Chase, James E. Jr.
Clow, James L.
Deason, Robert L.
Gumper, Victor W.
Johnson, Dean B.
Johnston, Charles W.
Jordon, Richard W.
McKitrick, Michael L.
McMenamy, Charles W.
Rouse, Glenn R.
Salsman, Berney
Shreck, Raymond D.
Shriver, Jerry
Sturm, Henry B.
Tocci, Mark A.
Young, James W.

1967
Anderson, Roger L.
Andree, Martin E.
Arrants, Jerry C.
Ballou, Richard D.
Bardsley, Richard W. Jr.
Barnes, James M.
Blake, John H. III
Lane, William K. Jr.
Lavaud, Jean P.
Brooks
Castillo, John J.
Daly, John J.
Everett, James L.
Freedman, Lawrence
Geronime, John F. II
Gilmore, Gordon S.
Goff, Robert E. Jr.
Goodwin, Donald J.
Herbert, John
Homitz, Ronald D.
Jackson, Hugh
Jarvies, James Y.
Kentopp, James M.
Key, John C.
King, Roy
Koch, Paul L.
Lee, Wilbur L.
Madera, Edward
Miller, James H. Jr.
Morace, Albert T. Jr.
Munoz, Ferdinand
Noe, Frank R.
Puckett, Wayne R.
Reynolds, Robert W.
Sanderson
Sotello, Juan
Stewart, Mitchell G.
St. Martin, Joseph E.
Sullivan, Michael E.
Dinnel, Michael L.
Ditton, William L.

The Men of Special Forces Detachment A-502

York, Larry K.

1968

Allen, Manuel B.
Armstrong, Edwin D.
Bachelor, Hardy E. Jr.
Beeler, David E.
Brandon, John C.
Brown, Edward
Burruss, Tommy
Caldwell, Herschel E.
Campbell, Charles E.
Cheston, Elliott B. Jr.
Childs, Benjamin B.
Darragh, Shaun M.
Dawkins
Drennan, Dennis P.
Dubovick, Richard R.
Dukovic, Gary V.
Egan, Jan C.
Gray, Darrell W.
Harrell, Robert L. Jr.
Harris, Edward D.
Hawley, Robert L. Jr.
Hicks, Archibald G.
Hilliard, Sidney H. III
Hines, Robert M. Sr.
Holland, James D. Jr.
Hubbard, Lyman L.
Juncer, Dennis A.
Kerestes, Paul A.
Knorr, James R.
Land, Kenneth D.
Lane, Terry V.
McGill, Charles A.
McKay
Ochsner, Robert L.
Olt, Timothy F.
Oxenham, Randall
Palmer, Charles P.
Phalen, William C.
Phillips, William J.
Pope, Alonzo D.
Robertson, Juan P.
Ross, Thomas A.
Rupp, John N.
Sanford, H. C. Jr.
Sellers, Lawrence P.
Sheppard, Andrew D.
Sipots, Carl A.
Strong, Tully F.
Trujillo, Louis A.
Webb, Carlton E.
Weller, Richard O.
Wilson, Thomas E.

1969

Abraham, Anthony
Bemis, Donald W.
Blancarte, Edward A.
Carlson, John E.
Cooper, Gerald L.
Cottrel, George A. Jr.
Cottrel, John R.
Crabtree, Donald L.
Crockett, Charles D.
Deschamps, John T.
Dinnel, Michael L.
Downs
Eastburn, David R.
Estrada, Pedro B.
Funk, George C.
Gebhardt, John L.
Gigliotti, John L.
Guerrero, Francisco T.
Hearst, John R.
Hefferman, William F.
Hein, Charles
Hoffman, George P.
Horne, Freddy A.
Jenkins, Larry D.
Jones, James H.
Kemmer, Thomas J.
Kirby, Wickliffe B. III
Lindsey, Gene B.
Martin, John R.
McBride, John B.
McCandless, Kerry E.
Merletti, Lewis C.
Mika, Michael J.
Miller, Franklin D.
Mitchem, James W.
Olivera, Gilbert G.
Overby. Morris C.
Payne, Thomas R.
Roush, James E.
Saganella, Eugene V.
Sheridan, William E.
Short, Harlow C.
Shutley, George F. Jr.
Stucki, Gary W.
Tolbert, James E.

CPSIA information can be obtained
at www.ICGtesting.com
Printed in the USA
BVHW051154100121
597425BV00002B/3